D1045224

Gerontology for Health Professionals

A Practice Guide

2nd Edition

Edited by

Florence Safford
George I. Krell

NASW PRESS
National Association of Social Workers
Washington, DC

Jane Browning, *Director, Member Services/Publications*

Nancy Winchester, *Executive Editor*

Sarah Lowman, *Staff Editor*

Christine Cotting, UpperCase Publication Services, *Project Manager*

Louise Goines, *Copyeditor*

Patricia Borthwick, *Proofreader*

Robert Elwood, *Indexer*

First impression, September 1997
Second impression, March 1998
Third impression, April 2001

Library of Congress Cataloging-in-Publication Data

Gerontology for health professionals : a practice guide / edited by Florence
Safford, George I. Krell. -- 2nd ed.
p. cm.
Includes bibliographical references and index.
ISBN 0-87101-283-9 (alk. paper)
1. Geriatrics. 2. Gerontology. 3. Aged--Health and hygiene.
I. Safford, Florence. II. Krell, George I.
[DNLM: 1. Health Services for the Aged. 2. Aged. 3. Social Work.
WT 31 G377 1997]
RC952.G446 1997
618.97--dc21
DNLM/DLC
For Library of Congress 97-36941
CIP

Printed in the United States of America

To our respective spouses,
Aaron Berkowitz and Constance V. Krell,
for their professional wisdom, assistance, and
loving support

Contents

Introduction

"How can I know if my client's problem is related to the medications he or she is taking?" "How do I know if my client is depressed or showing symptoms of dementia?" "What do I need to know to determine if my client can safely remain in the community?" "At what point might my client need a guardian?" "How far should I go in advocating for or against treatment if my client is terminally ill?"

Practitioners providing services to the elderly ask questions such as these on a daily basis. No field is more complex and challenging than the field of health, concerned with life and death issues for people of every stage and station of life. As new knowledge relentlessly grows in the technical domain of medicine, new knowledge is demanded in the social and psychological domains. This book is intended to provide the gerontological knowledge needed by interdisciplinary practitioners to answer these types of questions.

The workers for whom this book is intended represent a number of different specialties in the field of health and aging services. They include social workers, case managers, senior center personnel, recreation workers in adult day care centers, hospice care workers, and ancillary therapists such as occupational and physical therapists, as well as nurses, hospital intake workers, nutritionists, and physician assistants. For convenience, throughout the book the authors primarily use the term "practitioner," but the guidance being provided applies equally to social work practitioners and those other workers listed above.

Health care professionals as a group are committed to helping people prevent or minimize illness and disability or, when necessary, to maximize their coping abilities. This humane goal is increasingly difficult as the advances of science and technology propel us into a constantly changing world in which patients and their families need all the help they can get to understand and benefit from these advances.

One of the most significant social changes that has resulted from the many miracles of modern science is the phenomenally rapid increase in the number of people who survive to old age. Because health problems accrue as people age, a large proportion of the patients seen by health care professionals are elderly.

Although the basic principles that guide our practice are generic to all ages, certain special characteristics of the aging experience must be understood for us to be effective helpers to this population.

This book grew from the perceived practice needs for gerontological knowledge in a hospital social work department. The social workers selected several areas of direct applicability: understanding the process of aging; the context of practice in a rapidly changing health care system; knowledge of health and illness in later life; knowledge of medication use and misuse in elderly people; assessment skills in differentiating depression, dementia, and other mental impairments; assessment skills and knowledge for effective case management practice; family issues in practice with elderly people; understanding ethnic influences in practice with elderly people; ethical dilemmas in issues of autonomy versus protective services; and death and bereavement issues with elderly people. The principles that are developed herein to maximize individual potential in each of these special areas are transferable to the entire range of gerontological practice.

From the vast body of gerontological research that has grown since that discipline's beginning 50 years ago, the authors have selected those issues that are most relevant to a humanistic perspective in health care for the aging. The humanistic perspective, centered on humane values, asserts the dignity, worth, and boundless capacity of each individual, even into advanced old age. Humanness is thus seen as having the potential for a constant process of becoming, of developing in a constantly changing environment (Whittaker, 1974).

The issues chosen are those that provide a knowledge base for understanding some of the most common problems that challenge the growth potential of the aging, such as supportive family relationships, mental impairment, urinary incontinence, loss and bereavement, and the need for case management.

A humanistic approach demands sensitivity and knowledge about ethnic and cultural influences in the use of services. The authors have selected blacks and Hispanics as particular groups to illustrate the need for culturally specific knowledge. The principles given can be applied to all minorities, such as Native Americans, Jews, and Asians.

The above topics were the basis of training workshops presented by members of the faculty of Florida International University for the Social Work Department of Mt. Sinai Hospital in Miami Beach through the generosity of the Samuel D. and Isabel May Fund of the Greenberg–May Foundation. Such collaborations between academia and agency staff are mutually beneficial. Through testing of theoretical knowledge by direct practitioners, each profession is better informed. The systematic evaluation of such informed health care practice in geriatrics is a challenge that is only now beginning to receive sufficient attention.

The authors compiled this second edition because of the continuing rapid expansion of knowledge and the increasing challenges confronting health care professionals trying to work effectively with the new elderly population. Although some gerontologists emphasize the need to recognize the strength and creativity of older people (Cohen, 1993), a view to which the authors fully subscribe, the reality is that health care practitioners more often must grapple with the ethical dilemmas related to the frail and impaired. Therefore, three new chapters have been added to address some of the most troubling concerns: elder abuse, AIDS and the elderly, and the need for clarity regarding the usefulness of advance directives.

This book reflects the diverse views of its editors and contributors, views that are nevertheless unified by a common focus on developing an interdisciplinary understanding of elderly people in the hard-to-understand world of health care.

REFERENCES

Cohen, G. (1993, Winter/Spring). Comprehensive assessment: Capturing strengths, not just weaknesses. *Generations, 17*, 47–50.

Whittaker, J. K. (1974). *Social treatment.* New York: Aldine.

Working with the Old, Older, and Oldest: Understanding the Experience of Aging in America

Florence Safford

How does it feel to be old in a modern society? Developing that insight is one of the most important tasks for social work practitioners and other health care professionals working with elderly people. To be able to understand and empathize with elderly clients calls for an awareness of one's own attitudes about aging as well as knowledge about the attitudes and beliefs of others, including elderly people themselves.

As a first step in identifying some common biases in relation to aging, consider the issue of chronological age. In the author's gerontology course, when the students are asked to introduce themselves and to give their ages, there is always some embarrassment and nervous laughter, with at least one student refusing to disclose his or her age. It is an important lesson that teaches us that although many people are comfortable with their age, and identification with that age, many others are not.

What is it about chronological age that can make people uneasy? Age is a status that carries many social connotations, roles, and expectations, according to the particular culture. And the more technically advanced a society is, the lower the status of the elders (Cowgill & Holmes, 1972). If a society ascribes negative attributes to an age stage, the occupants of the age stage will be forced to overcome the stigma, cognitively and emotionally, to accept themselves as they are.

AGEISM

When people are viewed or treated negatively because of their age, they are victims of "ageism," a term coined to describe this prejudice (Butler, 1974). A person can feel the effects of ageism relatively early in life, depending on the extent to which the society values physical appearance and accomplishments and on the nature of the demands of the person's career.

The portrayal of elderly people in the media in U.S. society both reveals the low social position they occupy and reinforces it. Elderly people are usually depicted as troubled, needy, helpless, sick, constipated, incontinent, befuddled, and with slipping dentures. Only recently have some magazines and advertisers begun to target young retirees with positive images of healthy, vital, attractive older people. Despite some outstanding literature, television programs, and films—such as *On Golden Pond*—that treat elderly people honestly and with respect for their individuality, the vast majority of the media images of elderly people lack dignity (Cirillo, 1993; Gerbner, Gross, Signorelli, & Morgan, 1980; Loughman, 1977; Sohngen, 1977).

These negative, biased images are shared by many older people themselves. Many people are so concerned with wanting to seem younger that they will forgo "senior citizen" discounts rather than identify themselves as seniors. And professionals working with elderly people frequently encounter obviously elderly people who will not consider participation in senior programs because they "don't want to be around all those old people." Indeed, many practitioners who do not want to work with elderly people express similar biases.

There is so much concern in modern society about the physical appearance of aging that increasing numbers of people are subjecting themselves to expensive face-lifts, hair transplants, and other procedures to regain a youthful image. Some of these actions are motivated by an internalization of society's gerontophobia, whereas others reflect a realistic attempt to remain competitive in the world of business, which also judges people based on age.

Ageist stereotypes can also be expressed through excessive praise of older people who exhibit positive traits or criteria that are unexpected at their age. For example, someone expecting markedly decreased ability in older people might express surprise and amazement in the company of a vital, active, mentally sharp octogenarian. But aging is highly individualized, and there are many healthy, capable, independent people of very advanced ages. And although some older people may enjoy recognition for vigor and productivity in their 80s and 90s, as more and more reach that stage in good health and with positive attitudes, vitality will become the norm rather than the exception.

In addition to avoiding biases based on chronological age, practitioners must also understand the impact on the majority of older people of the accumulation of insults to the older ego. Even an integrated, stable personality is susceptible to regressive self-doubting in the face of such massive negative attitudes. Knowledge of the widespread aversion to the process of aging, and the subtleties of its expression, is essential in assessing the coping capacity of the older client.

Why is aging so denigrated in modern society? One of the most accepted explanations is that the aged remind us of the inevitability of our own death, which for most people produces anxiety and denial (Becker, 1973; Weisman, 1972). Some of this anxiety may be relieved through the distancing technique of ageism. Knowledge about the psychosocial aspects of dying and acceptance of the natural occurrence of death may help reduce the prevalence of ageism.

Aging anxiety is also related to the anticipation of cumulative losses that people may experience in the social and psychological domain. Even though many of the losses are realistic and inevitable, others are preventable through counseling or can be delayed or mediated by compensatory behaviors or social supports.

HOW OLD IS OLD?

Old age is a category that is defined socially. In the United States, the age most frequently used to establish eligibility for benefits that begin in old age, such as pensions and health benefits, is 65. It is also the age at which people had been forced to retire from work until mandatory retirement was abolished legally in 1978 for most occupations. Although 65 may be the most common age used to define the beginning of old age, it is merely an arbitrary choice, and many other chronological ages are used to define old, depending on the purpose of the definition. For example, many social programs define seniors as those over age 55 or 60. The wide range of ages used by different government and local community programs demonstrates a lack of agreement about when individuals typically become old (Atchley, 1987). So although it is necessary to use chronological age for legal or economic purposes, the basis for using it to define old age is clearly controvertible.

During the past 40 years, there has been a growing awareness of the rapidly increasing number of older people in society, and a concomitant growth in the systematic study of gerontology. One of the most important facts for health care professionals, in terms of the growing number of older people, is the unprecedented rate of growth. At the turn of this past century, the average life expectancy for an individual was only 47 years. The percentage of older people (over 65) in the entire population was 4 percent, or 3 million. By 1975, the average life expectancy was 72 years, and there were 20 million older people, or 10 percent of the whole population. At that time, demographers were concerned about the social impact of this rapid increase of elderly people and warned that by the year 2000, there would be 28 million older people, representing 12 percent of the population (Hendricks & Hendricks, 1986). The projection of 28 million was in fact reached in 1984, when older people represented 11.9 percent of the population and had a life expectancy at birth of almost 75 years (American Association of Retired Persons [AARP], 1987). Since 1990 the number of older Americans increased by 7 percent, compared to an increase of only 4 percent for the population under 65. And as of 1994, the 33.2 million elderly people made up 12.7 percent of the population. The fastest growing segment of elderly people is currently the 75-plus segment of the population, with an explosive growth rate for those over 85.

Because the demographics of aging change constantly, practitioners should keep themselves informed by reading the invaluable pamphlet, *A Profile of Older Americans,* which is published annually by the AARP. Throughout this book, the terms "aged" and "older persons" refer, for convenience, to that segment of the population that is over 65, and, unless otherwise noted, statistics are based on data from *A Profile of Older Americans* (AARP, 1995).

Because of the speed with which these increasing numbers of people are surviving to old age, we are not prepared for the changes in family structure nor for the changes in social and health services that this new reality requires. Elderly people have been called "modern pioneers" (Silverman, 1987) in recognition of this population revolution, which is causing a reshaping of society.

As more and more people survive to very advanced chronological old age, we must differentiate the generations that now make up the elderly populace. Gerontologists refer to the segment of elderly aged 60 to 75 as the "young-old" and to those of 75-plus as the "old-old" (Neugarten, 1974). And as the 85-plus segment increases exponentially, there is a need to further differentiate with the classification "oldest-old" (Bould, Sanborn, & Reif, 1989). It is necessary to categorize the young-old, the old-old, and the oldest-old because of their increasing differences as younger cohorts enter this stage of the life cycle in better health, more educated, and better off financially than those who have gone before (AARP, 1995).

Practitioners with the aging are familiar with the growing phenomenon of elderly clients who have living parents and even grandparents. The potential for stress and crisis is apparent, because the probability of illness, disability, and dependency increases in very advanced old age. This phenomenon of generations of elderly people leads to other concepts about age, such as functional age or perceived age.

Functional age is sometimes measured as a profile of an individual's biological capacity. Such an index of function of heart, lungs, muscles, and all other bodily systems does not help to assess overall capacity or to predict longevity any better than chronological age because of the incalculable variability of aging within each person as well as from one person to another (Hendricks & Hendricks, 1986).

Functional age also refers to an individual's capacity to manage physically, socially, and psychologically in comparison with what would be widely perceived as a typical level of capacity for the particular age cohort (Atchley, 1987). For example, most people have some notion of how a person in his or her 60s, 70s, or 80s looks and acts.

These notions do not always conform to the person's own perception, however. Perceived age is the internalized sense of age each person develops as part of his or her self-image. Many people don't perceive themselves as old or elderly until they note a marked slowing down in functioning.

Recent research reports have indicated that even "middle age" is growing older, as definitions of age categories are modified by changing attitudes. Respondents to a national survey of more than 1,200 people identified middle age as the ages between 46 and 66. Many of the perceptions of what constitutes middle age or old age were functional in their definition. For example, 63 percent of those surveyed agreed that people are probably not old until they feel too tired to participate in enjoyable activities. The researchers concluded that "the longer we live, the longer we are likely to feel 'middle-aged'" (Naunton, 1990, p. G1). There is obviously no one answer to the question "how old is old?"

SELECTED DEMOGRAPHICS OF AGING

The demographic characteristics of the aging in America that are particularly relevant for practitioners are those that help to break down the stereotypes about this highly differentiated population. The discussion below focuses on economics, marital status, living arrangements, education, and racial and ethnic demographics.

Economics

The economic condition of the majority of social security recipients has improved in the past 15 years, since legislation increased benefits to compensate for the rate of inflation, which had previously pushed many retirees into poverty. Automatic cost-of-living adjustments (COLAs) now protect most beneficiaries from the unrelenting trend of inflation. But the burden of increased social security taxes on current workers has led to the emergence of a new stereotype of aging people. Having once been viewed as a frail, poor, dependent homogeneous mass, they are now stereotyped, equally misleadingly, as carefree, healthy, and frolicking every morning on the golf course (Pollack, 1985).

The reality is that many old people are still poor, with 19 percent of elderly people living in poverty, or near poverty. The poorest elderly are black women who live alone, 54 percent of whom live below the official poverty index. The median income of older people in 1994 was $15,250 for males and $8,950 for females. This fact provides another illustration of the principle that economic disadvantage continues into old age.

Although many elderly people are poor and eligible for a broad range of social welfare entitlements, many do not receive them. Only 4 percent (1.34 million) of elderly people receive supplementary security income (SSI) and only 7 percent receive food stamps. Some possible explanations are the following: (1) many older people are unable to initiate and follow through the bureaucratic requirements to establish their eligibility, (2) many are unaware of these benefits, and (3) many will not apply for them because of an ethic that rejects what may be perceived as charity. By being particularly sensitive to these needs and attitudes, practitioners who work with these poor elderly through outreach and advocacy can ensure that they receive all the benefits to which they are entitled and that are often prerequisites to basic health and safety.

Marital Status

Almost half (47 percent) of all older women are widowed, compared with 13 percent of older men. Forty-three percent of older women are married, 4 percent single (never married), and 6 percent are divorced. By contrast, 77 percent of all older men are married. Some consequences of the extensive social and personal losses represented by widowhood are discussed in chapter 7.

Living Arrangements

One of the myths about older people is that they are isolated and lonely, extruded from their families, with a large proportion ending up in nursing homes. The reality is that at any point in time only 5 percent of elderly people are living in institutions (Hendricks & Hendricks, 1986). The majority (68 percent) of the noninstitutionalized live in a family setting: 75 percent of men with their spouses and 41 percent of women with their spouses. Six percent of men live with other relatives, and 19 percent live alone. Seventeen percent of women live with other relatives, and 42 percent live alone.

The data are somewhat different for black elderly people. Because more older blacks are widowed, divorced, or separated than are whites, a smaller proportion live with their spouses.

However, sharing a home with a grown child, usually a daughter, is a common living arrangement.

Education

The educational level of the older population has been steadily rising since the turn of the century. Each aging cohort has a higher average number of schooling years completed. As of 1994, more than half of all older people (62 percent) were high school graduates, and about 13 percent had a bachelor's degree or higher. There was still a profound difference for members of racial and ethnic minorities, however, with only 37 percent of older blacks and 30 percent of older Hispanic people having completed high school.

Racial and Ethnic Demographics

In 1994, about 85 percent of older people in the United States were white, 8 percent were black, and less than 3 percent were Asian or Pacific Islanders, Native Americans, or Native Alaskans. Hispanic elderly (who may be white or black) represent 4 percent of the aged. (Currently, in the general population 12 percent of the people are black and 8 percent are Hispanic.) This disproportionately lower percentage of minorities reflects lower life expectancy, which results from socioeconomic disadvantage and unequal access to health care. In 1990 the life expectancy at birth for white men was 71.8 years, whereas black men could not even expect to live to collect their social security, with 64.5 years as their life expectancy. Black women fared better, with 73.6 years, although that was still 5 years fewer than white women, whose life expectancy at birth was 78.8 years (National Center for Health Statistics, 1995).

A further indicator of this inequality is reflected in the percentage of each racial and ethnic group that is over 65: As of 1994, 12.7 percent of white people; 8 percent of black people; 7 percent of Asian/Pacific Islanders, Native Americans, and Native Alaskans; and 5 percent of Hispanic people.

These data should alert each practitioner to the pressing challenge to identify those older clients who are at risk for serious health problems and to assist them through counseling, information and referral, outreach, and advocacy. Our professional ethic of social justice demands that the least advantaged be given priority in terms of commitment and energy. Clearly, the elderly minorities require such attention.

AGING AS A BIOPSYCHOSOCIAL PASSAGE

Aging is the most complex of processes, consisting of, and affected by, biological, psychological, and social factors. Each person experiences social and physiological aging in the context of his or her own culture, race, and sex. This experience is further influenced by the values, attitudes, and beliefs of the cohort, or generation, of which the individual is a member, as well as by the particular historical events during which the aging process proceeds.

Despite the obviously unique aspects of each individual's aging process, there exists a tendency to universalize the process of aging. We discuss the aging, or elderly people, as though they were a homogeneous group, when in fact there is no group that is more heterogeneous. We have only recently begun to acknowledge the differential aspects of aging (Dannefer, 1988; Maddox & Douglass, 1974; Moody, 1994; Schaie, 1981).

Biological Factors

The biological or physiological aspect of aging is influenced first by the unique genetic heritage of each individual. With the remarkable recent findings in the study of genes, scientists are identifying inherited causes or predispositions to an increasing range of conditions, including personality traits. Thus, the aging process is uniquely programmed for each individual from birth.

Physiological aging is further affected both positively and negatively by countless environmental factors, such as climate, lifestyle habits (such as whether the person is sedentary or active, smoking or nonsmoking), and nutrition.

That emotion can have an effect on physical health is common knowledge, but this relationship has particular relevance for elderly people because they are subject to multiple losses, all with emotional consequences (Stenback, 1975). These emotional responses to multiple stressors have a more pronounced impact on the physically vulnerable older person than they might on a younger, more resilient person. However, caution is urged with regard to making premature assumptions about an older person's adaptability, or lack of it, as evidence is rapidly accumulating that demonstrates the extreme variability of individual responses (Dannefer, 1988).

Because all aspects of an individual's life are affected by his or her social and family systems, which have psychological and emotional consequences, it is apparent that the biological, social, and psychological variables are all inextricably related.

Social Factors

Social changes in the life cycle of aging are often viewed as a series of cumulative losses. Significant social roles may be lost through the major transitions of retirement or widowhood or through the limitations imposed by chronic illnesses. Loneliness is a serious problem for many older people whose support networks thin out as families move to distant locations and friends move away or die. In addition, economic and social disadvantages tend to persist and worsen in old age. The impact of race can place the person in "double jeopardy," and race and gender can produce "triple jeopardy," through lifelong decreasing access to economic opportunities that is aggravated by age (Hendricks & Hendricks, 1986).

Paradoxically, the process of aging may also include the accumulation of advantages. The roles and statuses attained in maturity are influenced by early life characteristics and socioeconomic opportunities as well as constraints (Dannefer, 1988).

Furthermore, the diverse adaptive capabilities each person develops add to the differential experiences of aging. Another immeasurable and often overlooked variable in the dynamics of aging is the role of luck or chance in an individual's life (Maddox, 1987a). This humbling factor puts the importance placed on volition and planning in a realistic perspective and is an essential insight to use in counseling elderly people, who may suffer from low self-esteem as a consequence of ageist attitudes.

To illustrate how a social transition can have different effects on different people, consider the fairly recent phenomenon of retirement. The oldest-old cohort has had little preparation for retirement, which has become a possibility only during the past 50 years with the advent of social security pensions. For the old-old, the world of work was primal, and leisure an unaccustomed respite. The young-old, on the other hand, who were born in the 1920s, were socialized to value leisure more and to anticipate retirement as an entitlement.

But what is the experience of the new role of retiree? For some, it brings freedom from difficult or stressful occupations. For others, it represents the loss of a valued, enjoyable occupational status. For some, it brings adequate pensions and dividend income. For others, it brings financial hardship. For some, the first few years are like a prolonged honeymoon, the opportunity for fulfillment of dreams, followed by a period of boredom and time that seems endless. For others, the first few years are marred by depression, because of difficulty in adjusting to an unstructured time span, without satisfying roles to replace the occupational roles. For some couples, retirement brings emotional satisfaction and renewed intimacy. Other couples may need help in adjusting to their new roles.

For many, retirement is becoming a longer and longer span of the life cycle. As increasing numbers survive to very old age, they may spend 20 to 40 years as retirees. Older people's needs will change over this significant period of time, and many of them are not at all prepared for the biopsychosocial adjustments that will have to be made.

Practitioners working with this segment of the population can intervene positively in the challenge of the increasing length of retirement. They can assist through individual, family, and group counseling, preretirement training with attention to family relations and personal growth (as well as the usual focus of financial planning), community education programs, and health promotion programs.

The same methods can be used in helping elderly people adjust to other major transitions, such as the loss of a spouse and the frequent development of chronic health conditions in advanced old age. Because each person meets the challenge of each social transition uniquely, the practitioner must first discard all preconceived ideas about the impact of widowhood, chronic illness, or other major changes. Only then can he or she begin to understand the meaning of the experience to the older person.

Psychological Factors

Psychological aspects of aging are concerned with perception, reaction time, learning and memory, developmental tasks over the life cycle, personality and coping styles, and mental health in later life. These are also experienced uniquely by each individual, although generalized patterns have been identified by gerontologists. Kuypers's (1978) discussion of ego functioning in old age summarized many of the pertinent influences of an individual's past.

> Archetypes transmit psychological dispositions; genes transmit messages of size, shape, and color; early material or maternal deprivations affect later emotionality and psychological health. Early advantages of health and economics determine later aspects of adaptability and personal strength. The parenting styles experienced in childhood determine subsequent character and philosophy. Historical emphases of value, custom, and ideology are taught, absorbed, and changed. These, in part, determine behavior of the present, demanding that new forms of thought and action spring from older forms. Each of these explanations defines its own boundaries and tries to measure its influence against that of others—genetics vs. environment—race vs. culture—personal reinforcement histories vs. free will. (p. 111)

One of the early contributions to our understanding of the developmental tasks in late life was made by Robert Havighurst in 1952 (cited in Silverman, 1987) and is still a relevant formulation today. Havighurst suggested that a person must satisfactorily resolve the following tasks to age successfully:

- adjust to decreasing physical strength and health
- adjust to retirement and reduced income
- adjust to death of one's spouse
- establish an explicit affiliation with one's age group
- adopt and adapt social roles in a flexible way (by expanding or slowing down one's activities involving family, community, or hobbies)
- establish satisfactory physical living arrangements.

This list is intended as a guide and was not meant to be exhaustive. The tasks listed here will vary in type, number, and meaning across various ethnic groups, genders, and cohorts.

The many theories of psychodynamics of later life are beyond the scope of this chapter. A synthesis of present knowledge of psychological changes from midlife to old age presents three basic models for adult development: (1) adult stability model, (2) irreversible decrement model, and (3) decrement with compensation model. The third model is perhaps the most relevant to mental health professionals, in that such a model allows for variations in fluid intelligence, temperament, and other personality traits (Schaie, 1981), which can show the compensatory effects of changes in social support systems and educational practices, for example.

The behavior of older adults is, in fact, more plastic and varied than is generally inferred from psychological assessment instruments that are based on stereotypic assumptions. Regarding age differences in learning and memory, as measured by standard tests, older people do seem to be at a disadvantage with respect to short-term memory, but there are no age differences with respect to retention in long-term memory. This latter decrement can be compensated for by the use of material that is meaningful to the older learner, or by allowing for encoding the material in more than one sensory modality, such as learning from visual material and auditory material.

Regarding intelligence, if older people are assessed according to their competence in managing problems of daily living, there is relatively minor decline in healthy older adults. Schaie (1981) pointed out that what is often characterized as decrement in intellect is really the result of the enormous pace of sociocultural change, which can be remedied by educational interventions.

Personality styles that develop in midlife will tend to be maintained into old age, "unless non-normative individual experiences determine otherwise" (Schaie, 1981, p. 57).

Of particular interest for health professionals is the observation that older adults become more cautious in risk-taking behavior, which may result in an unnecessary lowering of expectation levels. Schaie recommends that one of the most important clinical interventions in early old age may be to help counteract the lowering of the willingness to take risks and explore new solutions, which is so necessary for continued high-quality living.

One of the most useful formulations on the unique psychology of old age is the concept of personhood, and the preservation of the self as the primary adaptive task of elderly people. Based on his decades of experience and research, Tobin (1991) offers the health professional knowledge and insights on the psychological dialectic of gerontology, through utilitarian discussion and excellent case vignettes. In direct practice, the reader will find eminently helpful the concepts Tobin presents about how elderly people cope with changes such as the blurring of past and present, or "mythicizing" the past, as they cut across class, culture, and gender.

Because one of the specific interventions in work with elderly people is the use of reminiscence and oral histories in developing a sense of coherence, the practitioner will find Tobin's text, *Personhood in Advanced Old Age,* invaluable.

BASIC NEEDS FOR SATISFACTION IN OLD AGE

The earliest studies in gerontology were concerned with adjustment to aging and life satisfaction. The *Encyclopedia of Aging* (Maddox, 1987b) cites several criticisms of this past research, such as (1) the measurement of life satisfaction did not capture the daily experiences of life (cited in Gubrium & Lynott, 1983), and (2) the wide range of nominal definitions for the constructs of adjustment, life satisfaction, and morale lead to invalid comparisons (Lohman, 1980). The usefulness of the life satisfaction research on the whole has been found questionable.

A meaningful construct for practitioners in considering the experience of aging was offered by the geriatric psychiatrist Stanley Cath in 1963 and is still timely. He stated that as all people grow old, they share a need for basic anchorages, which include (1) an intact body and body image, (2) an acceptable home, (3) a socioeconomic anchorage, and (4) a meaningful identity and purpose in life:

> From a combination of very early experiences centering on physical care and psychological well-being, and the personal history of accidental trauma or injury, an

> anchorage of basic personal and physical security is or is not established which is related to the capacity to bear anxiety and stress. . . . From the security of the intact home one learns or derives those facets of personality related to trust, tenderness, self-control and autonomy (in contrast to their opposites, mistrust, exploitation, shame, and doubt) as delineated by Erikson. The social anchorage is based upon these early phases and includes friendships or object relationships in which trust, faith, constancy, and the like are tested and experienced in school and away from home. Finally, by achievement of an inner identity through the adolescent years, one may achieve the "meaningful purpose," which may be one's family, science, art, literature, religion, or other sublimated activities that give life its purpose and flavor. (p. 174)

Cath's contribution to our understanding of the challenges of the transitions and crises of aging in terms of the loss or threat of loss of these basic anchorages is clear. As the multiple biopsychosocial losses accrue, as discussed earlier in this chapter, older people and those who care about them are required to creatively find compensations to restore stability. Cath described a construct of the omniconvergence ("omnicon") of multiple losses or depletions for which restitution must be found.

Finally, it is important to note the need for an integration of social and psychological theories across the life span. Just as there is no unified theory of the life course, there are no single social or psychological theories to explain the nature of aging (George, 1996). What is needed is the recognition and appreciation of the links between the biological, social, and psychological aspects of life's transitions on individuals as members of particular cohorts or generations. Cross-fertilization of theories is necessary for the development of the interdisciplinary perspective that is essential for gerontology.

This chapter selectively highlights some of the significant gerontological discourse in order to present a balanced view of the complex aging experience, in which biological, psychological, and social events accumulate over a lifetime to produce highly diverse sets of experiences. The following chapters explore in depth many of these issues.

REFERENCES

American Association of Retired Persons. (1987). *A profile of older Americans*. Washington, DC: Author.

American Association of Retired Persons. (1995). *A profile of older Americans*. Washington, DC: Author.

Atchley, R. C. (1987). *Aging: Continuity and change*. Belmont, CA: Wadsworth.

Becker, E. (1973). *The denial of death*. New York: Free Press.

Bould, S., Sanborn, B., & Reif, L. (1989). *Eighty-five plus: The oldest old*. Belmont, CA: Wadsworth.

Butler, R. N. (1974). *Why survive: Being old in America*. New York: Harper & Row.

Cath, S. (1963). Some dynamics of the middle and later years. *Smith College Studies in Social Work, 33*(2), 174–190.

Cirillo, L. (1993). Verbal imagery of aging in the news magazines. *Generations, 17*(2), 91–93.

Cowgill, D. O., & Holmes, L. (1972). *Aging and modernization*. Englewood Cliffs, NJ: Appleton-Century-Crofts.

Dannefer, D. (1988). Differential gerontology and the stratified life course. In G. L. Maddox & M. P. Lawton (Eds.), *Annual review of gerontology and geriatrics: Vol. 8. Varieties of aging* (pp. 3–36). New York: Springer.

George, L. K. (1996). Missing links: The case for a social psychology of the life course. *Gerontologist, 36*, 248–255.

Gerbner, G., Gross, L., Signorelli, N., & Morgan, M. (1980). Aging with television: Images on television drama. *Journal of Communication, 30*(1), 37–47.

Gubrium, J. F., & Lynott, R. J. (1983). Rethinking life satisfaction. *Human Organization, 42*, 30–38.

Hendricks, J., & Hendricks, C. D. (1986). *Aging in mass society*. Boston: Little, Brown.

Kuypers, J. A. (1978). Ego functioning in old age: Early adult life antecedents. In J. Hendricks (Ed.), *Being and becoming old*. New York: Baywood.

Lohman, N. (1980). Life satisfaction research in aging. In N. Datan & N. Lohman (Eds.), *Transitions of aging* (pp. 27–38). New York: Academic Press.

Loughman, C. (1977). Novels of senescence. *Gerontologist, 17*, 79–84.

Maddox, G. L. (1987a). Aging differently. *Gerontologist, 27*, 557–564.

Maddox, G. L. (Ed.). (1987b). *Encyclopedia of aging*. New York: Springer.

Maddox, G. L., & Douglass, E. (1974). Aging and individual differences. *Journal of Gerontology, 29*, 558–563.

Moody, H. R. (1994). *Aging: Concepts and controversies.* Thousand Oaks, CA: Pine Forge Press.

National Center for Health Statistics. (1995). *Vital Statistics of the United States, 1990, Vol. II. Mortality. Part I.* Washington, DC: U.S. Government Printing Office.

Naunton, E. (1990, February 4). Middle age is growing ever older. *Miami Herald,* p. G1.

Neugarten, B. (1974). Age groups in American society. *Annals of the American Academy of Political and Social Science, 415,* 187–198.

Pollack, R. F. (1985, March 14). A wrong way to see the aged. *New York Times,* p. A27.

Schaie, K. W. (1981). Psychological changes from midlife to early old age. *American Journal of Orthopsychiatry, 51,* 199–218.

Silverman, P. (Ed.). (1987). *The elderly as modern pioneers.* Bloomington: Indiana University Press.

Sohngen, M. (1977). The experience of old age as depicted in contemporary novels. *Gerontologist, 17,* 70–78.

Stenback, A. (1975). Psychosomatic states. In J. J. Howells (Ed.), *Modern perspectives in the psychiatry of old age* (pp. 269–289). New York: Brunner/Mazel.

Tobin, S. S. (1991). *Personhood in advanced old age: Implications for practice.* New York: Springer.

Weisman, A. (1972). *On dying and denying.* New York: Behavioral Publications.

2 Health and Illness in the Later Years: Range of Normal and Pathological

Florence Safford

An elderly square dancer went to his doctor because of pain in his left knee. It was causing him so much discomfort that it was keeping him from his favorite weekly dance group. The doctor smiled at the very old man and went into a long discourse on the process of aging. He explained that cells break down, muscles lose elasticity, resistance to movement in the connective tissues around joints and muscles increases, and joints become tender because of changes in the synovial fluid and weakened cartilage; "you see," he added "it's all part of normal aging." "But, doctor," exclaimed the patient, "my right knee is as old as my left knee, and it doesn't hurt at all."

This classic gerontological story, although humorous, is one of the best illustrations of how difficult it is to know what constitutes "normal aging," as differentiated from pathology. Evidence is continuously appearing that calls into question the norms of physiological aging. It is difficult to measure the rate of aging, and there is controversy about how much of the observed decline is a result of aging as opposed to disease, misuse, or disuse (Jahnigen, 1987).

In general, physiological aging involves a gradual decline in bodily functions, a loss of cells, and a slowing down of cell and tissue activity and response time. Homeostatic mechanisms that keep all systems in balance—such as body temperature, fluids, and electrolytes—decline in their capacity, which leads to decreased ability to respond to physical and emotional stress and to reestablish equilibrium (Weg, 1975). The immune system becomes less vigorous, which leads to a decline in the ability to fight infections or even to fight cancer cells.

However, research continues to document that each individual ages uniquely, and, within each individual, aging varies from system to system. The benefits of lifestyle changes in preventing and even reversing the effects of aging and illness are increasingly described in professional and popular literature, as more and more middle-aged and older people are changing their diets, not smoking, and exercising regularly. Although there are not enough long-term studies of the benefits of such changes for scientists to declare that they are "proved," there is enough face validity in the range of reported studies for practitioners to adopt such preventive, healthy lifestyles for themselves and to encourage older clients to follow suit. Among the most enthusiastic exponents of exercise, for example, are T. Franklin Williams, former director of the National Institute on Aging, an avid cyclist and runner, and cardiologist Paul D. Thompson, a veteran of 16 Boston Marathons (Stockton, 1990).

Not everyone has to be fit enough to jog or run marathons to benefit. The largest study measuring physical fitness ever carried out, studying more than 13,000 men and women for an average of eight years, suggests that even modest amounts of exercise can substantially reduce a person's chance of dying prematurely of heart disease, cancer, or other causes (Hilts, 1989). Furthermore, and of particular interest for those working with the oldest, most frail clients, it has been demonstrated that even loss of muscle mass is reversible with regular weight-training regimes. A Boston research group taught nursing home residents to lift weights, demonstrating that people as old as their 90s can become stronger and increase the size of their muscles. Some of the elderly patients increased their strength by as much as 200 percent, and in some cases their muscle mass increased by as much as 15 percent. There was dramatic improvement in mobility as measured by how long it took to stand up from a chair or how long it took to walk 20 feet (Stockton, 1988).

Recent research at a nutrition site for rural-community elderly people demonstrated that even a low-intensity physical exercise program twice a week produced significant health benefits, such as increased flexibility, muscle strength, and walking speed (Sharpe et al., 1997).

Geriatric health care professionals who are aware of these findings and how they qualify traditional assumptions about the inevitable decline that comes with aging can provide better information in their role as health educators with elderly clients. Despite these positive new indicators, however, health problems continue to increase with age. The more knowledgeable the professional is about these health problems, the more effective he or she will be. Following the health and science section of a major daily newspaper is a good way to keep current regarding new findings, as well as regularly reading some major gerontological journals. An excellent recent source in the journal *Generations* titled "Progress in Geriatrics: A Clinical Care Update" (1996) is comprehensive and very relevant to the most serious and frequent health concerns of elderly people.

MAJOR DISEASES IN ELDERLY PEOPLE

The three major causes of death for people 65 years and over are cardiovascular disease (50 percent), cerebrovascular disease (14 percent), and cancer (15 percent), accounting for 79 percent of all deaths (Ham, Holtzman, Marcy, & Smith, 1983).

Cardiovascular Disease

Cardiovascular disease appears in two common forms: (1) coronary artery disease (arteriosclerosis ["hardening of the arteries"] or atherosclerosis [fatty plaque and cholesterol buildup on the inside walls of arteries]) and (2) hypertension (high blood pressure).

Coronary artery disease interferes with adequate circulation, causing ischemia, or inadequate oxygen to cells. This sometimes causes angina, which is characterized by chest pain, sometimes extending into neck, jaw, or shoulders or down the arms. Angina is generally treated first with medications such as nitroglycerin, which relaxes the arteries so more blood can flow, or with various heart medications such as beta blockers and calcium channel blockers, which slow the heart rate, causing it less stress. Most cardiologists recommend small doses of aspirin to thin the blood. Medical treatment should also include lifestyle counseling on methods to reduce risk of heart attack, such as prudent diet, elimination of smoking, moderate exercise, and reduced personal stressors. If treatment is not effective, then surgery may be indicated. Coronary artery bypass surgery (particularly for middle- and upper-class males) has become so widely available that deaths from heart disease have been remarkably reduced, for those whose insurance covers it.

High blood pressure, twice as prevalent among black people as among white people, affects an estimated 37 million Americans (Bigger, 1985). Blood pressure is the amount of force exerted by the blood on the artery walls as it is pumped from the heart and through the circulatory system. If blood pressure is too high for a long period of time, the arteries will be damaged, predisposing the formation of blood clots and placing the person at risk for heart attack or stroke. Hypertension is often called an insidious disease, because in the early stages there are no apparent symptoms.

If older people are screened for hypertension, it can be detected and treated. Like coronary artery disease, it can be controlled with lifestyle changes, low-sodium diet, and medications. There is considerable risk, however, because elderly people are particularly susceptible to side effects from the medications, and these can lead, for example, to hypotension and risk of falling. They are also at risk for central nervous system side effects such as depression and confusion from certain of the hypertension drugs. Therefore drugs are not recommended for long-term use in most cases.

Myocardial infarction (heart attack) occurs when the heart muscle is damaged from lack of blood supply. This is often caused by a coronary thrombosis, or blood clot, that blocks one of the two arteries that supply the heart. The symptoms of heart attack in elderly people are often dizziness and shortness of breath (dyspnea) instead of the excruciating pain that is characteristic in younger patients.

One of the most prevalent chronic cardiac conditions in older people is congestive heart failure. When the heart fails to pump enough blood to meet the system's need, the patient experiences shortness of breath, fatigue, weakness, and edema (accumulation of fluids in ankles, lungs, or other parts of the body). Congestive heart failure is usually treated successfully with rest, salt restriction, and diuretics (Cape, 1978).

Elderly people are also especially susceptible to changes in the normal rhythm of the heartbeat. Cardiac arrhythmias, or irregular heartbeats, can be caused by a number of factors, such as cigarette smoking, anxiety, certain drugs, and excessive caffeine. Most arrhythmias are temporary and benign. However, some are chronic and life threatening and require treatment. They are treated with a variety of drugs, including digitalis, guianidine, beta blockers, calcium channel blockers, and atropine.

One of the major breakthroughs in the treatment of heart conditions has been in existence for only three decades—the implantation of an electronic pacemaker to regulate the heartbeat. Pacemakers operate from long-lived batteries, which can last for seven or eight years, placed under the skin (Bigger, 1985).

Heart valve disease is another problem frequently seen in elderly people. The valves, which control the flow of blood into and out of the heart, may have been damaged by earlier conditions or may be congenitally defective. Again, medications are very effective in controlling symptoms. When the condition requires surgical intervention, artificial valves, developed from animal parts and/or plastic and metal, can be used.

Cerebrovascular Disease

Cerebrovascular disease can lead to stroke or cerebral vascular accident (CVA). This is a sudden neurological disorder due to the disruption of the blood supply to part of the brain. Strokes are caused by the following:

- thrombus formation, or thrombosis, which is an obstruction within an artery from the buildup of plaque formed by fat and cholesterol
- embolism, which is an obstruction that formed elsewhere in the body and floated free in the circulation until it lodged in the artery, where it blocks flow of blood to the brain
- hemorrhage resulting from the rupture of an intracranial blood vessel—the blood that erupts may destroy normal brain cells.

Symptoms of a stroke depend on the artery involved and the area of the brain affected by the lack of blood supply and may include partial or complete paralysis of the face, arm, and leg on the opposite side of the body from the occluded artery. It may affect vision and speech (aphasia). It may include double vision, slurred speech, uncoordination, difficulty swallowing, and various patterns of weakness (Bigger, 1985).

Treatment of stroke is primarily on a preventive level, including control of blood pressure, weight reduction, elimination of smoking, and proper diet and exercise. Recognition that transient ischemic attacks (TIAs, also called "little strokes") are warnings of impending full-blown strokes can prevent the progression to the more serious, disabling, and sometimes fatal stroke if such preventive treatment is begun. TIAs are not easy to recognize, however. Symptoms might include very transient weakness or numbness on one side, double vision, a brief spell of confusion, or dizziness. Treatment may require medication to reduce blood clots in narrowed arteries. Aspirin is considered helpful in preventing platelet aggregation, and warfarin (Coumadin), which is an anticoagulant, is also commonly used.

Surgery to remove the arteriosclerotic blockage is sometimes recommended, as is a new technique that connects superficial arteries in the scalp directly to intracranial vessels, providing additional blood flow to the brain.

Once a stroke has occurred, physical, occupational, and speech therapies are all important for rehabilitation. Stroke is both emotionally and physically devastating to the family and the patient. Treatment should therefore include counseling and support groups for all involved.

Cancer

Cancer, the second leading cause of death for elderly people, increases in frequency with aging, although the reason for this is debatable and not completely understood (Meyer, 1987). The most prevalent sites of cancer in older men are the lung, colon, rectum, prostate, and bladder. Older women are more likely to have cancer in the breast, colon, rectum, lung, pancreas, and uterus. Unfortunately, elderly people are least likely to be screened, and therefore cancer is often not detected until it has metastasized. One of the reasons for the lower rate of screening in the older age group is the cost of such procedures, many of which may not be covered by insurance unless symptoms are already present. Another reason is that some older people may be considered too frail to tolerate the screening procedures. When cancer is diagnosed, surgery and radiation or chemotherapy may be effective.

Cancer, like stroke, is a disease that is emotionally and physically devastating for the patient and the family. Attention to the emotional as well as the physical needs requires counseling, education, and support programs. For terminal patients, a hospice may offer the most compassionate care and humane palliative treatment rather than continuing aggressive therapy. A hospice's primary concerns are to keep the patient free of pain and to treat the family system (Buckingham, 1983). Practitioners will find many services available through the American Cancer Society and useful resources available through the National Cancer Institute.

COMMON HEALTH PROBLEMS IN ELDERLY PEOPLE

Although heart disease, stroke, and cancer cause most deaths in elderly people, death rates have been decreasing because of improved medical and surgical care. But because they are living longer, there is an increasing prevalence of chronic health problems in elderly people (Mader & Ford, 1987).

Osteoarthritis

One of the most common chronic problems is osteoarthritis, a degenerative joint disorder, primarily in weight-bearing joints such as the knees, hips, and spine. It is also common in the distal joints of the fingers. Although it produces pain and stiffness, only 5 percent of elderly people are incapacitated significantly. The association between arthritis and old age is striking; however, it should not be assumed that arthritis is caused by normal aging. Common types of arthritis seem to be due to secondary causes, such as trauma related to certain occupations. Men and women are equally affected.

Clinically, osteoarthritis presents as pain, loss of motion, and deformity. Pathological changes initially involve the cartilage. Although it is primarily a degenerative disease, it has been shown that drugs that relieve pain and have anti-inflammatory properties are best because joint inflammation is often present.

Management of arthritis involves physical therapy, medication, and, when the condition is severe, surgical procedures. Joint replacements represent some of the modern miracles for elderly people. Although drug therapy is most widely used, all three rehabilitative methods can offer relief to patients. Because of the long-term need for drugs with arthritis, the practitioner must be particularly vigilant for possible side effects of all medications, as discussed more fully in chapter 4 on medication usage.

In addition to direct treatment of the patient, assistive devices can be helpful, such as easy-opening jar devices, raised toilet seats, and canes, all of which serve to decrease stress on specific joints (Nickerson, 1987).

Osteoporosis

Another common health problem for elderly people is osteoporosis, which heads the list of musculoskeletal diseases that cause debility in elderly women, particularly white women of the middle and upper classes. With osteoporosis, bone tissue is diminished, resulting in less dense, more porous bones. This structural change makes bones weaker and more prone to fracture.

One of the most serious fractures with osteoporosis is hip fracture, which often occurs in the absence of significant trauma. Fractures sometimes seem to occur spontaneously, when a person is stepping off a curb, for example, or getting out of bed. Many clinicians believe that the person falls after the fracture, rather than the fracture occurring as a result of the fall. Hip fractures used to be a common cause of death for elderly women, often related to the prolonged immobility that was required for treatment. Newer surgical techniques, such as internal fixation ("hip pinning"), have made it possible for patients to ambulate shortly after surgery, reducing considerably the mortality for this disorder.

Osteoporosis, which can dramatically deform the appearance of elderly women (as with "dowager's hump"), is painful and can severely limit daily activities. Sometimes just bending, sneezing, or coughing can cause fractures of the ribs and vertebrae. Its cause is related to loss of calcium, hormonal changes after menopause, and amount of exercise. There has been ongoing debate about the effectiveness of adding calcium and other nutritional supplements to the diet. There is also debate about estrogen therapy. Concerns for increased cancer risk with hormone therapy make this a problematic treatment for some women. Although osteoporosis is a progressive disorder, there is general agreement about the benefits of adding calcium, vitamin D, and fluoride to the diet as a preventive measure, and increasing exercise seems to promote denser bones (Notelovitz & Ware, 1982).

Falls

Another serious health problem among the aged population is the effects of falls. Treatment of injuries resulting from falls is one of the main components of geriatric medicine, and accidents are the sixth leading cause of death among elderly people (Ham et al., 1983). It is estimated that one of every four elderly patients is admitted to a hospital for an injury caused by falling (Paige, 1990).

Falls usually result from a combination of factors, including problems with equilibrium and decreased vision. According to research at Washington University School of Medicine in St. Louis, balance systems deteriorate with age. Paige (1990) studied the vestibulo-ocular reflex (VOR), a critical component of balance and spatial orientation that keeps the eyes positioned on visual targets as the head and body move, and found a marked decline in VOR performance among elderly people.

About half of all falls stem from diagnosable medical conditions, such as irregular heart rhythm leading to sudden loss of consciousness or dizziness, or hypotension, as discussed earlier. One-third of falls arise primarily from environmental hazards, such as poor lighting and loose scatter rugs. The causes of the balance of falls are unclear, even after thorough examination (Dobkin, 1989).

Falls can have a profound psychological effect on elderly people, particularly those living alone, who may feel totally isolated after falling and not being able to get up until someone finds them. The lack of confidence that develops often hastens the end of independent living. Dobkin called for a preventive approach to this problem, through diagnosing reversible medical causes, encouraging exercise and fitness, which increases strength and improves coordination, and correcting architectural hazards.

Malnutrition

Another common health problem, often overlooked, is malnutrition, which is possibly the cause of many other problems and may have a significant role in the decline of the body's immune system. Several researchers have concurred that about 50 percent of elderly Americans consume insufficient levels of calories or of micronutrients such as calcium, iron, the B vitamins, and vitamin C (Eckholm, 1985). Ranjit K. Chandra of Canada (cited in Eckholm) said that as a conservative estimate, "15 percent to 20 percent of those over 65 in North America are malnourished. For those at special risk—those with chronic diseases or who have lost their spouses, or are poor—the rate is higher" (p. C1). Chandra has shown in experiments that nutritional supplements can partly restore the immune systems of malnourished elderly patients and can improve their responses to vaccines for influenza, tetanus, and pneumonia, bolstering their resistance to disease (cited in Eckholm). Chandra's work is one more example of findings of factors that can maintain or improve functions that had been assumed to be deteriorating as part of the aging process.

Nutritional patterns are influenced by many social, psychological, and physiological factors, which lead to the prevalence of malnutrition. William Bateman, of the Montefiore Medical Center in New York, found that people who are fighting disease need additional protein (cited in Eckholm, 1985). But high-protein items such as meat are expensive and hard to chew, so they may be avoided by elderly people. Furthermore, few elderly eat enough dairy products to get sufficient protein. Even among healthy older people, decreases in the senses of taste and smell lead to loss of interest in food. This is compounded by the fact that many diseases and drugs alter taste and smell (Eckholm, 1985). As noted in chapter 5, depression, another frequent problem of elderly people, also alters appetite. Lonely older people are known to skimp on meals and survive on "tea and toast."

Practitioners who are knowledgeable about geriatric nutritional needs can help their elderly clients both to prevent many of the problems that come with aging and to reverse many others.

CONCLUSION

Some of the health problems discussed in this chapter were selected because of their prevalence and morbidity and others because they are likely to be overlooked. Some of the more common problems that tend to be overlooked or misdiagnosed are discussed more fully in separate chapters—incontinence (chapter 3), medications (chapter 4), and dementia and depression (chapter 5). There are many other problems that require understanding, such as constipation, sleep disorders, skin conditions, and problems with hearing and vision, which are devastating and potentially isolating for large numbers of elderly. The practitioner is referred to one of the comprehensive texts on geriatrics (Kane, Ouslander, & Abrass, 1990; Libow & Sherman, 1981; Lonergan, 1996; Wei & Sheehan, 1996) as well as to the specialized large foundations, such as the Lighthouse for the Blind, that provide up-to-the-minute information about clinical and social aspects of these disorders and information on the many services that are available.

One of the myths about elderly people is that they complain all the time. According to Ham et al. (1983), the fact is that many elderly people wrongly tolerate disabling or isolating symptoms, accepting illness as part of growing old. Diseases such as osteoarthritis, hearing loss, and even congestive heart failure are tolerated far too long because of their insidious nature and because loss of function is regarded as an inevitable consequence of increasing age.

It is probable that as the young-old become more elderly, they will continue to lead the healthier lifestyles that are becoming more common. Health promotion and wellness programs have been increasing, although they generally do not reach more than 50 percent of the target population (Hooyman & Kiyak, 1996). A healthy lifestyle, which includes preventive medical care, health-inducing nutrition, exercise, weight control, satisfying social supports, an active sex life, and attention to reducing stress, will make the increase of longevity worthwhile.

REFERENCES

Bigger, J. T. (1985). Heart and blood vessel disease. In D. F. Tapley, R. J. Weiss, & T. Q. Morris (Eds.), *Columbia University College of Physicians and Surgeons complete home medical guide* (pp. 362–394). New York: Crown.

Buckingham, R. W. (1983). *The complete hospice guide.* New York: Harper & Row.

Cape, R. (1978). *Aging: Its complex management.* New York: Harper & Row.

Dobkin, B. (1989, August 27). Challenge of gravity. *New York Times Magazine*, p. 36.

Eckholm, E. (1985, August 13). Malnutrition in elderly: Widespread health threat. *New York Times*, p. C1.

Ham, R. J., Holtzman, J. M., Marcy, M. L., & Smith, M. R. (1983). *Primary care geriatrics*. Boston: John Wright.

Hilts, P. (1989, November 3). Exercise and longevity: A little goes a long way. *New York Times*, p. 1.

Hooyman, N., & Kiyak, H. A. (1996). *Social gerontology* (4th ed.). Boston: Allyn & Bacon.

Jahnigen, D. (1987). Introduction: Progress in clinical care of the elderly. *Generations, 12*(1), 5.

Kane, R. L., Ouslander, J. G., & Abrass, I. B. (1990). *Essentials of clinical geriatrics* (2nd ed.). Hightstown, NJ: McGraw-Hill.

Libow, L. S., & Sherman, F. T. (Eds.). (1981). *The core of geriatrics medicine: A guide for students and practitioners*. St. Louis: C. V. Mosby.

Lonergan, E. T. (1996). *Clinical manual of geriatrics*. Stamford, CT: Appleton and Lange.

Mader, S. I., & Ford, A. B. (1987). Morbidity and mortality trends among the aged. *Generations, 12*(1), 5–7.

Meyer, T. J. (1987). Cancer in the elderly. *Generations, 12*(1), 20–24.

Nickerson, P. E. (1987). Osteoarthritis. *Generations, 12*(1), 8–11.

Notelovitz, M., & Ware, M. (1982). *Stand tall: The informed woman's guide to osteoporosis*. Gainesville, FL: Triad.

Paige, G. D. (1990, May). Equilibrium research at Washington University School of Medicine in St. Louis. *Gerontology News*, p. 7.

Progress in geriatrics: A clinical care update. (1996). *Generations, 20*(4, Winter 1996–1997).

Sharpe, P. A., Jackson, K. L., White, C., Vaca, V. L., Hickey, T., Gu, J., & Otterness, C. (1997). Effects of a one-year physical activity intervention for older adults at congregate nutrition sites. *Gerontologist, 37*(2), 208–215.

Stockton, W. (1988, November 28). Can exercise alter the aging process? *New York Times*, p. C19.

Stockton, W. (1990, April 29). The trick of growing older. *New York Times Magazine*, pp. 55–76.

Weg, R. (1975). Changing physiology of aging: Normal and pathological. In D. Woodruff & J. Birren (Eds.), *Aging: Scientific perspectives and social issues* (pp. 242–284). New York: Van Nostrand Reinhold.

Wei, J. Y., & Sheehan, M. N. (1996). *Geriatric medicine: A case-based manual*. New York: Oxford University Press.

3 Helping the Incontinent: A Biopsychosocial Challenge

Florence Safford

One of the most dreaded and misunderstood problems of elderly people is urinary incontinence, commonly referred to as loss of bladder control. Like mental impairment, it is not a disease but a syndrome that is caused by numerous conditions. Also like mental impairment, it is often seen as a normal and irreversible consequence of the process of aging and illness. This negative belief is held not only by the general public but also by many professionals, including physicians (Brocklehurst, 1990; Campbell, 1988).

A variety of disorders can cause incontinence, including disorders of the lower genitourinary tract and nervous system, cognitive impairment, impaired mobility, psychological disturbances, and environmental obstacles. This broad range of possible causes demonstrates the multisystemic nature of geriatric conditions (Cape, 1978; Ouslander, 1996).

Because incontinence is embarrassing to admit and hard to define, prevalence estimates are extremely variable. However, several studies have estimated that between 10 and 40 percent of noninstitutionalized elderly people have some problem with urinary incontinence and at least 50 percent of those in institutions (Angier, 1990; Diokno, Brock, Brown, & Herzog, 1986; Mitteness & Wood, 1986). The National Institutes of Health estimates that at least 10 million Americans are affected by urinary incontinence that is extreme enough to cost $10.3 billion annually to manage the problem (Angier, 1990). Community care accounts for $7 billion of these direct costs, and nursing homes account for $3.3 billion for an estimated 800,000 incontinent patients (Hu, 1990).

Although this condition is often not reported, it can cause social isolation or ostracism, depression, sexual difficulties, and a cycle of negative consequences. Relationships with relatives, friends, and particularly with spouses may be negatively affected. Victims of incontinence may give up traveling, vacations, entertainment events, hobbies, physical recreation, church attendance, and shopping trips. In attempting to keep incontinence a secret, some frail elderly become virtually imprisoned by their management strategies, such as avoiding visitors who might notice evidence of their problem, and by the need to be near a toilet at all times. Such strategies can have long-term consequences of loneliness and anxiety as well as low self-esteem (Mitteness, 1987; Wyman, Harkins, & Fante, 1990). At the same time, it has been estimated that from 70 percent to more than 90 percent of those afflicted can be helped with proper diagnosis and treatment (Brocklehurst, 1984; Brody, 1985; Leary, 1992; Ouslander, 1996). Unfortunately, however, half of all people with incontinence do not get help because they think it is untreatable (Burgio, Pearce, & Lucco, 1989).

Incontinence is often cited as a precipitating cause of institutionalization, although conclusive evidence is not apparent from existing studies (Herzog, Diokno, & Fultz, 1990). Whether it is the primary cause, or merely a related problem, it is still a significant challenge in caring for the more than 50 percent in nursing homes who reportedly suffer from incontinence.

Practitioners can play a significant role in uncovering the problem and in helping the patient through the process of diagnosis and treatment. First, it is necessary to recognize the extent of stigma and blame that are associated with bladder control problems, and then it is important to learn something about the causes of the condition and some treatment options.

CONTINENCE

Before incontinence can be discussed, continence—or the control of the act of micturition (urination) must be understood. The normal physiological process of control of micturition is summarized in Ronald Cape's (1978) excellent book, *Aging: Its Complex Management*. Urine flows from the kidneys in a steady trickle into the bladder. The bladder is a muscular organ that stores the urine until it is convenient to void. Maintaining complete control of the act of micturition involves a complex series of neurologic centers and pathways. Thus, continence and micturition depend on a normally functioning lower urinary tract and intact nervous system.

The wall of the bladder contains a series of stretch receptors that respond to the increasing volume of urine in the organ by stimulating the bladder center in specific segments of the spinal cord. Contraction of bladder muscle, the internal and external sphincter, and voiding follows by reflex. This is the total controlling mechanism in infants. As children develop, an afferent pathway is established from the sacral cord to the center in the brain that makes them aware of the bladder filling. As children learn the social advantage of remaining dry and controlling the time of bladder emptying, they develop another center in the brain related to motor control that enables them to inhibit the sacral reflex action. These two components of voluntary inhibition of micturition enable the individual to control the act and remain continent.

DEFINITION AND CAUSES OF INCONTINENCE

What is urinary incontinence? One definition is the involuntary loss of urine, of sufficient amount or frequency to be a social or health problem. According to the International Continence Society Standardization Committee, it is "a condition in which involuntary loss of urine is a social or hygienic problem, and is objectively demonstrable" (Herzog et al., 1990, p. 75). Bladder capacity declines as part of normal aging, from the ability to hold up to a pint of urine to the ability to hold only half a pint. In addition, the signal to urinate does not occur until that capacity is nearly reached. These two factors lead to problems of frequency and urgency. Incontinence also refers to such problems as dribbling, or leakage, and may be temporary and transient or chronic and established.

There are several common types of urinary incontinence in elderly people:

- *Detrusor instability*. The most common type of urinary incontinence is caused by the instability of the detrusor, which is the bladder muscle. This is characterized by urgency, frequency, nocturia, small volume voiding, and the experience of loss of large amounts of urine, often after laughing, sneezing, or coughing.

- *Overflow incontinence.* This is caused by spontaneous bladder contractions to empty the bladder when it is filled to capacity. People with this problem frequently do not receive the signal to void, so they lose control when it fills. Diabetics, or others with conditions that damage nerves, may suffer from this type of incontinence. Many can manage this problem if they can remember to schedule regular toileting.
- *Stress incontinence.* In women, this is associated with loss of muscle tone related to childbearing as well as age. The symptom is a loss of small amounts of urine when coughing, sneezing, laughing, or straining.
- *Functional incontinence.* This occurs in people who are normally continent but are unable to reach a toilet in time to avoid an accident. This can be the result of arthritis or other mobility limitations or of being in an unfamiliar environment or being dependent on someone else for assistance to the toilet, bedpan, or urinal.
- *Iatrogenic incontinence.* This is caused by medical treatment for other conditions. For example, incontinence can result from fast-acting diuretics, it can be a side effect of some psychotropic drugs, or it can be the unintended consequence of urologic or gynecologic surgery.
- *Uninhibited neurogenic bladder.* One common breakdown in the nervous pathway between the brain and the sacral micturition center (in the spinal cord) results in the uninhibited neurogenic bladder. This affects the majority of very old people and is the primary cause of increase of incontinence in advanced old age. A possible explanation is that the cortical cells in the frontal lobe that are responsible for the inhibition of bladder contractions may be damaged. Recognition of bladder filling is present, although usually late, but the ability to inhibit contraction by the bladder muscle is lost. There is also a marked precipitancy of micturition, which, combined with the slow pace of elderly people, often results in incontinence.
- *Bladder outlet obstruction.* Another physical cause of many cases of urinary incontinence is obstruction of the bladder

outlet, resulting in a dribbling incontinence. This is most common in elderly men with enlarged prostates (prostatic hypertrophy). It may also occur in women with pelvic pathology, such as fibroid tumors or urethral strictures. In both sexes, it may also occur as a result of chronic fecal impaction.

Other possible causes of incontinence also exist. Research in brain function has identified urinary incontinence as a common symptom of basal ganglion disorders, which may be secondary to an imbalance of catecholamine neurotransmitters (Ambrosini, 1985). Drugs that increase the dopamine activity of the brain may be therapeutic for persons suffering this type of incontinence.

In this past decade, the functions of many neurotransmitters have been discovered. These are enzymes or chemicals that transmit impulses or messages from one cell to another. Bladder function depends on normal activity of the neurotransmitter acetylcholine (Bennett, 1987). Normal activity of acetylcholine depends on adequate supplies of choline, which may be reduced by anticholinergic drugs. There are over 800 prescription and nonprescription products in the United States that have anticholinergic properties (Pepper & Robbins, 1987). These include antihistamines (such as Benadryl and Dramamine), antispasmodics (such as Donnatal), antidepressants, and antipsychotics. Older persons may be taking several anticholinergic drugs simultaneously, which can have many adverse effects (Blazer, Federspiel, Ray, & Schaffner, 1983), including dryness, constipation, and urinary retention, because they affect bodily secretions. But we may infer that they can also lead to incontinence, if they reduce the amount of choline needed for normal acetylcholine to transmit the neural messages to and from the bladder.

Many psychoactive drugs, such as the phenothiazines (for example, Compazine, Sparine, Stelazine, Chlorpromazine, and Thorazine), can impair normal attention to bladder cues and therefore cause incontinence.

Several types of medications commonly used to control high blood pressure may also cause incontinence. These include muscle relaxants or sympathetic blockers, which can produce sphincter weakness. The commonly prescribed tranquilizer diazepam (Valium) is primarily a muscle relaxant and should be questioned if incontinence develops in a long-term user of this drug.

In addition, certain fast-acting diuretics may lead to functional urinary incontinence. Elderly incontinent patients who are taking reserpine (Chloroserpine, Diupres, Diutensen, and Hydropres), guanethidine (Esimil and Ismelin), methyldopa (Aldoclor, Aldomet, and Aldoril), or fast-acting diuretics such as furosemide (Lasix) may need to have these drugs changed or monitored or the dosages adjusted.

PRACTITIONER'S ROLE IN THE TREATMENT OF INCONTINENCE

Practitioners who are knowledgeable about and sensitive to the special concerns of geriatric patients can fulfill a significant role in treating urinary incontinence and in preventing and minimizing chronic incontinence.

An important variable in understanding the impact of incontinence is the severity of the condition in terms of the psychological and economic consequences. Severity is typically measured in research studies by the frequency of incontinence episodes or by the frequency of difficulties with controlling urine (Fultz & Herzog, 1993; Herzog et al., 1990). Some studies have measured severity by the quantity of loss. A survey of patients referred to an outpatient continence clinic revealed that it was the amount, or quantity, of urine loss rather than frequency that was more upsetting (Ouslander & Abelson, 1990).

Through understanding the extent of embarrassment for the older patient and his or her family, and through careful history taking, clues can be obtained that can assist the physician in diagnosing this complex condition. This is no easy task, as there is no condition more demoralizing than incontinence. It can cause feelings of shame, helplessness, hopelessness, and depression. Even the most tactful, sensitive handling may not be enough to overcome the intense stigma felt by both the older person and his or her relatives. The condition is often denied or covered up with rationalizations and excuses.

One of the first steps in cutting through the embarrassment is to learn to talk about incontinence in understandable terms and in a nonjudgmental manner. Health professionals generally discuss these conditions with technical terms, such as "voiding schedules" and "incontinence of urine or feces," to which there are no feelings attached. These terms are inappropriate for most clients. Questions such as "Do you have a problem in getting to the bathroom on time?" are relatively nonthreatening and may help ease into the discussion.

Role playing a counseling session with a colleague in which incontinence is the presenting problem is an effective technique in practicing expressions and terms that will make the encounter more comfortable for client and practitioner. For example, one could assume the role of a director at a senior center whose members have complained about one participant who is obviously incontinent, smells of stale urine, and occasionally leaves a wet chair. The members are demanding that the offending member be expelled from the program, and the director must discuss this with the embarrassed member, who denies the problem. Such a role play provides a vivid learning experience in preparing to discuss this typically taboo topic.

Hospital workers often find that admission to a hospital because of an acute illness may result in incontinence in an elderly person for whom bladder control had been precarious but manageable. For example, the person who is used to emptying his or her bladder one or more times during the night will wind up with wet sheets if put in a hospital bed with siderails, given a sedative, and left until 6 A.M. Such a patient may be labeled incorrectly as incontinent and treated inappropriately, for example, with a catheter. A thorough social and behavioral history taken by the social worker, case manager, or other service provider can help to minimize treatments that ignore the customary habits of the elderly patient.

Because many medications can cause incontinence in elderly people, in addition to those that affect the neurotransmitters previously discussed, and many older persons take a great number of drugs prescribed by several different physicians, as well as over-the-counter preparations, the referring professional or intake worker must check the current drugs and provide this information to the primary physician. Medication-induced incontinence is easily reversible. (See chapter 4 on medications for further clarification of this significant problem.)

Practitioners must also be knowledgeable about the many underlying conditions that can cause urinary incontinence and advocate for their treatment in cases in which therapeutic pessimism prevails because of the advanced age of the patient.

Infections such as cystitis or prostatitis, chronic urinary tract infections, and chronic bladder infections are frequently treatable causes (Chalker & Whitmore, 1990). The increased incidence of urinary tract infections among elderly people may be related to incomplete emptying of the bladder, which results from the decreased elasticity and diminished muscle tone of the bladder, ureters, and urethra that accompanies the normal aging process. It is important to educate elderly people about the need to take extra time when urinating to empty the bladder consciously.

Because fecal impactions can obstruct the ureters and result in urinary incontinence, as discussed above, it is important to include questions about constipation when taking a history from the elderly patient.

Stress incontinence in women is one type of incontinence that can often be cured through behavioral changes such as Kegel exercises to strengthen the pelvic floor muscles and increase sphincter tone (Brody, 1985; Burgio et al., 1989; Kegel, 1948). Counselors can provide an invaluable service to women with stress incontinence by distributing the following information on exercises to strengthen pelvic muscles:

- Kegel: a series of 20 to 30 contractions of the muscles of the pelvic floor, as though holding back from urinating and defecating at the same time. Contractions are held only a few seconds, but the series must be repeated at least three times a day for a total of at least 100 contractions.
- Squeeze vaginal muscles. Hold each contraction for 10 seconds, five or six times each, repeating two or three times a day.
- Draw up or contract the rectum as though ending a bowel movement. Repeat as for the second exercise above.
- Squeeze the lower buttocks muscles to draw up the genital area. Repeat as for the second exercise above.
- When urinating, squeeze or contract the muscles to interrupt the flow temporarily. Repeat as for the second exercise above.

It usually takes several weeks to notice an effect.

Another problem of postmenopausal women is incontinence due to urethral stiffness and irritability. This can be relieved with vaginal estrogen cream therapy, if the problem is identified through sensitive discussion and then referred to a gynecologist who cares about older women.

Many cases of incontinence (for example, overflow incontinence) can be managed by urinating every two to four hours. In institutions, many patients whose incontinence is managed with pads can benefit from behavior modification techniques wherein records are maintained of the timing and frequency of incontinence episodes. A method of "prompted voiding," in which nursing aides regularly offer to assist the patient to the toilet and chart the frequency of urination, can lead to fewer incidences of incontinence (Schnelle, 1991; Schnelle et al., 1993).

Bladder retraining, in which the patient is put on a voiding schedule with gradual increases in the amount of time between visits to the toilet, is another highly effective treatment for the institutionalized aged, which may be overlooked for the elderly people in the community. Bladder training aims at identifying a predictable pattern of urination through maintaining a "voiding chart" and then consciously increasing the span between scheduled urinating (Chalker & Whitmore, 1990).

Many incontinent older persons can be helped by surgical intervention, such as for enlarged prostate, to correct a weak sphincter, to reposition the bladder or other organs, or to remove an obstruction. It is one of the tragedies of aging that countless victims of incontinence are doomed to restricted, socially impoverished lives because this option is not even considered. Their incontinence is simply attributed to old age by both patients and their health professionals.

Other incontinent persons may be helped with drug therapies using anticholinergic drugs in dosages that cause urinary retention. For example, some of the tricyclic antidepressants, when used in smaller doses than are therapeutic for depression, can control certain types of urinary incontinence.

If the problem is with the bladder, other drugs may reduce the tendency for the bladder to contract or may improve the tone of the muscles at the opening of the bladder. However, some of these drugs produce unpleasant side effects, such as a dry mouth or irritability (Libow, 1986).

Finally, when other treatment has failed, management of incontinence with pads, catheters, and other devices may be necessary. As more elderly people with chronic medical problems are surviving into advanced age, there is more public awareness of some of the attendant problems, including incontinence. The visibility of advertisements and articles in magazines and on television for incontinence products demonstrates a growing public recognition of this predicament. ("The Last of the Closet Issues," 1986). A negative consequence of the media battle for this billion dollar market is the portrayal of active, attractive young elders who remain involved in life with the help of adult diapers, which reinforces the myth that incontinence is a normal part of aging. Rather than seeking medical help, countless consumers are lured into a management strategy that currently costs $100 per month.

Patients can now be referred to a self-help and patient advocacy group (Help for Incontinent People, or HIP) that provides information and encouragement and lists resources. HIP also publishes a newsletter, the *HIP Report* (Department RBC, P.O. Box 544, Union, SC 29379; telephone [800] 585-8789).

Another important referral source is the Simon Foundation, which publishes a newsletter, *The Informer* (Box 815, Wilmette, IL 60091). In addition, the president of the Simon Foundation, Cheryl Gartley (1985) has written *Managing Incontinence: A Guide to Living with Loss of Bladder Control*. More recent contributions include *Staying Dry: A Practical Guide to Bladder Control* (Burgio et al., 1989), *Overcoming Bladder Disorders* (Chalker & Whitmore, 1990), and *Managing Urinary Incontinence in the Elderly* (Schnelle, 1991).

It is important to include the family in all of the suggestions cited. Because of the private nature of the problem, the incontinent person often attempts to hide the condition from even close family members. The empathetic practitioner can work toward more open communication within the family, because the family is a potential source of help and support for the older person whose self-esteem is lowered and who probably suffers from self-consciousness.

For those family members who serve as caregivers to their elderly relatives, the educational guides mentioned above can provide important strategies to lessen the burden. For example, caregivers to the mentally impaired incontinent older person can learn behavioral techniques to monitor and prompt their relatives about toileting. Those whose relatives are mentally intact, but physically impaired, may benefit from information on adaptive clothing, use of commodes, and other environmental aids. Such practical information can lead to more effective caregiving skills and a decreased sense of burden and can possibly reduce the rate of nursing home placement (Noelker, 1987; Schofield & Wheaton, 1992).

Practitioners must take a leadership role in educating the public and in advocating for elderly people in obtaining appropriate treatment. A special issue of the *Journal of the American Geriatrics Society* (volume 38, number 3, 1990) reports on a Consensus Development Conference sponsored by the National Institutes of Health that offered practitioners up-to-date information on prevention and treatment of urinary incontinence.

At the same time, there is a need for developing "continence clinics" modeled after the pioneering programs at the University of Michigan and the University of California, Los Angeles (Brink et al., 1987; Ouslander, 1984). Such programs feature "urodynamic" measurements of bladder and sphincter function, with safe and painless procedures. These new techniques are leading to improved classification of symptoms and more precise knowledge of the origin and causes of the symptoms and therefore to better treatment.

Another model to be replicated is the development of a new specialty, continence advising, which emerged from Great Britain's interdisciplinary approach to incontinence care. There is now an International Association of Continence Advisors representing professionals from several disciplines, which has led efforts to include more information on incontinence in the curricula of medical and nursing schools, as well as continuing education courses and public education materials (Wyman, 1991).

Finally, two other recent developments offer hope for improving the quality of life for many sufferers: the confirmation by research of the effectiveness of nonsurgical and nondrug treatments, such as pelvic exercises, with or without biofeedback. Also promising is the approval by the U.S. Food and Drug Administration of collagen injections to add bulk to the urethra, which increases resistance to leakage (Eastman, 1994).

Through expansion of such programs, and through greater sensitivity, practitioners will be better able to refer incontinent clients for accurate diagnosis, treatment, and support.

REFERENCES

Ambrosini, P. J. (1985). A pharmacological paradigm for urinary incontinence and enuresis. *Journal of the American Geriatrics Society, 4,* 247.

Angier, N. (1990, October 25). New focus on urinary incontinence. *New York Times,* p. B7.

Bennett, W. (1987, December 13). Monitoring drugs for the aged. *New York Times Magazine,* pp. 73–74.

Blazer, D., Federspiel, C., Ray, W., & Schaffner, W. (1983). The risk of anticholinergic toxicity in the elderly. *Journal of Gerontology 38*(1), 31–35.

Brink, C. A., Wells, T. J., & Diokno, A. C. (1987). Urinary incontinence in women. *Public Health Nursing, 4,* 114.

Brocklehurst, J. C. (Ed.). (1984). *Urology in old age.* New York: Churchill-Livingstone.

Brocklehurst, J. C. (1990). Professional and public education about incontinence. *Journal of the American Geriatrics Society, 38*(3), 384–386.

Brody, J. (1985, June 5). Personal health. *New York Times,* p. C10.

Burgio, K. L., Pearce, K. L., & Lucco, A. J. (1989). *Staying dry: A practical guide to bladder control.* Baltimore: Johns Hopkins University Press.

Campbell, E. (1988). Coping with incontinence. In *Health issues for housing managers* (pp. 1–21). Madison: University of Wisconsin, Center for Health Sciences.

Cape, R. (1978). *Aging: Its complex management.* New York: Harper & Row.

Chalker, R., & Whitmore, K. E. (1990). *Overcoming bladder disorders.* New York: Harper & Row.

Diokno, A. C., Brock, B. M., Brown, M. B., & Herzog, A. R. (1986). Prevalence of urinary incontinence and other urological symptoms in the noninstitutionalized elderly. *Journal of Urology, 136,* 1022–1025.

Eastman, P. (1994, July–August). A problem no one wants to talk about: New treatments offer hope to the millions with incontinence. *AARP Bulletin, 35*(7), 16–17.

Fultz, N., & Herzog, A. (1993). Measuring urinary incontinence in surveys. *Gerontologist, 33*(6), 708–713.

Gartley, C. (1985). *Managing incontinence: A guide to living with loss of bladder control.* Ottawa, IL: Jameson.

Herzog, A. R., Diokno, A. C., & Fultz, N. H. (1990). Urinary incontinence: Medical and psychosocial aspects. In C. Eisdorfer (Ed.), *Annual review of gerontology and geriatrics: Vol. 11* (pp. 74–119). New York: Springer.

Hu, T.-W. (1990). Impact of urinary incontinence on health care costs. *Journal of the American Geriatrics Society, 38*(3), 292–295.

Kegel, A. H. (1948). Progressive resistance exercise in the functional restoration of the perineal muscles. *American Journal of Obstetrics and Gynecology, 56,* 238–248.

Leary, W. (1992, March 24). U.S. issues guidelines on bladder problems, *New York Times,* p. B6.

Libow, L. S. (1986, April). New pills for old ills: Pharmacology and pharmacy for the elderly. *Pharmacy Times,* 112–120.

Mitteness, L. (1987). The management of urinary incontinence by community-living elderly. *Gerontologist, 27,* 185–193.

Mitteness, L., & Wood, S. (1986). Social workers' responses to incontinence, confusion and mobility impairments in frail elderly clients. *Journal of Gerontological Social Work, 9*(3), 63–77.

Noelker, L. (1987). Incontinence in elderly cared for by family. *Gerontologist, 27,* 194–200.

Ouslander, J. (1984). Incontinence clinics: A new approach to diagnosis and management. *Generations, 8*(4), 18–19.

Ouslander, J. (1996). Geriatric urinary incontinence. *Generations, 20*(4, Winter 1996–1997).

Ouslander, J. G., & Abelson, S. (1990). Perceptions of urinary incontinence among elderly outpatients. *Gerontologist, 30,* 369–372.

Pepper, G., & Robbins, L. (1987). Improving geriatric drug therapy. *Generations, 12*(1), 57–61.

Schnelle, J. (1991). *Managing urinary incontinence in the elderly.* New York: Springer.

Schnelle, J., Newman, D., White, M., Abby, J., Wallston, K., Fogarty, T., & Ory, M. (1993). Maintaining continence in nursing home residents through the application of industrial quality control. *Gerontologist, 31,* 114–121.

Schofield, A., & Wheaton, C. (1992). Support/education groups for people with urinary incontinence. *Australian Social Work, 45*(4), 31–40.

The last of the closet issues. (1986, October 6). *Time,* p. 69.

Wyman, J. (1991). Urinary incontinence in the community-dwelling elderly population. *Family and Community Health, 14*(2), 35–47.

Wyman, J. F., Harkins, S., & Fante, J. A. (1990). Psychosocial impact of urinary incontinence in the community-dwelling population. *Journal of the American Geriatrics Society, 38,* 282–288.

Medication and the Elderly

Mary Helen Hayden and Florence Safford

A growing body of evidence compiled over the past 10 years indicates that medication problems of elderly people constitute a critical health care issue, sometimes called "the nation's other drug problem." The problems cited in a report by the inspector general of the U.S. Department of Health and Human Services include inadequate training of doctors in geriatrics, prescriptions of the wrong drug or dosage, faulty testing of medications, inadequate information on labels, and misuse of drugs by elderly people themselves (cited in Johnson, 1989). The editor of the *Harvard Medical School Health Letter* stated that "warnings have been appearing in medical journals, and research . . . indicates that over-medication and adverse reaction to drugs are not only prevalent, but have probably become epidemic among the elderly" (cited in Bennett, 1987, p. 73). There is clearly a need for increased knowledge and concern about drugs and their effects on elderly people by physicians, drug manufacturers, and pharmacists, as well as by patients and their families.

Practitioners who provide direct services to elderly people can play a significant role in educating, counseling, and monitoring the effects of medications and in detecting when unexpected physical or emotional changes in the client may be the result of medications. An obvious barrier to fulfilling this role is the issue of professional responsibility and expertise. It is generally assumed that physicians, who prescribe medications, have total responsibility in this area and that it is presumptuous for nonphysicians to raise questions. Many patients, particularly elderly people, have been socialized as well to believe that it is improper to question their physician—trust and compliance are supreme values in the patient–doctor relationship. However, recent trends in medical training include patient education as an integral part of preventive care and therapeutic success. An informed, caring physician will welcome the interest, observations, and questions raised by any member of the health care team. Therefore practitioners (as well as family members) must learn to overcome feelings of intrusiveness in exploring the realm of medication effects on their elderly clients.

A dramatic illustration of the need for monitoring medication effects was presented in an article in *The New York Times* (Brody, 1988) that described the frightening experience of Mary Calderone, a well-known research physician in her 80s. When Calderone complained of extreme sleepiness, lassitude, loss of balance, memory problems, weakness, difficulty concentrating, unease, and depression, the many physicians she consulted could find no explanation and attributed the symptoms to her advanced age. Calderone knew there must be some reason for the sudden decline in vitality, and after several serious falls she began to systematically stop her medications. One was Elavil, an antidepressant that had been prescribed many years previously in a small nightly dose to help her sleep more soundly. Two days after cutting out the Elavil, Calderone began to feel normal again, with energy, no memory impairment, and no imbalance or unsteadiness.

This is a particularly vivid example because the victim of many physicians' oversight in detecting a drug as the cause of the presented symptoms is herself a physician, and one might have anticipated collegial concern. It demonstrates that many physicians are biased against elderly people, assuming too many symptoms to be due to age, rather than to specific pathology or adverse drug effects. A frequent scenario is that rather than review the patient's drugs, the physician "may add a new drug to combat side effects not recognized as coming from another—say an antidepressant to relieve the blues caused by a blood-pressure drug. Just because a drug has been taken comfortably for months or years does not automatically mean that it is innocent" (Bennett, 1987, p. 73).

Many of the symptoms of adverse reactions to medications that commonly occur in elderly people may be overlooked because they can also result from many other physical or emotional conditions. These include, but are not limited to, anorexia (loss of appetite), confusion, forgetfulness, tremor, constipation, diarrhea, and urinary retention, in addition to the depression, weakness, and lethargy Calderone experienced (Simonson, 1983). Whenever an elderly client has such symptoms, possible causes by medications should be thoroughly explored with a physician.

EXTENT OF THE PROBLEM

Although older Americans make up 12 percent of our population, they use nearly 25 percent of all prescription drugs, and by the year 2000, with a projected increase in the elderly population to over 35 million, they will use nearly 50 percent of all prescriptions (Wolfe, Fugate, Hope, Hulstrand, & Kamimoto, 1993). People over the age of 60 have 40 percent of all adverse drug reactions, and one-sixth of all hospital admissions for patients over the age of 70 are for medication problems. A study conducted in San Francisco found that a person over the age of 60 was 15 times more likely to be admitted for a medication-induced illness than a younger person (Brody, 1988). At the same time, nearly 25 percent of the elderly patients discharged from the hospital received six or more prescriptions to take home, a fact that is compelling evidence of the need for vigilance regarding the patient's capacity to take the drug properly and the possibility of side effects.

Additional data were provided by Wolfe et al. (1993), who raised the question of whether older adults were prescribed too many drugs. Using age 60 and over to define "older adults," the authors (who represent the Public Citizen Health Research Group in Washington, DC) pointed out that in 1986 older Americans obtained 613 million prescriptions at retail drug stores, an average of 15.5 prescriptions per person, or almost 40 percent of all prescription drugs dispensed outside of institutions. Some of the 15.5 prescriptions per person were refills, but a survey of the 65-plus population living in the community found that 61 percent received three or more different prescription drugs in a year, 37 percent received five or more, and 19 percent received seven or more different drugs (Ray, 1986). The opportunity for elderly people to be poisoned mounts with each drug added. *Polypharmacy* is a term used to describe the excessive and inappropriate use of medications, which can result from many factors (Simonson, 1983).

A study conducted by medical researchers at Harvard University documented the vast extent of medication problems, concluding that almost 25 percent of the population over age 65 are being prescribed drugs that have been deemed dangerous for older people. The researchers, as well as geriatric specialists, indicate that excessive drug prescribing stems from gaps in doctors' knowledge about the effects of drugs on elderly patients. In addition, one of the Harvard study's authors blames the problem on aggressive marketing by drug companies, which spend about $10 billion each year in promoting new drugs to physicians (Los Angeles News Service, 1994).

The foregoing examples clearly support the argument for vigilance in monitoring the ability of elderly people to keep track of their medication regimes, as well as the need for systematic assessment of the effectiveness of the drugs.

MOST FREQUENTLY USED DRUGS

The largest category of drugs prescribed for older adults are drugs for heart disease, hypertension, and blood vessel diseases, accounting for 46 percent of all prescriptions (Wolfe et al., 1993). Many of these drugs pose unnecessary risks for older people when dosages and side effects are not monitored closely. Drugs for hypertension (high blood pressure) have been shown to be overprescribed, and often unnecessary if other methods of treatment are used, such as salt restriction and lifestyle modifications. M. D. Blumenthal (1980), a noted geriatric psychiatrist, stated that overtreated hypertension is a common cause of depression in elderly people and that the depression can often be solved by taking the patient off the antihypertensive drug, particularly those containing reserpine (that is, Ser-ap-es, Diupres, and Hydropres).

The second largest category of drugs are analgesics for pain and for arthritis. Many of these are also implicated as possible causes of depression, as well as psychoses, delirium, hallucinations, confusion, and dementia (Wolfe et al., 1993).

These reversible symptoms of mental impairment are called *pseudodementia*. Although the practitioner cannot expect to be knowledgeable about all of the benefits and dangers of the thousands of prescription drugs that are used by elderly people, awareness of the frequency of probability that elderly clients are taking many different drugs can lead to a more complete history in assessing problems that are presented.

The third largest category of drugs, psychotropic medications, includes tranquilizers, sleeping pills, antipsychotic drugs, and antidepressants, which, according to the Public Citizen Health Research Group, is probably the group of drugs most likely to victimize elderly people. One-half of all sleeping pills, for example, are prescribed for older adults, and well over one-third of all minor tranquilizers, with adverse effects very common (Wolfe et al., 1993).

The vast majority of minor tranquilizers (antianxiety drugs) and sleeping pills belong to the same family of chemicals, benzodiazepines, such as Valium (diazepam), Librium (chlordiazepoxide), Xanax (alprazolam), Tranxene (clorazepate), Dalmane (flurazepam), Restoril (temazepam), and Halcion (triazolam). Because elders are more sensitive to the effects of these drugs than younger adults, they are at significantly increased risk of adverse effects, such as unsteady gait, dizziness, falling, impairment of mental abilities, and addiction (Wolfe et al., 1993). The extent of usage and the degree of risk amount to a major public health problem. Practitioners can develop better assessment skills and intervention techniques with the help of a new text, *The Social Worker and Psychotropic Medication*, by Bentley and Walsh (1996).

Another serious problem is the extent of usage of nonprescription drugs, the over-the-counter (OTC) drug business. About one-third of all expenditures for medications used by the elderly population is for OTC products. One factor that contributes to the problems related to OTC drug usage is the perception that those drugs must be harmless because they are readily available to all consumers. In fact, they can be very dangerous to elderly people because of the possibility of adverse effects, as well as the risk of synergistic side effects when interacting with prescription drugs or alcohol (Coons, Hendricks, & Sheahan, 1988). For example, many cold remedies contain ingredients that stimulate the sympathetic nervous system and can cause nervousness, insomnia, and heart irregularities in the susceptible older person. OTC cold and allergy preparations also contain antihistamines and belladonna alkaloids, which are effective in drying secretions but can cause older people to experience rapid heartbeat, increased ocular pressure (dangerous for those with glaucoma), urinary retention, constipation, blurred vision, dizziness, and a sedative effect on mental function (Coons et al., 1988).

The most frequently used OTC medications that can cause problems are analgesics, laxatives, antacids, and sedatives. Aspirin, for example, often used by elderly people for arthritis, can be toxic in high doses. This toxicity may manifest itself as confusion, irritability, tinnitus (ringing in the ear), blurred vision, or vomiting and diarrhea. Long-term use of aspirin or aspirin taken in combination with alcohol can also cause gastrointestinal bleeding (Coons et al., 1988).

Antacids, needed in increasing amounts as an elderly person ages because of changes in gastric acidity, may cause constipation and, by causing an acid-base imbalance in the intestines, may interfere with the absorption of certain prescribed drugs. The use of laxatives, especially their overuse and dependence on them, can cause constipation by reducing muscle tone and reflexes in the large bowel. The practitioner can offer a much better solution by suggesting increased fiber in the individual's diet (Giannetti, 1983).

PHYSIOLOGICAL CAUSES OF ADVERSE DRUG EFFECTS

The major factors in the sensitivity of older people to the effects of drugs relate to *pharmacokinetics,* that is, the absorption and distribution of the drug, drug disposition at the receptor site, and excretion of the drug. The elderly have decreased lean body and muscle mass, decreased total body water, and increased body fat in relation to total weight. These physical changes result in a difference between elderly people and young people in the distribution and absorption of many drugs within the body, potentially leading to excessively high serum levels of the drugs in some elderly patients (German & Burton, 1989).

The kidneys and liver basically process and clear drugs from the body. Many drugs are metabolized in the liver, but changes in the liver's enzymes may prevent total drug clearance. The rate at which the kidneys filter and excrete wastes tends to decrease with aging, and this decrease can also result in higher levels of drugs in the bloodstream. In addition to normal changes with age, some elderly have liver or kidney disease, which further diminishes the ability to process drugs. Also, some drugs, such as aspirin and anticoagulants, tend to bind to proteins. Their effectiveness depends on how much active (unbound) drug is available at a specific site. In elderly patients, a decline in serum or plasma albumin (a form of protein) results in a higher percentage of active drug and therefore a greater possibility of toxicity (Teusink & Shamoian, 1983).

Other physiological changes that affect drug distribution in the body include altered intestinal functions; increased gastric acidity, or, conversely, a decrease of hydrochloric acid in the stomach, which affects the solubility of drugs and slows the rate at which the stomach empties; cerebrovascular disease, which diminishes blood flow; and respiratory disease. Despite all of these physiological changes, adjustments for dosages that are primarily tested on younger patients, are not often made.

POLYPHARMACY AND POLYMEDICINE

The terms *polypharmacy* and *polymedicine* are used in geriatrics to emphasize the problems related to a patient's use of multiple drugs, often prescribed by several physicians. Because of the trend toward specialization in modern medicine, older patients with, typically, multiple chronic and acute conditions must be treated by several physicians. When care is divided in this way, it is often not coordinated, with inadequate attention to the possibility of duplication of prescriptions or adverse effects of some drug interactions.

The older consumer and his or her family must become knowledgeable about all of the medications prescribed and any OTC medications used. The older patient may need help in communicating with his or her physicians and in making sure that all of them are aware of all of the drugs being taken. The family is the usual source of help in these matters, but the family may also need help in learning the role of advocate or counselor to the elderly member (Klein, German, McPhee, Smith, & Levine, 1982). Social workers, nurses, case managers, and family therapists can

TABLE 4-1

The Family Caregiver and the Patient's Medications

Caregiver Function	Percent Performing
Picks up medication from pharmacy	77.1
Reminds recipient of purpose	77.3
Sets out medications	50.0
Assists with medication taking	75.0
Administers medications	38.5
Checks that medication is taken	38.5
Reminds of need for refills	67.3

SOURCE: Lamy, P., Godnek, K., Feinberg, M., Yachmetz, B., & Oed, M. (1991). The family caregiver. *Eldercare News, 1*(3), 17–24. Reprinted with permission of Madeline Feinberg, Editor, *Eldercare News.*

provide counseling and role modeling in communicating with the physicians. They can also provide community education programs, based on some pilot programs that have developed manuals suitable for training elderly people and their families (Eng, 1982; Lamy & Feinberg, 1983). The importance of targeting the family in education programs about medication may be inferred from Table 4.1, which is based on a report of the Maryland Caregiver Program (Lamy, Godnek, Feinberg, Yachmetz, & Oed, 1991). In addition to the functions shown in Table 4.1, many caregivers may observe and monitor the use of OTC drugs and preparations, and these activities should therefore also be part of the training (Lamy et al., 1991).

Another important role for the case manager or responsible health practitioner or responsible relative is to make sure that accurate medication information is provided when an elderly client is hospitalized. Elderly clients who have no difficulty in following their complex medication regimens are often unable to give a comprehensive list of their medications. A study found widespread errors in drug histories taken for hospital admission, with a 60 percent error rate in listing important medications that elderly patients were taking ("Wide Errors Found in Drug Histories," 1990). This statistic emphasizes the significant part played by the family or health practitioner in gathering information on drug usage for the hospital admission process.

NONCOMPLIANCE WITH MEDICATION REGIMES

Discussions of geriatric drug problems usually include the problem of noncompliance with medication regimes. Estimates of noncompliance range from 25 percent to 50 percent (Giannetti, 1983; Shimp & Ascione, 1988). Patients may be noncompliant either intentionally or unintentionally. Increasing forgetfulness, confusion, failing eyesight, hearing impairment, lack of understanding of therapeutic intent, and multiple drug therapy can all contribute to errors, omissions, misunderstanding, and a failure to maintain the prescribed drug regime. Furthermore, elderly people who are least able mentally and physically to follow their regimen are those who are most likely to be in need of the drug therapy (Conrad & Bressler, 1982).

Noncompliance may also include taking medication that was not prescribed or taking medication in incorrect dosages. These activities may lead to exacerbation of illness when the dosage is insufficient for a therapeutic response or to toxic reactions when unprescribed drugs are taken or dosages are too high. On occasion, noncompliance may be related to financial constraints, prompting elderly people to delay treatment while medicating themselves, to save medication for another episode of illness, or to share medications with other elderly friends. Still another factor in noncompliance may be social isolation. Many elderly people lack a significant other who is concerned about their medications or who is capable of monitoring their regimens (Giannetti, 1983).

Although it is generally agreed that patient compliance in drug therapy needs to be improved, it is also recognized that physicians and pharmacists need to take a more active role in making sure that the patient understands the purpose of the drugs, the precise methods of taking them, the time period involved, and the possible side effects.

Finally, there is growing sentiment that blaming the patient for noncompliance is too limited a view of medication misuse—the patients' rights in making decisions about their drug intake must be considered. Practitioners are urged to effectively communicate information about medication that will assist consumers in making informed decisions (LeSage & Zwygart-Stauffacher, 1988).

ALCOHOL ABUSE

According to research, neither alcohol use nor abuse rates are high among older adults; however, it does not follow that drinking problems are inconsequential. Alcohol use poses special risks for older drinkers; they include increased incidence of alcohol-induced disease, interaction with prescribed and OTC drugs, and increased risk of falls and accidents (Maddox, 1988). Those risks call for vigilance on the part of practitioners in assessment of the elderly client who may use alcohol as a means of coping with the many stressors and losses that eventually accumulate in a long lifetime.

THE PRACTITIONER'S ROLE

Social workers, nurses, case managers, and senior center and housing managers have an important role with regard to the use of medication by elderly people. They can help by detecting problems, communicating their observations to the physician, and educating elders and their families. The Council on Social Work Education presented two interactive national videoconferences—*Psychopharmacology: The Social Work Agenda* (1991, April 11) and *Psychopharmacology: Social Work Practice with Adults* (1992, April 2)—legitimizing social work's role in educating and advocating for better medication management of the client within the health care system.

Practitioners first have a responsibility to acquire sufficient knowledge to fulfill this role. Several books on the effects of medications on elderly people are available, along with the *PDR Pocket Guide to Prescription Drugs* (1996) (Bentley & Walsh, 1996; Graedon & Graedon, 1989; Gurnack, 1997; Wolfe et al., 1993).

Practitioners can help overcome medication problems by asking the following questions on drug selection of the prescribing physician or pharmacist (adapted from a checklist developed by the Up Front Drug Information Center in Miami, Florida; National Council on Patient Information and Education, 1987):

- Is there a documented need for the drug?
- Could presenting symptoms be the result of side effects from other drugs?
- Is there a better drug?

- Are there any contraindications or problems with other illnesses?
- Does the patient have impaired liver or kidney function?
- What is the smallest dose that will provide the desired effect?
- What other prescription and nonprescription drugs is the patient taking?
- Are all these drugs still needed?
- Is an easy-to-administer form of the drug available?
- Is a once-a-day form available?
- Is the patient's nutritional status adequate?
- Are there other indications that food-drug interactions may be a problem?

The following questions (also from the Up Front Drug Information Center) on monitoring drug therapy are also appropriate:

- What laboratory tests will be needed to evaluate the effect of the drug?
- Have side effects occurred with this patient?
- Is the patient taking the drug as directed?
- Is the drug producing the desired effect?
- Is it still needed?

Because of his or her knowledge of the older client's personal history, cultural preferences, and attitudes, the practitioner can suggest changes in the medication regimen that would make it fit more easily into the client's lifestyle and therefore more likely to be followed.

Another important way in which the practitioner could help would be by learning which pharmacies maintain computerized customer profiles and alert physicians and patients about potentially dangerous drug combinations or inappropriate dosages; elderly clients could be referred to those pharmacies. Also, many educational programs on understanding medications and their effects are offered by drug companies, senior organizations (such as the American Association of Retired Persons [AARP]), and community colleges to which clients can be referred. An up-to-date knowledge of resources such as these is an essential practice tool. Networking with colleagues and studying the literature on aging can keep this knowledge current. AARP's bimonthly magazine, *Modern Maturity,* is an inexpensive way to learn of new resources for elderly people. Another resource is volume 18 of *Generations* ("Pharmacology and Older People," 1994) which presents the most current concerns for practitioners.

Finally, the practitioner, with advice from a pharmacist, can assist the client in setting up a system for taking drugs safely, either with color-coded reminders or a network of relatives to monitor the patient's actions. Clients should also be encouraged to keep a personal record of all prescription and OTC medications taken on a regular basis.

It is in the area of medication use that the practitioner can provide one of the most critical services to elderly clients. By knowing about medications and exchanging information with other health professionals working with the client, the practitioner can be instrumental in preventing unnecessary suffering for elderly people and promoting optimal health care.

REFERENCES

Bennett, W. I. (1987, December 13). Monitoring drugs for the aged. *New York Times Magazine,* pp. 73–74.

Bentley, K. J., & Walsh, J. (1996). *The social worker and psychotropic medication: Toward effective collaboration with mental health clients, families, and providers.* Pacific Grove, CA: Brooks/Cole.

Blumenthal, M. D. (1980). Depressive illness in old age: Getting behind the mask. *Geriatrics, 35*(4), 35–43.

Brody, J. (1988, November 10). Personal health: An alert for older Americans about preventable adverse reactions to many common drugs. *New York Times,* p. B20.

Conrad, K., & Bressler, R. (1982). *Drug therapy for the elderly.* St. Louis: C. V. Mosby.

Coons, S. I., Hendricks, J., & Sheahan, S. L. (1988). Self-medication with non-prescription drugs. *Generations, 12*(4), 22–26.

Council on Social Work Education. (1991, April 11). *Psychopharmacology: The social work agenda* [videoconference]. Alexandria, VA: Author.

Council on Social Work Education. (1992, April 2). *Psychopharmacology: Social work practice with adults* [videoconference]. Alexandria, VA: Author.

Eng, K. (1982). *Preventing geriatric medication misuse: A manual for developing a model program.* San Francisco: Department of Public Health.

German, P. S., & Burton, L. C. (1989). Medication and the elderly. *Journal of Aging and Health, 1,* 4–34.

Giannetti, V. J. (1983). Medication utilization problems among the elderly. *Health and Social Work, 8,* 262–270.
Graedon, J., & Graedon, T. (1989). *50-Plus, the Graedons' people's pharmacy for older adults.* New York: Bantam.
Gurnack, A. M. (Ed.). (1997). *Older adults' misuse of alcohol, medicines, and other drugs: Research and practice issues.* New York: Springer.
Johnson, J. (1989, February 15). Widespread drug lapses found among elderly. *New York Times,* p. A1.
Klein, L. E., German, P. S., McPhee, S. J., Smith, C. R., & Levine, D. M. (1982). Aging and its relationship to health knowledge and medication compliance. *Gerontologist, 22,* 384–387.
Lamy, P., & Feinberg, M. (1983). *The Elder-Health Program: A consumer drug education program.* Baltimore: University of Maryland, School of Pharmacy.
Lamy, P., Godnek, K., Feinberg, M., Yachmetz, B., & Oed, M. (1991). The family caregiver. *Eldercare News, 7*(3), 17–24.
LeSage, J., & Zwygart-Stauffacher, M. (1988). Detection of medication misuse in elders. *Generations, 12,* 32–36.
Maddox, G. (1988). Aging, drinking and alcohol abuse. *Generations, 12*(4), 14–16.
National Council on Patient Information and Education. (1987). *Talkabout prescriptions.* Washington, DC: Author.
PDR Pocket Guide to Prescription Drugs. (1996). New York: Pocket Books, Simon & Schuster.
Pharmacology and older people. (1994). *Generations, 18*(2).
Ray, W. A. (1986). Prescribing patterns for the elderly. In *Pharmaceuticals for the elderly* (p. 35). Washington, DC: Pharmaceuticals Manufacturers Association.
Shimp, L., & Ascione, F. (1988). Causes of medication misuse and error. *Generations, 12*(4), 17–21.
Simonson, W. (1983). Methods to insure proper medication use by older adults. *Generations, 8*(2), 42–45.
Teusink, J. P., & Shamoian, C. A. (1983). Understanding the body: Aging, illness and medications. *Generations, 8*(2), 6–9.
Wide errors found in drug histories. (1990, December 18). *New York Times,* p. A1.
Wolfe, S. M., Fugate, L., Hope, R. E., Hulstrand, E., & Kamimoto, L. (1993). *Best pills, worst pills. II.* Washington, DC: Public Citizen Health Research Group.

5 Differential Assessment of Dementia and Depression in Elderly People

Florence Safford

One of the most serious challenges to the health care community in geriatrics is to be able to tell whether an elderly patient with symptoms of mental and physical impairment is suffering from dementia, depression, or the normal results of aging. Accurate diagnosis calls for an enlightened interdisciplinary team assessment in response to the multicausal aspects of geriatric problems, including the physical, psychological, and social (Katzman, 1986).

Until the 1960s, elderly patients whose main complaint was mental deterioration had been traditionally viewed as "senile," demented, and untreatable. With increasing numbers of elderly patients, physicians became aware of the need for more careful assessments. These mental symptoms were identified as resulting from organic brain disease, and the symptoms were classified as resulting from organic brain syndrome (Busse & Pfeiffer, 1973; Butler & Lewis, 1982). In the mid-1970s, this terminology was replaced by the category of dementia, as medical advances continued to increase knowledge of brain physiology.

The American Psychiatric Association has promoted greater specificity in the classification and nomenclature of mental disorders in the *Diagnostic and Statistical Manual of Mental Disorders*, fourth edition (DSM-IV) (1994). One of the most important criteria in the classification system is the qualifier that the diagnosis of dementia or depression cannot be made unless all other possible causes of the syndrome have been excluded.

Unfortunately, in spite of the advances in the DSM-IV, there are still many obstacles to the goal of accurate diagnosis. Some of the most obvious are the following:

- attitudinal bias about treating the very old patient—"What do you expect at this age?"
- hospital stays that are too short, because of high cost of care, to investigate thoroughly the many possible causes
- difficulty in obtaining personal and medical history
- widespread lack of knowledge about geriatrics, although the specialty is slowly developing
- often confusing terminology used to describe dementia and the related syndrome of delirium.

Practitioners can fulfill a significant advocacy role with the frail older patient by being prepared to overcome these obstacles and learn what questions to raise to increase the likelihood of accurate assessment. When an older person presents signs of cognitive and emotional changes, questions must always be raised as to whether these are symptoms of dementia or of depression masking as dementia. When the symptoms presented are physical, questions must also be raised. Is it depression masking as somatic illness? Are the symptoms caused by specific medical problems such as cardiovascular illness? Are the symptoms caused by drugs? Or by a combination of the above?

A first consideration in defining dementia, delirium, or depression is to note that these are syndromes rather than diseases. A syndrome is a cluster of symptoms that can have a variety of causes. After the practitioner identifies which syndrome is present, the next steps for assessment and treatment can follow. The differential definition of these three syndromes is summarized as follows (Zarit, Orr, & Zarit, 1985):

1. *Dementia.* A syndrome involving memory and other impairments in cognition and behavior, usually gradual in onset over a period of months or years. Dementia may be irreversible, when caused by a degenerative brain disease, or potentially reversible, when caused by treatable conditions such as metabolic or toxic disorders.
2. *Delirium.* A syndrome involving fluctuating mental function and disturbances of consciousness, attention, and cognition, of acute onset, usually hours or days. Delirium can be caused by many conditions, including drugs, infections, fractures, metabolic disorders, malnutrition, and environmental stress.

3. *Depression.* A syndrome involving persistent feelings of sadness or dysphoric mood; often accompanied by lack of energy, loss of appetite, insomnia, or withdrawal from usual activities. In elderly people, depression sometimes presents without overt complaints of sadness.

SYMPTOMS OF MENTAL IMPAIRMENT

Because the many possible symptoms that appear with dementia, depression, and other mental disorders are similar, it may be preferable to call them symptoms of mental impairment. The use of this more general term emphasizes the need for more specificity before settling on a diagnosis.

The following is a classification of the broad range of symptoms that can appear—either singly or in combination, either gradually or abruptly—and that can help identify the problem (Safford, 1986). The symptoms of mental impairment fall into three categories: cognitive, psychological, and behavioral.

Cognitive Symptoms

The cognitive symptoms of mental impairment include the following:

- memory loss—severe forgetfulness, serious enough to interfere with independent functioning. Immediate and recent memory is affected first, and then remote or distant memory. With loss of memory, words are lost, recognition of close kin may be lost, and old skills are lost. In its final, extreme form, the self is lost (Eisdorfer & Cohen, 1986).
- loss of orientation—for time (day, hour, year), place (house, city, country), or person (understanding of who people are).
- the combined effect of memory loss and disorientation is described by the term *confusion,* which results from the fragmentation of mental processes, leading to an inability to make the connections to be coherent or to be aware of time, place, or person.
- loss of comprehension—as memory impairment worsens, the symptoms include inability to comprehend or understand what is being said, what is being read, and what is

seen. New information cannot be learned, and things previously understood may become incomprehensible.

- lack of concentration—noticeable reduction of attention span.
- loss of general information—first, lack of awareness of current events; later, commonly known facts disappear as well.
- loss of insight and logic—inability to make the mental connections to think abstractly. This limitation to concrete thoughts precludes an ability for everyday problem solving.
- loss of judgment—although not always recognized as a symptom of mental impairment, this follows from the loss of insight and can be a serious impediment to an older person's ability for self-care.
- formation of delusions—in some cases, the disordered thoughts that result from loss of memory, confusion, disorientation, and lack of judgment can lead to the formation of delusions. Without insight and the ability to distinguish between real events and thoughts, it is understandable that delusions may occur. These may be visual delusions, auditory delusions, or a system of ideas that explains events that otherwise do not make sense.

Psychological Symptoms

It is obvious that people who suffer mental losses may respond with fear, anger, frustration, sadness, hostility, and depression. These emotional reactions may appear in addition to similar symptoms caused directly by impaired brain function. Emotional behavior involves physiological, biological, and chemical responses to external events and interpersonal situations. These responses are processed by particular centers in the brain. Impaired function of any part of the chain of reactions can trigger an unusual emotional response. Some of the most common personality changes are the following:

- emotional lability—mood swings; includes temper outbursts and disproportionate rage.
- lack of emotional response—flatness of affect.
- anxiety—related to many possible causes but also possibly caused by breakdown of brain and central nervous system function.

- irritability—possibly related to mental impairment when it is a change from the person's usual behavior and out of proportion to provocation.
- hostility—when brain centers that process socially learned responses fail, instinctive hostility, belligerence, or aggression may be expressed if the older person feels attacked or overwhelmed.
- stubbornness—obstinate behavior; often shows up as insistence on being right; frequently a characteristic of those trying to maintain control as their capacity for independence slips away.
- loss of sense of humor—many older people maintain a good facade, despite serious mental impairment, through a conditioned pattern of humor, using humor to relieve anxiety; others may have a total personality change and lose their customary sense of humor.
- suspiciousness—when out of proportion to actual events or uncharacteristic; in its extreme, suspiciousness is expressed as paranoia.
- jealousy—irrational reversion to primitive instincts.

Behavioral Symptoms

Many of the following changes in behavior may not seem to be symptoms of mental impairment and may mistakenly be considered normal signs of aging. It is important that practitioners recognize these changes as symptoms:

- loss of initiative—lack of spontaneity; needs directions for most activities.
- inability to follow through—may start activity but may be unable to finish.
- loss of interest—withdraws from social relationships; is unresponsive or apathetic.
- personal neglect—sometimes this is the first clue to the seriousness of the mental changes.
- restlessness—in contrast to apathetic behavior, some confused, forgetful older people become restless or hyperactive, rummaging through drawers or shuffling papers; restlessness can lead to wandering behavior.

- verbal changes, including confabulation, perseveration, and irrelevancies—practitioners need to develop skills in interpreting the meaning of what seems to be nonsense.
- loosening of inhibitions—reflects damage in the brain center that controls learned social behavior.
- impulsiveness—may not be noticeable unless related to important imprudent decisions.
- hoarding—some older people develop a compulsion to accumulate and save things; it is not known if this is caused by physiological change or emotional need.
- perceptual changes—if there is no other apparent physical reason, these are probably related to impaired brain function.
- incontinence—again, if there is no other apparent physiological reason, such as prostate enlargement or urinary tract infection, it could be related to mental impairment.

Each person is unique in terms of which symptom(s) may appear, how it is expressed, for what length of time and how often, and what condition or conditions may be causing it.

Assessment for Dementia

The most common assumption about the older patient who presents with some or all of these symptoms is that he or she is suffering from dementia. Because of the negative attitude about aging that still prevails in society, and because a thorough diagnosis is a time-consuming process, too often the label of dementia is used as loosely as the term *senility* has previously been used, or as quickly as the term *Alzheimer's disease* is still being used. Because as many as 30 percent of patients regarded as demented have potentially treatable and reversible disorders (National Institute on Aging Task Force, 1980), practitioners must be particularly alert when taking the history to help identify when a patient has been misdiagnosed.

The steps and principles of assessment for dementia have been outlined in many books and articles. A comprehensive assessment requires careful personal and medical history, administration of a mental status examination, and thorough physical and psychiatric evaluations, including laboratory findings.

There are so many assessment tools available that an entire book and journal have been devoted to describing them (Kane & Kane, 1981; Generations, 1997).

Among the most useful assessment tools for social workers and allied health professionals are the models described by Cohen (1988); Gallo, Reichel, & Anderson (1988); Toseland, Derico, & Owen (1984); and Zarit et al. (1985). These authors suggest the value of brief screening tests to identify the possibility of dementia and more extensive testing to differentiate among the various types of dementia. The brief screening instruments most commonly used are the Mental Status Questionnaire (Kahn, Goldfarb, Pollack, & Peck, 1960), the Short Portable Mental Status Questionnaire (Pfeiffer, 1975), and the Mini-Mental State (Folstein, Folstein, & McHugh, 1975), which has become the most popular.

These instruments generally test for remote and recent memory, orientation, comprehension, and general information, with such questions as, What is the date? Where are we? and Who is the president of the United States? The Pfeiffer and Folstein et al. instruments also test for the ability to concentrate on simple arithmetic by asking the client to count backward by threes or sevens.

Another validated six-item test is the Orientation–Memory–Concentration Test (Katzman et al., 1983). This convenient test includes a phrase that the client is asked to memorize and repeat at the end of the session. It also includes an item in which the client must name the 12 months in reverse order. It has been shown that these two items are among the first to be answered incorrectly as dementia progresses, and therefore this screening test may be particularly sensitive for detecting dementia early in its course.

It is important for practitioners to become skillful in administering at least one of these mental status examinations because self-reports about memory function are often inaccurate. Mentally impaired clients may be oblivious to their faulty memories, or they may cover up their memory problems with rationalizations, quips, or fabrications. Objective measures are therefore essential.

Asking the questions on standardized instruments that seem too simple—such as, What year is this?—may at first cause discomfort for the professional and anxiety for the client. It is less threatening when the interviewer puts the client at ease with some introductory remarks to the effect that the questions may seem obvious and silly, but they are part of a routine that everyone goes through. Then the client will usually cooperate.

If the screening test indicates mental impairment, the next step is to ensure a complete enough workup, based on as accurate a history as possible, that the cause of the impairment may be identified. This is no easy matter, as there are more than 60 or 70 possible causes of dementia (Cohen, 1988; Katzman, 1986).

Current estimates indicate that Senile Dementia Alzheimer's Type is the most common cause of diagnosed dementias, accounting for approximately 50 percent of the cases; about 20 percent are caused by strokes or vascular disease (multi-infarct dementia); approximately 18 percent are caused by a combination of Alzheimer's disease and multi-infarct dementia; and the remaining 12 percent are caused by a growing list of miscellaneous conditions, such as tumors, toxins, infections, and metabolic disorders, with the most recent being AIDS.

Differentiating Dementia from Depression and Other Conditions

Those conditions whose symptoms mimic dementia but are potentially reversible when treated have been called pseudodementia. Up to 20 percent of depressed elderly people have been misdiagnosed as suffering from dementia. Other common examples of pseudodementias are those that are due to drug side effects, nutritional deficiencies, or cardiovascular problems.

Because of the difficulty in identifying possible causes of mental impairment, it is essential to involve the family in obtaining an accurate history and to coach family members or significant others in developing skills to uncover the kind of facts that may be important in diagnosis. Family members are often in a crisis when the elderly relative shows signs of mental impairment, and they may need help and encouragement in assuming a responsible role toward their older relative and specific suggestions as to how they can obtain the needed information. For example, family members are in the best position to identify the onset of symptoms, to learn what drugs the patient is taking, and to observe signs of incontinence and constipation, which may be clues to other drugs and nonprescription preparations that may be implicated. Using a crisis intervention approach reframes the problem in terms of partial goals and tasks of limited duration so that even family members who live at a distance or have been estranged can be encouraged to take part in the diagnostic assessment (Kirschner, 1979; Silverstone & Burack-Weiss, 1983). In the absence of family members, practitioners often take on the role of detective, gathering evidence from neighbors, friends, or any source that can provide information.

Practitioners must also be aware that many common drugs for heart conditions or hypertension are safely taken for years by older people but can build up in the system and become toxic, leading to symptoms of mental impairment. It is important for the practitioner, as part of the assessment team, to raise this possibility, even though questioning medication is not always welcomed by the physician. What may seem to be a gradual deterioration of cognitive function and accepted as a symptom of dementia may in fact be a reaction to the gradual toxic buildup of a drug taken over a long period of time for a chronic condition such as hypertension. (An extensive discussion of medication issues appears in chapter 4.)

Furthermore, these same causes can surface as depression, but it is more common for older patients to be labeled demented than depressed. The complexity of establishing an accurate diagnosis of dementia or depression in elderly people cannot be overstated.

To differentiate between dementia and depression as a cause of the presenting symptoms of mental impairment, the following list is a helpful beginning (Ham, Holtzman, Marcy, & Smith, 1983):

Dementia	*Depression*
insidious onset	abrupt onset
fluctuating mood	constant mood
"near-miss" answers	"near-miss" answers
conceals disabilities	highlights disabilities
stable cognitive loss	fluctuating cognitive loss
memory loss occurs first	depressed mood occurs first

These features are more common:
unsociability
uncooperativeness
hostility
emotional instability
confusion
disorientation
reduced alertness

These features are more common:
depressed or anxious mood
sleep disturbances
appetite disturbances
suicidal thoughts

Assessment for Depression

Although there is a lack of consensus on the prevalence of depression in elderly people, it is generally recognized as the psychiatric illness that occurs most commonly in old age, outnumbering all forms of dementia and psychoses (Frengley, 1987). However, studies have shown that depression among elderly patients is often undetected (Goleman, 1988).

Once depression is recognized and not assumed to be a normal reaction to the many losses and stressors in old age, it is eminently treatable (see the section below on treatment). According to Blazer (1986), paradoxically, where there is depression, there is hope.

Some symptoms of depression, such as guilt, feelings of persecution, and lack of self-esteem that are commonly seen in younger patients, may be absent in elderly people. More characteristic symptoms in elderly people are the following:

- withdrawal
- self-neglect
- sleep disturbances
- aches and pains
- emotional changes
- difficulty in concentration
- pessimism
- sadness
- fatigue
- slowness of thought and action
- change in appetite
- lack of libido

- hopelessness
- agitation.

Ham et al. (1983) suggested the following questions in diagnosis:

- Is there sadness of mood out of proportion to circumstances?
- Has there been a loss of interest in life?
- Have friends and social contacts been given up?
- Has there been a change in appetite?
- Have there been suicidal thoughts, plans, or attempts?
- Has there been a loss of libido?
- Has sleep been disturbed?
- Has there been a slowing down of thought or action?
- Have there been difficulties in concentration or memory?

The answers to these questions, by either the patient or knowledgeable family members, help to specify the depth and duration of depressive symptoms and establish the possibility of a diagnosis of depression.

The next important concern in terms of treatment is to distinguish the type of depression. Traditionally, depressions had been identified as "endogenous" (an intrinsic biological state unrelated to circumstances) or "reactive" (related to a specific situation or unresolved conflict). This distinction was discarded in the 1980 DSM-III.

Depression is now described in four ways: major depression, adjustment disorder, minor depression, and bereavement reaction. Reactive depression is no longer considered a clinical entity; the implication of this change is that depression is an illness unto itself and should not be thought of as part of another illness or as a situational response (Frengley, 1987).

According to the DSM-IV, the diagnostic criteria for major depressive episodes are now classified under the section "Mood Disorders," previously called "Affective Disorders." Major depression consists of the following:

1. dysphoric (depressed or sad) mood or loss of interest and pleasure in most usual activities, nearly every day
2. duration of at least two weeks, with at least four of the following symptoms to a significant degree:

   - poor appetite or significant weight loss when not dieting or increased appetite or significant weight gain

- insomnia or hypersomnia nearly every day
- loss of energy or fatigue nearly every day
- psychomotor agitation or retardation nearly every day
- loss of interest or pleasure in usual activities nearly every day or decrease in sexual drive
- feelings of worthlessness or excessive or inappropriate guilt nearly every day
- diminished ability to think or concentrate nearly every day
- suicidal ideation.

In addition, the patient does not have symptoms suggestive of other psychotic disorders.

For elderly patients, four additional criteria are included: (1) an increase in psychosomatic complaints; (2) an increase in complaints about cognitive abilities; (3) a loss of interest associated with apathy, often compounding a sense of worthlessness and guilt; (4) and an increase in alcoholism (Frengley, 1987).

Reviewing the criteria as defined by the DSM-IV reveals that many of these symptoms may also occur as a direct consequence of physical illness or as a result of the treatment of a physical illness. The difficulty in disentangling symptoms of depressive illness from symptoms of a chronic disabling disease in an elderly individual reinforces comments above about the difficulties in differential diagnosis.

Another important consideration regarding differential diagnosis is that often patients are plagued by a combination of depression and conditions other than physical illness. There has been an emphasis on uncovering pseudodementia when it is depression masking as dementia. The reality, according to Blazer (1986), is that most persons exhibiting a depressed affect associated with cognitive impairment are plagued by both depression and chronic dementia. Treatment of the depression should be pursued, because it is often effective, even though the cognitive difficulties are not eliminated.

Despite progress in diagnostic specificity represented by the DSM classifications, there is still no complete agreement on how to differentiate various depressions. Depression has no single cause, and there is no one depressive syndrome (Klerman, 1983).

Indeed, a large number of elderly depressed patients do not fit the DSM classifications at all. They are the clinically suspected

3 to 4 percent who suffer a transient but severe depressive disorder. Although they may suffer obvious losses or stress, these external events are not in proportion to the severity of the symptoms. In addition, the symptoms cause significant impairment, but because they are transient, lasting only two weeks or so, they do not meet the criteria for a diagnosis as a major depressive episode. The DSM-IV would cover these disorders as presenting "with atypical features"; however, they are not at all atypical in their frequency (Blazer, 1986).

Geriatric research has expanded our understanding of the nature and number of categories of depression. Because of the prevalence of depression in elderly people that is associated with physical illness and drug side effects, a major classification scheme for distinguishing different types has now been formulated as primary versus secondary depressive disorders (Klerman, 1983). Primary depressive disorders are those occurring in people without other illnesses. Secondary depressive disorders are manifested typically in those who have a physical illness or are having an adverse drug effect. The high frequency of medical disorders and medication usage among elderly people has increased the visibility of secondary depression. This differentiation has greatly increased understanding of depression and led to improvement in treatment approaches for numerous elderly people (Cohen, 1988).

Some of the medical problems that can produce secondary depressive disorders include: electrolyte disturbances; endocrine disorders, such as thyroid disease or diabetes; anemia; Parkinson's disease; uremia; systemic lupus erythematosus; congestive heart failure; malignant disease (particularly carcinoma of the pancreas, leukemia, and brain tumors); renal failure; hearing loss; vision loss; malnutrition; chronic infections (urinary tract infection and tuberculosis); liver disease; alcoholism; malabsorption syndromes; chronic obstructive pulmonary disease; and influenza (Ham et al., 1983; Klerman, 1983).

It has often been observed that depressed elderly people may be reluctant to admit feelings of dysphoria and that such depression may be masked and present itself primarily as somatic concerns (Gurland, 1976). Various somatic and autonomic symptoms, such as pain, hypochondriasis, obsessional states, and even accidents, have been proposed as "depressive equivalents" (Spar,

1988). Practitioners must be alert to the possibility that such symptoms may be clues to the presence of depression.

Some commonly used drugs that are known to cause depression include the following:

- barbiturates such as phenobarbital
- tranquilizers such as diazepam (Valium) and triazolam (Halcion)
- heart drugs containing reserpine (Serpasil and others)
- beta blockers such as propranolol (Inderal)
- high blood pressure drugs such as clonidine (Catapres), methyldopa (Aldomet), and prazosin (Minipress)
- drugs for treating abnormal heart rhythms, such as disopyramide (Norpace)
- ulcer drugs such as cimetidine (Tagamet) and ranitidine (Zantac)
- anti-Parkinsonians such as levodopa (Dopar) and bromocriptine (Parlodel)
- corticosteroids such as cortisone and prednisone
- anticonvulsants such as phenytoin (Dilantin), ethosuximide (Zarontin), and primidone (Mysoline)
- antibiotics such as cycloserine (Seromycin), isoniazid (INH), ethionamide (Trecator-SC), and metronidazole (Flagyl)
- diet drugs such as amphetamines (during withdrawal from the drug)
- painkillers or arthritis drugs such as pentazocine (Talwin), indomethacin (Indocin), and ibuprofen (Motrin, Rufen, Advil, Nuprin)
- others drugs, including metrizamide (Ampaque), a drug used for diagnosing slipped discs, and disulfiram (Antabuse), the alcoholism treatment drug (Wolfe, Fugate, Hope, Hulstrand, & Kamimoto, 1993).

Although it may seem that a comprehensive geriatric assessment calls for a great deal of specialized knowledge, practitioners can become sufficiently conversant with the principal categories of drugs and illnesses that may cause depression, dementia, or pseudodementia to be able to identify the possible associations and raise the issue with the appropriate physician.

There are still many contradictions in theories about biologic causes or predispositions to depression in elderly people. Studies of the aging brain had indicated the role of increased levels of monamine oxidase as interfering with the activity of other neurotransmitters, specifically norepinephrine and serotonin, which affect moods. However, although depression is prevalent in the elderly, most elderly people are not depressed despite the changes in neurotransmitter levels. More recent research is investigating the mechanisms that regulate neurotransmitter activity and interactions rather than their levels in the body (Cohen, 1988; Maas, Katz, Frazer, & Bowden, 1991; Richelson, 1991; Rossen & Buschmann, 1995; Shelton, Hollon, Purdon, & Loosen, 1991). The effect of age on hormone levels, such as those from the adrenal, thyroid, and pituitary glands, is also being investigated widely, as is the relationship to vascular disease. These studies offer promise of greater understanding of biologic determinants of depression in the next few years (Baldwin & Tomenson, 1995; Billig, 1987).

TREATMENT OF DEMENTIA AND DEPRESSION

Approaches to treatment of these disabling conditions are the subject of many specialized books. For practitioners, the important principle is that assessment, diagnosis, and treatment tasks are all essentially interdisciplinary.

Dementia caused by drugs, other illnesses, or neglect can be reversed. Depression, if diagnosed accurately, can be treated with appropriate drugs, individual and group psychotherapy, environmental adjustments, or electroconvulsive therapy.

Suicide can be the ultimate consequence of missing the seriousness of depressive symptoms in vulnerable older people. Elderly Americans have suicide rates that are twice the national average, with white males at the highest risk, at four times the national average (Mercer, 1989). These figures are low; elderly suicide is consistently underreported because many self-inflicted deaths are not officially documented as such. Because of the stigma attached and guilt for the family, or the institution where it occurred, other causes are often listed officially on death certificates (Kornblum, 1989).

Risk factors for suicide should be part of the knowledge base for all health professionals. These factors include physical illness, previous attempts or gestures, bereavement, isolation and loneliness, use of alcohol, and psychiatric disorders. It is estimated that 50 to 70 percent of late-life suicide victims have had significant depression (Katz, Curlik, & Nemetz, 1988).

A difficult judgment call in assessing the elderly client who refuses treatment, medication, or food is the weight of his or her autonomy, the right to refuse treatment, or even the right to die, versus his or her right to protective care. At issue is usually the competence or capacity of the client to make this decision. If the decision is made while the client is clinically depressed or otherwise mentally impaired, then involuntary hospitalization and treatment might be required, because the client's right to freedom or self-determination must be based on the mental capacity to choose (Lewis, 1984).

Finally, even with conditions that are chronic and irreversible, careful, individualized assessment, along with the new medications, techniques, interventions, and supports that are continually appearing, can ease the problems for the patients and their families. As Cohen (1988) wrote, "Symptoms and suffering can be diminished, coping skills assisted, the dignity of the patient and family preserved" (p. 140). These treatment goals should be the model for all chronic disorders but are particularly relevant for mentally impaired elderly people and their families.

REFERENCES

American Psychiatric Association. (1994). *Diagnostic and statistical manual of mental disorders* (4th ed.). Washington, DC: Author.

Baldwin, R. C., & Tomenson, B. (1995). Depression in later life: A comparison of symptoms and risk factors in early and late onset cases. *British Journal of Psychiatry, 167*(5), 649–652.

Billig, N. (1987). *To be old and sad.* Lexington, MA: Lexington Books.

Blazer, D. (1986). Depression: Paradoxically a cause for hope. *Generations, 10*(3), 21–23.

Busse, E. W., & Pfeiffer, E. (1973). *Mental illness in later life.* Washington, DC: American Psychiatric Association.

Butler, R. N., & Lewis, M. J. (1982). *Aging and mental health* (3rd ed.). St. Louis: C. V. Mosby.

Cohen, J. D. (1988). *The brain in human aging.* New York: Springer.

Eisdorfer, C., & Cohen, D. (1986). *The loss of self.* New York: W. W. Norton.

Folstein, M., Folstein, S., & McHugh, P. R. (1975). Mini-Mental State: A practical method for grading the cognitive state of patients for the clinician. *Journal of Psychiatric Research, 12,* 189–198.
Frengley, J. D. (1987). Depression: Interplay with other chronic illnesses of old age. *Generations, 12*(1), 29–33.
Gallo, J., Reichel, W., & Anderson, L. (1988). *Handbook of geriatric assessment.* Rockville, MD: Aspen.
Generations. (1997, Spring). Using assessment to improve practice: New developments and measures. *Journal of the American Society on Aging, 21*(1).
Goleman, D. (1988, December 22). Depression among elderly patients is often undetected, study finds. *New York Times,* p. 25.
Gurland, B. (1976). The comparative frequency of depression in various adult age groups. *Journal of Gerontology, 31,* 283–292.
Ham, R. J., Holtzman, J. M., Marcy, M. L., & Smith, M. R. (1983). *Primary care geriatrics.* Boston: John Wright.
Kahn, R. L., Goldfarb, A. I., Pollack, M., & Peck, A. (1960). Brief objective measures for the determination of mental status of the aged. *American Journal of Psychiatry, 117,* 326–328.
Kane, R. A., & Kane, R. L. (1981). *Assessing the elderly: A practical guide to measurement.* Lexington, MA: D. C. Heath.
Katz, J. R., Curlik, S., & Nemetz, P. (1988). Functional psychiatric disorders. In L. Lazarus (Ed.), *Essentials of geriatric psychiatry: A guide for health professionals* (pp. 113–137). New York: Springer.
Katzman, R. (1986). Alzheimer's disease. *New England Journal of Medicine, 314,* 964–973.
Katzman, R., Brown, T., Fuld, P., Peck, A., Schechter, R., & Schimmel, H. (1983). Validation of a short orientation–memory–concentration test of cognitive impairment. *American Journal of Psychiatry, 140,* 734–739.
Kirschner, C. (1979). The aging family in crisis: A problem in living. *Social Casework, 60*(4), 209–216.
Klerman, G. L. (1983). Problems in the definition and diagnosis of depression in the elderly. In L. D. Breslau & M. R. Haug (Eds.), *Depression and aging* (pp. 3–19). New York: Springer.
Kornblum, A. (1989, July 23). Elderly suicide: Confronting its reality. *Miami Herald,* p. 5C.
Lewis, H. (1984). Self-determination: The aged client's autonomy in service encounters. *Journal of Gerontological Social Work, 7*(3), 51–64.
Maas, J., Katz, M., Frazer, A., & Bowden, C. (1991). Current evidence regarding biological hypothesis of depression and accompanying pathophysiological processes: A critique and synthesis using clinical and basic research results. *Integrative Psychiatry, 7*(3–4), 155–169.

Mercer, S. O. (1989). *Elder suicide: A national survey of prevention and intervention programs.* Washington, DC: American Association of Retired Persons.

National Institute on Aging Task Force. (1980). Senility reconsidered—Treatment possibilities for mental impairment of the elderly. *JAMA, 244,* 259–263.

Pfeiffer, E. (1975). A short portable mental status questionnaire for the assessment of organic brain deficit in elderly patients. *Journal of the American Geriatrics Society, 23,* 433–441.

Richelson, E. (1991). Biological basis of depression and therapeutic relevance. *Journal of Clinical Psychiatry, 52*(Suppl.), 4–10.

Rossen, E., & Buschmann, M. (1995). Mental illness in late life: The neurobiology of depression. *Archives of Psychiatric Nursing, 9*(3), 130–136.

Safford, F. (1986). *Caring for the mentally impaired elderly.* New York: Henry Holt.

Shelton, R., Hollon, S., Purdon, S., & Loosen, P. (1991). Biological and psychological aspects of depression. *Behavior Therapy, 22*(2), 201–228.

Silverstone, B., & Burack-Weiss, A. (1983). *Social work practice with the frail elderly and their families.* Springfield, IL: Charles C Thomas.

Spar, J. (1988). Principles of diagnosis and treatment in geriatric psychiatry. In L. Lazarus (Ed.), *Essentials of geriatric psychiatry* (pp. 102–112). New York: Springer.

Toseland, R. W., Derico, A., & Owen, M. L. (1984). Alzheimer's disease and related disorders: Assessment and intervention. *Health and Social Work, 9*(2), 212–226.

Wolfe, S. M., Fugate, L., Hope, R. E., Hulstrand, E., & Kamimoto, L. (1993). *Best pills, worst pills. II.* Washington, DC: Public Citizen Health Research Group.

Zarit, S. H., Orr, N. K., & Zarit, J. M. (1985). *The hidden victims of Alzheimer's disease.* New York: New York University.

6 Case Management with the Elderly

Karen M. Sowers-Hoag

The origins of case management are rooted in the early development of the profession of social work at the beginning of the 20th century in the Charity Organization Societies and the Settlement House movement (Austin, 1988). From the beginning of its history to the present, case management has had two sets of goals—one set related to service coordination, including the quality and effectiveness of service, and the other set related to accountability and the cost-effective use of resources (Weil & Karls, 1985).

Certain social currents have stimulated the emergence of case management. In the gerontology field it was advances in medical science, resulting in prolonged life expectancies and diminished responsibility on the part of families to attend to elderly people that accentuated the need for professional continuing care (Rothman, 1991). A fragmented services delivery system and increasing demands on limited resources (Sizemore, Bennett, & Anderson, 1989) further underscored the need for case management services. Such programs have been developed throughout the country in every conceivable setting, from hospitals to private practice. Both public and private sectors have supported implementation of case management, which is widely seen as an effective method of delivering services, especially with long-term care needs (White, Goldis, & Cebula, 1989).

Case management is the coordination of a specified group of resources and services for a specified group of people (Kane, 1988). It is a mechanism designed to produce multiple services to clients with complex needs in a timely fashion (Cabot, Cannon, & Cannon, 1987; Seltzer, Ivry, & Litchfield, 1987). Social workers, as case managers, play a critical role in the successful integration of formal services and services provided by families and other primary groups (Moore, 1990). Social workers serve as enablers, maximizing the potential of individuals and primary groups to function independently and as facilitators, negotiating and providing a liaison among social institutions, organizations, agencies, and people in need (Lowry, 1985).

The increasing emphasis on the use of case management in the delivery of social services is an attempt to provide a strategy that will overcome the neglect and fragmentation of the provision of services to multiproblem or profoundly impaired clients from communitywide multiservice providers (Cabot et al., 1987). The designation of one person as the case manager is an attempt to ensure that one person is responsible and accountable for the provision of quality services addressing all needs within the client system (Miller, 1983) and to ensure that clients do not "fall through the cracks" of the service delivery system. The role of case manager involves not only providing direct services but also assuming responsibility for linking the client to diverse resources and ensuring that the client receives needed services in a timely fashion (Austin, 1988; Johnson & Rubin, 1983; Lamb, 1980; Rothman, 1991; Steinberg & Carter, 1983). Case management is a highly individualized approach in that it assesses the unique needs of each client, and, at the same time, it provides a holistic orientation that views all aspects of the client system, including the client, family, friends, their situation, and their environment.

Since the beginning of this century, the proportion of people over 65 years of age has changed from one out of every 25 people to one out of every nine (Klein, 1989). By the year 2020, this proportion may be as high as one person in five (Neugarten, 1982). With the "graying" of America and the increasing life expectancy for elderly people and developmentally disabled people, we can expect that the role of case management will become increasingly important.

STEPS OF CASE MANAGEMENT

The sequential tasks of case management include case finding or screening to identify people in the target population who may require services; comprehensive, multidimensional assessment to determine any individualized unmet needs; care planning, which requires decisions about how the needs identified in the assessment can be met; implementation of the plan; monitoring both the progress of the client and the adequacy of the services given under the plan; and formal reassessment at intervals to gauge continuing need (Kane, 1988; White, 1987) and advocacy (Rothman, 1991).

The role of the case manager is multifaceted and requires problem-solving skills. Depending on the agency setting, the case manager may assume a wide range and level of responsibility, including counselor, problem solver, mediator, resource allocator, goal keeper, data collector, program changer, services manager, negotiator, consultant, documenter, and advocate (Rothman, 1991; White, 1987). All of these roles are directed toward using the services available to an individual as fully as possible to maintain or improve that person's ability to be independent.

Case Finding

Because case management is not appropriate for all elderly people in need of social or health services, education of social services and health-related personnel is crucial in promoting appropriate referrals. Case management is appropriate for those clients who present complicated interacting problems, who need services that cross organizational lines, or who lack the capacity to gain access to services unaided (Kane, 1989). The typical case management client is an older person with multiple chronic functional impairments associated with late life (Gwyther, 1988), including chronic illness, infirmity, and impaired vision or hearing (Hepworth & Larsen, 1986). Often having restricted financial resources and limited mobility, elderly people can become socially isolated to the extent that life becomes barren and empty (Gallos, 1982).

Assessment

Assessment is the bedrock of the helping process that ultimately informs the care planning and implementation stage of practice (Hepworth & Larsen, 1986). The assessment may be performed by a health or social services professional or by an interdisciplinary team. The overall goal of assessment is to develop an individualized treatment plan for the client or family. Assessment in case management is complex with elderly clients (Kane, 1990). The interconnections of the medical, psychological, and social factors in elderly people make assessment the most complicated phase of the treatment process (Morrow-Howell, 1992). Although the assessment procedures in case management differ with the purpose and agency setting, in general, clinical assessment in case management differs from other assessments in that it is more problem-focused than descriptive. Emphasis in the assessment is placed on the history, etiology, restorative potential, and professional judgments that summarize conclusions for other service providers (Gwyther, 1988). There has been a gradual trend in many fields of practice to ensure that assessments are multidimensional, and thus capture data on client performance in a wide variety of life spheres. Additionally, there has been increased emphasis on the assessment of strengths as well as deficits (Hepworth & Larsen, 1986; Saleebey, 1992). Case managers are expected to remain aware of their clients' comprehensive needs as well as their current and potential strengths and weaknesses (Cabot et al., 1987; Intagliata, 1982).

The assessment should be comprehensive, listing and describing all problem areas. Comprehensive assessment typically involves a face-to-face interview between the client and case manager at the client's home. During this meeting, which generally lasts two or three hours, the case manager collects information about the client, using a standardized assessment instrument or form. Data are collected about the client's health, emotional–behavioral status, functional capacity, cognitive capacity, support system (family, friends, neighbors), environment, and financial status (Quinn, 1995). The assessment should include a listing of problems that may or may not be addressed in the care plan, and the rationale for not including these problems in the care plan should be well documented.

Care Planning

Care planning is at the core of case management (Intagliata, 1982; Miller, 1983). *Care planning* is defined as "the process of developing an agreement between client and case manager regarding identified client problems, outcomes to be achieved, and services to be pursued in support of goal achievement" (Schneider, 1988, p. 16). The case manager is the one practitioner who assumes responsibility for ensuring that the plan is implemented in a timely fashion and as intended.

Typically, case managers are expected to develop an overall care plan for each client system. The care plan focuses on the progression of services to be provided over time and the linkages among them and between them and the informal support system (Cabot et al., 1987). Services required often include shopping, housekeeping, personal care, transportation, and bookkeeping.

Planning addresses immediate needs and anticipated needs for such services over time. Careful attention should be paid to determining the priority of problems to be addressed, with an outline of goals, objectives, and tasks clearly delineated throughout the care plan. Designation of responsibility for carrying out tasks and expected time frames for completion should include incorporating the client, family, and other supports participating (when appropriate) in carrying out the care plan.

Standard features of the care plan include a comprehensive and prioritized list of problems; stated operational and measurable expected outcomes for each problem; the anticipated amounts and types of services needed to achieve each desired outcome; an estimation of the costs of providing the listed services; and a contractual agreement with the client, case manager, and other parties assuming responsibility for the care plan.

One of the most challenging and often neglected aspects of the care plan is the element of creativity and individualization required of the case manager in addressing the assessed needs. To individualize a care plan, following a problems-based assessment, is to specifically tailor a configuration of specialized services to match the identified need (Sullivan & Fisher, 1994). Good care plans should take consumer preferences into account, including their cultural beliefs and language (Quinn, 1995). However, all too often, programs' care plans reflect a startling sameness. Creative responses to the assessment data are seldom seen (Kane, 1989). Care planning should not be viewed as simply ordering basic or available services. Reliance on formal available services is often not adequate to address all the client's needs. In such instances, the case manager should seek nonservice solutions, by seeking assistance from the informal and volunteer care network (Lieberman & Borman, 1979) and care available from other service systems (Schneider, 1989). A client who has a leaky roof, for instance, may test the case manager's ability to creatively seek a volunteer organization that will donate funds, labor, or supplies on a one-time basis but does not want to make a long-term commitment. Likewise, when the case manager determines that a client requires more services per week than formal entitlements permit, the case manager should seek help from volunteer organizations, friends, or family to augment the services offered by the formal system.

Plan Implementation

Implementation of the care plan requires knowledge and use of a wide range of services from various sources and emphasizes the access and coordination of excising services appropriate for the client's needs. Since case managers are expected to link clients with appropriate services and entitlements, the case manager must know about all available services and informal support networks (Cabot et al., 1987). It is essential that case managers maintain a complete roster of service agencies and organizations in the community, know what each service provides and its policies and procedures, and develop ongoing professional relationships with appropriate personnel in the referring agencies. The personal use of self by the case manager in establishing and maintaining linkages with personnel in referral agencies is of critical importance. The informal relationships, the give and take between agency personnel, and the level of respect held by others for the case manager often affect the extent of willingness on the part of others to "go the extra mile" to help find community resources for the case manager's clients. Reciprocity, collegiality, and respect developed between and among personnel will dramatically influence the success of a case manager's ability to access needed services from formal and informal organizations.

In addition to identifying appropriate referral sources, the case manager must help clients access the services and when necessary serve as an advocate for the client. These duties may include assisting clients in overcoming barriers such as lengthy or difficult form completions, applying for and attending hearings when clients are denied entitlement payments, interceding when undue delays in services persist, and so on. Similarly, the case manager must anticipate and be prepared to provide appropriate supports to help clients in implementing the care plan when clients are resistant or in danger of dropping out of services. Careful attention to incorporating the client and his or her family into the decision-making process during the development of the care plan aids in preventing the development of plans that are unacceptable to the client.

Monitoring

The care plan is the mechanism by which resources in the program or the system are allocated. Even in programs that do not fund services, the care plan is intended to influence the use of resources of other agencies (Schneider, 1988). Thus, monitoring must be applied at the client level and system level.

On the client level, case managers should evaluate the progress of the client throughout the care plan for each stated problem. Monitoring of progress remains the responsibility of the case manager, even for services provided for by other service agencies or contractual providers. The case manager, therefore, oversees and evaluates the effectiveness and affect of all services received by the client. Client problems cannot be viewed discretely because most problems are interactive. Because failure to resolve one problem area may very well have an impact on other problems and perhaps the entire care plan, monitoring must be continuous throughout the care plan process. Monitoring should include the use of objective repeated measures to assess ongoing progress (see Bloom, Fischer, & Orme, 1994). Service providers may be valuable assets in the development of the monitoring plan and may participate in the monitoring process through the collection and reporting of progress data. The case manager is also responsible for monitoring the progress of the client. In cases in which the amount and quality of services are being delivered as required but the clients are not progressing toward the stated goals, the case manager must reassess the viability and appropriateness of the care plan and consider possible alternatives that may be more effective in addressing the client's problems (Corcoran, 1988; Nurius & Hudson, 1993).

Systematic monitoring of client progress has become more simplified in the last 10 years. The introduction of the use of practice technology to assess client progress through the use of single-system designs and the proliferation of reliable and valid instruments to use with elderly clients has increased our ability in the field of gerontology not only to evaluate ongoing client progress but also to identify selections of appropriate programs of intervention by clarifying the relevant factors involved in the problem (see, for example, Austin, 1981; Gambrill, 1985; Linsk, Howe, & Pinkston, 1975). Through the development and wide dissemination of realistic, accurate, and practical measures of change, practitioners now can fulfill the requirements of accountability as well as their own growing sense of personal obligation to their clients to evaluate their intervention. This proliferation of brief, rapid assessment instruments that are easy to administer and score now allows practitioners to use objective, quantifiable indicators of progress in a manner that can be accomplished in several minutes.

As in most human services areas, the field of gerontology has witnessed the development of rapid assessment instruments designed specifically for use with elderly people. Examples of the breadth of content covered by available assessment instruments include the Geriatric Depression Scale (Yesavage, Brink, Rose, & Leirer, 1983), the Hypochondriasis Scale for Institutional Geriatric Patients (Brink et al., 1978), Attitude Toward the Provision of Long-Term Care (Klein, 1992), Caregiver Strain Index (Robinson, 1983), Caregiver's Burden Scale (Zarit & Bach-Peterson, 1980), Concern about Death-Dying and Coping Checklists (Fry, 1990), Irritability/Apathy Scale (Burns, Folstein, Brandt, & Folstein, 1990), Memory and Behavior Problems Checklist (Zarit & Zarit, 1985), and Realizations of Filial Responsibility (Seelbach, 1978).

Other rapid assessment instruments for adults that may be appropriate for use with elderly people but have not been normed on geriatric populations include such scales as the Adult Health Concerns Questionnaire (Spoth & Dush, 1988), Death Depression Scale (Templer, LaVoie, Chalgujian, & Thomas-Dobson, 1990), Emotional/Social Loneliness Inventory (Vincenzi & Grabosky,

1987), McGill Pain Questionnaire (Melzack, 1975), Multidimensional Scale of Perceived Social Support Scale (Zimet, Dahlem, Zimet, & Farley, 1988), Social Avoidance and Distress Scale (Watson & Friend, 1969), and Trust in Physician Scale (Anderson & Dedrick, 1990). Many other useful and appropriate indexes and scales are readily available for practitioner use. In the past, instruments were widely scattered throughout the literature. Practitioners found it difficult and time consuming to attempt to locate and access the measurement instruments. A book entitled *Measures for Clinical Practice* (Fischer & Corcoran, 1994) is a useful ready reference sourcebook that presents the most up-to-date and satisfactory measures of change for almost any problem a practitioner might encounter. This book should be on the shelf of every case manager and social services practitioner working in a human services setting. Through the use of this book, case managers will be able to meet the growing demands for accountability.

The increasing concern for accountability on the part of funding sources and services consumers will continue to demand a greater use of systematic outcome procedures. With the proliferation of managed care providers and tightened government regulation in the social services, case managers in all fields will feel the increased demand to evaluate what they do. Case managers and agencies providing case management services will be required to document the effectiveness of their services to receive continued funding.

On the system level, case managers have a responsibility to make themselves aware of and identify gaps in the service delivery system (Schneider, 1988). Services that are not readily available because of lengthy waiting periods should also be identified. Case managers may act as advocates at the local, state, or national level to address service inadequacies within their community.

Formal Reassessment

Functional losses for elderly people are rarely static. Changes in the client's physical and emotional functioning may occur frequently. Similarly, the client's available support from family and friends may fluctuate over time. These anticipated changes in the life of elderly people underscore the importance of frequent formal reassessments. Reassessments should be conducted with emphasis on each problem area previously identified. New or emerging strengths and weaknesses should be carefully noted. In addition, the reassessment should attempt to isolate new problem areas. Changes in the status of the client system may require additions or adjustments to the care plan. Any additions or adjustments must be considered in light of the interactive effect these changes may have on the overall care plan.

CLINICAL ASPECTS OF CASE MANAGEMENT WITH ELDERLY PEOPLE

Until recently, the majority of literature on case management with elderly people has focused on the coordination of services as the central function. The theory of case management—focusing on systems, networks, supports, linkages, and tracking—has not addressed many of the clinical aspects of case management. While there may be situations where the case manager simply or easily links clients with resources, the real world of case management is usually much more complex. Good clinical skills are essential for effective case management. Case managers cannot function without performing direct care tasks and using specialized direct service knowledge and skills (Intagliata, 1982; Lamb, 1980; Lourie, 1978; Miller, 1983). Clinical skills are necessary to understand and deal with the client's resistances, ambivalence, and dependency issues (Soares & Rose, 1994). The clinical aspects of case management focus on the roles of the elder, the family, and the practitioner in a reciprocal process over time (Burack-Weiss, 1988). Clinical skills such as development of the client–worker relationship, interviewing, assessment, and problem solving are crucial elements in the development and implementation of an accurate, adequate, and successful care plan. In case management with elderly people, a clinical understanding is especially important because the clients may be quite frail and at great risk, creating an urgency to intervene. Clients are faced with loss and grief, fears and anxieties, and unmet dependency needs. The role of the case manager necessitates understanding these issues and containing the clients' anxieties to help them come to terms with their lives and their losses, and finally, impending death (Soares & Rose, 1994).

Relationship Building

Case managers are often faced with clients who have strong personal values and preferences that may be in opposition to a proposed care plan. Additionally, some clients may be unwilling to accept formal help (White et al., 1989). Despite the quality of the assessment and care plan, these individuals may not follow through with the plan. Careful attention to the development of the worker–client relationship can enhance client follow-through (Burack-Weiss, 1988). The development of trust in the case manager promotes honesty in communication and allows the case manager to view the presenting problems from the client's perspective. Relationship building with the client and family members requires time on the part of the case manager. Although time is often at a premium for agency-based case managers, the rewards of a successful care plan are worth the time invested, especially when the waste of time involved in developing a care plan that is subsequently sabotaged by the client or family is considered.

Individualizing Care Plans

With the advent of case management, there has been an increasing tendency to focus on fitting the client to the existing community resources rather than focusing on the individuality of client needs and how best to tailor a program plan to meet them (Burack-Weiss, 1988). Individualization of care plans requires that the case manager establish rapport and trust with the client system. Careful and astute exploration during the assessment process aids in developing the client–worker relationship and gathering all information necessary to understand all the dimensions of the client's problems. To recognize the uniqueness and individuality of each client, the case manager must endeavor to understand the client's life experience, including thoughts, feelings, world views, daily stresses, joys, hopes, fears, disappointments, and all the myriad facets of human experience (Hepworth & Larsen, 1986).

Advocacy

Advocacy is an important, and often neglected, aspect of case management for elderly people (Rubin, 1987). Recent research indicated that when social workers provide case management services, there is a greater emphasis on the advocacy function (Douville, 1993). During the linking process, the client and case manager may encounter barriers to service. Advocacy involves an affirmative or assertive approach to assisting a client in receiving services or amenities that are being withheld unfairly (Rothman, 1991). Barriers can range from the more tangible problems of geographic inaccessibility to more subtle forms of practitioner resistance. To overcome these barriers, a case manager must have sound advocacy skills. Case managers must be able to move from thinking about barriers to services for a particular client (case advocacy) to a concern about how barriers can affect groups (class advocacy) (Dattalo, 1992). The case manager should be prepared to help the client move through bureaucratic rules and blocks and obtain benefits that are due (Rothman, 1991). Advocacy strategies range from discussion, persuasion, prodding, educating, campaigning, confrontation, and coercion.

Client Self-Determination

The medically oriented model of care used most frequently in case management assumes, somewhat paternalistically, that it is the professionals who can best evaluate the clients' needs and prescribe the appropriate interventions (Sabatino, 1989). At the same time, we have to recognize the autonomy of the client as crucial, especially because a major goal of care is to foster client independence and autonomy. Experience suggests that care plans may be well developed and thought through only to fail (Mosher & Burti, 1992). Often this occurs because the client was not instrumental in the development of the plan and, therefore, the final product does not reflect the stated problem or goals of interest to the client (Burack-Weiss, 1988).

A central value underlying case management practice is self-determination. This value has a bias toward least-restrictive environments. The fear of loss of control over one's life in later years is common. Fostering client participation in the assessment and care plan can offer to the elderly client the opportunity to continue to exercise choice and may reinforce feelings of competence and control. Similarly, when the client participates in the decision-making or problem-solving process, the chances for success are increased, and the likelihood of client sabotage is lessened. Social work case managers uphold the value of self-determination by recognizing the strengths of individuals and primary groups. When individuals and primary groups do as much as they can, formal services can be integrated in ways that complement rather than compete with informal systems of care (Moore, 1990).

CONCLUSION

Despite the fact that case management is still in its infancy, health and social services providers, especially in the field of aging, have embraced case management as the "new form of social work." Expectations of the role and functions of case management vary significantly among programs. There is also great variation in the level of education, skill, and experience expected of case managers. Recently, there has been a proliferation of agencies providing "case management services." However, merely designating staff members as case managers is no guarantee that case management aims will be achieved (Bachrach, 1983). Case management was developed to address specific problems in the delivery care system with specific types of clients. Care must be taken that case management does not become a trendy job title synonymous with social work. Although born from the social work profession, case management requires a specific set of skills and knowledge and assumes the combination of unique processes incorporating clinical, generalist, and administrative social work practice.

As the health care delivery system changes in response to technology, drug developments, and costs of care, many models of case management have emerged as part of the process of change. A review of the current literature on case management reveals that these various models, such as medical case management, social case management, vocational case management, and intensive case management, have developed to serve a variety of client populations, with a lack of attention to the applicability of these models to other populations. Agencies, without direction from governmental authorities, continue to develop their own models.

Evidence regarding the potential efficacy of case management programs was promising initially (Akabas, Fine, & Yasser, 1982;

Boone, Coulton, & Keller, 1981; Douville, 1993; King, Muraco, & Wells, 1984), although not every study of the use of case management with elderly people had positive results (Coulton & Frost, 1982). Caution must be exercised when interpreting the meaning of evaluations of case management programs and generalizing from them. Often, programs evaluated experimentally are implemented under ideal conditions that are not readily transferable to the field (Cabot et al., 1987). The lack of consistency in conforming to a professionally agreed on and accepted definition of case management services for elderly people by private and public health and social services providers presents additional obstacles in evaluating the effectiveness of their impact on service delivery (Douville, 1993). There clearly is a need for greater specificity in enunciating the roles and tasks of case management (Greenberg, Austin, & Doth, 1981) and the required qualifications of persons who fulfill these tasks. As though in response to the inherent inconsistencies reflected between the needs of vulnerable clients and the range of professionals deemed qualified, private geriatric case managers have formed an organization to address the need for professional standards of practice and have adopted the name "care managers" to emphasize the ethical imperative to individualize care, and not to treat clients as "cases." While the intent is commendable, there is considerable collaborative work necessary to reach consensus on appropriate goals and appropriate mechanisms for ensuring accountability (Steinberg & Carter, 1983).

The development of successful case management models will require substantial commitment to the care of older people within the community. Currently, federal budget restraints have limited most case management services to medically oriented agencies because they are reimbursed by Medicaid, Medicare, or private insurance (Wood & Estes, 1988). This situation may deter case managers from providing a holistic approach to assessing the client's problems (Roff & Atherton, 1989). In addition, case managers often find themselves functioning in a community with an inadequate social services delivery system and interfacing with programs unresponsive to the needs of elderly people.

Although case management is not needed by everyone, it shows promise with dependent populations such as the frail elderly. It has provided a means to assist many clients to maintain an optimal level of independence in the midst of a fragmented, duplicative, and confusing service delivery system (Morrow-Howell, 1992; White, 1987). Models of case management with the elderly that place primary emphasis on social services coordination have been developed (Sizemore et al., 1989). These models are typically found in programs in local agencies on aging under the department of social services, or within county or state health and welfare agencies (Crossman, 1986). Hospital-based case management is a recently developing model, encompassing the coordination and monitoring of health and social services, including in-home service providers, to reduce fragmented care. In the near future, we can expect further development of innovative models for geriatric case management, including private practice and community support models. The challenge for each community will be to provide uniform and comprehensive assessment, care planning and case management, information, referral, and brokering of services across the public and private sectors and across types of service providers. Gaps in the system that delivers services to elderly people must be documented and a united community effort mobilized to advocate for the needed services. Unless these goals can be accomplished, services to elderly people will remain fragmented and clients will continue to fall through the cracks despite the case manager's best efforts.

REFERENCES

Akabas, S. H., Fine, M., & Yasser, R. (1982). Putting secondary prevention to the test: A study of an early intervention strategy with disabled workers. *Journal of Primary Prevention, 2,* 165–187.

Anderson, L. A., & Dedrick, R. F. (1990). Development of the Trust in Physician Scale: A measure to assess interpersonal trust in patient–physician relationships. *Psychological Reports, 67,* 1091–1100.

Austin, C. D. (1981). Client assessment in context. *Social Work Research & Abstracts, 17,* 4–12.

Austin, C. D. (1988). History and politics of case management. *Generations, 12,* 7–10.

Bachrach, L. L. (1983). New directions in deinstitutionalization planning. In L. L. Bachrach (Ed.), *New directions in mental health services: Deinstitutionalization* (pp. 93–106). San Francisco: Jossey-Bass.

Bloom, M., Fischer, J., & Orme, J. (1994). *Evaluating practice: Guidelines for the accountable professional* (2nd ed.). Englewood Cliffs, NJ: Prentice Hall.

Boone, C. R., Coulton, C. J., & Keller, S. M. (1981). The impact of early and comprehensive social work services on length of stay. *Social Work in Health Care, 7*, 65–73.

Brink, T. L., Bryant, J., Belanger, J., Capri, D., Jascula, S., Janakes, C., & Oliveira, C. (1978). Hypochondriasis in an institutional geriatric population: Construction of a scale (HSIG). *Journal of the American Geriatrics Society, 26*, 552–559.

Burack-Weiss, A. (1988). Clinical aspects of case management. *Generations, 12*, 23–25.

Burns, A., Folstein, S., Brandt, J., & Folstein, M. (1990). Clinical assessment of irritability, aggression and apathy in Huntington and Alzheimer Disease. *Journal of Nervous and Mental Disease, 178*, 20–26.

Cabot, R. C., Cannon, I. M., & Cannon, M. A. (1987). Case management. In A. Minahan (Ed.-in-Chief), *Encyclopedia of social work* (18th ed., Vol. 1, pp. 212–222). Silver Spring, MD: National Association of Social Workers.

Corcoran, K. J. (1988). Selecting a measuring instrument. In R. M. Grinnell, Jr., (Ed.), *Social work research and evaluation* (3rd ed.). Itasca, IL: F. E. Peacock.

Coulton, C., & Frost, A. K. (1982). Use of social and health services by the elderly. *Journal of Health and Social Behavior, 23*, 330–339.

Crossman, L. (1986). Case management today and tomorrow. *Coordinator, 5*, 20–22.

Dattalo, P. (1992). Case management for gerontological social workers. In R. Schneider & N. Kroph (Eds.), *Gerontological social work* (pp. 138–169). Chicago: Nelson-Hall.

Douville, M. L. (1993). Case management: Predicting activity patterns. *Journal of Gerontological Social Work, 20*(3/4), 43–55.

Fischer, J., & Corcoran, K. (1994). *Measures for clinical practice: A sourcebook* (2nd ed.). New York: Free Press.

Fry, P. S. (1990). A factor analytic investigation of home-bound elderly individual's concern about death and dying and their coping responses. *Journal of Clinical Psychology, 46*, 737–748.

Gallos, F. (1982). The effects of social support networks in the health of the elderly. *Social Work in Health Care, 8*, 65–74.

Gambrill, E. D. (1985). Social skills training with the elderly. In L. Abate & M. Milan (Eds.), *Handbook of social skills training* (pp. 326–357). New York: John Wiley & Sons.

Greenberg, J., Austin, C., & Doth, D. (1981). *A comparative study of long-term care demonstrations, Vol. I: Lessons for future inquiry.* Minneapolis: Center for Health Services Research, University of Minnesota.

Gwyther, L. P. (1988). Assessment–content, purpose, outcomes. *Generations, 12*, 11–15.

Hepworth, D., & Larsen, J. (1986). *Direct social work practice: Theory and skills*. Chicago: Dorsey Press.
Intagliata, J. (1982). Improving the quality of community care for the chronically mentally disabled: The role of case management. *Schizophrenia Bulletin, 8,* 655–674.
Johnson, P., & Rubin, A. (1983). Case management in mental health: A social work domain. *Social Work, 28,* 419–425.
Kane, R. (1988). Introduction: Case management. *Generations, 12,* 5–6.
Kane, R. A. (1989). Introduction. In *Concepts in case management*. Unpublished manuscript, University of Minnesota, Long-Term Care Decisions Resource Center, Minneapolis.
Kane, R. (1990). Assessing the elderly client. In A. Monk (Ed.), *Handbook of gerontological services,* (2nd ed., pp. 55–89). New York: Columbia University Press.
King, J. A., Muraco, W. A., & Wells, J. P. (1984). *Case management: A study of patient outcomes.* Columbus: Ohio Department of Mental Health, Office of Program Evaluation and Research.
Klein, W. C. (1989). A generic model of long-term care for social work education. *Journal of Social Work Education, 25,* 224–234.
Klein, W. C. (1992). Measuring caregiver attitude toward the provision of long-term care. *Journal of Social Service Research, 16,* 147–162.
Lamb, H. (1980). Therapist-case managers: More than brokers of services. *Hospital and Community Psychiatry, 31,* 762–764.
Lieberman, M., & Borman, L. R. (1979). *Self-help groups for coping with crisis.* San Francisco: Jossey-Bass.
Linsk, N., Howe, M. W., & Pinkston, E. M. (1975). Behavioral group work in a home for the aged. *Social Work, 20,* 454–463.
Lourie, N. V. (1978). Case management. In J. A. Talbott (Ed.), *The chronic mental patient* (pp. 164–169). Washington, DC: American Psychiatric Association.
Lowry, L. (1985). *Social work with the aging: The challenge and promise of the later years* (2nd ed.). New York: Longman Green.
Melzack, R. (1975). The McGill Pain Questionnaire: Major properties and scoring methods. *Pain, 1,* 277–299.
Miller, G. (1983). Case management: The essential services. In C. J. Sanborn (Ed.), *Case management in mental health service* (pp. 3–16). New York: Haworth Press.
Moore, S. T. (1990). A social work practice model of case management: The case management grid. *Social Work, 35,* 444–448.
Morrow-Howell, N. (1992). Clinical case management: The hallmark of gerontological social work. In *Geriatric social work education* (pp. 119–129). New York: Haworth Press.

Mosher, L., & Burti, L. (1992). Relationships in rehabilitation: When technology fails. *Psychosocial Rehabilitation Journal, 15*(4), 11–17.
Neugarten, B. L. (1982). Older people: A profile. In B. L. Neugarten (Ed.), *Age or need?* (pp. 33–54). Beverly Hills, CA: Sage Publications.
Nurius, P., & Hudson, W. W. (1993). *Human sources: Practice, evaluation, and computers.* Pacific Grove, CA: Brooks/Cole.
Quinn, J. (1995). Case management in home and community care. *Journal of Gerontological Social Work, 24*(3/4), 233–248.
Robinson, B. C. (1983). Validation of a caregiver strain index. *Journal of Gerontology, 38,* 344–348.
Roff, L. L., & Atherton, C. R. (1989). *Promoting successful aging.* Chicago: Nelson-Hall.
Rothman, J. (1991). A model of case management: Toward empirically based practice. *Social Work, 36,* 520–528.
Rubin, A. (1987). Case management. In A. Minahan (Ed.-in-Chief), *Encyclopedia of social work* (18th ed., Vol. 1, pp. 212–222). Silver Spring, MD: National Association of Social Workers.
Sabatino, C. (1989). Home care quality. *Generations, 13,* 12–16.
Saleebey, D. (1992). *The strengths perspective in social work practice.* New York: Longman.
Schneider, B. (1988). Care planning—The core of case management. *Generations, 12,* 16–18.
Schneider, B. (1989). The process of care planning: How to do it. In *Concepts in case management.* Unpublished manuscript, University of Minnesota, Long-Term Care Decision Resource Center, Minneapolis.
Seelbach, W. C. (1978). Correlates of aged parents' filial responsibility expectations and realizations. *Family Coordinator, 27,* 341–350.
Seltzer, M. M., Ivry, J., & Litchfield, L. C. (1987). Family members as case managers: Partnership between the formal and informal support networks. *Gerontologist, 27,* 722–728.
Sizemore, M. T., Bennett, B. E., & Anderson, R. J. (1989). Public hospital-based geriatric case management. *Journal of Gerontological Social Work, 13,* 167–179.
Soares, H. H., & Rose, M. K. (1994). Clinical aspects of case management with the elderly. *Journal of Gerontological Social Work, 22*(3/4), 143–156.
Spoth, R. L., & Dush. D. M. (1988). The Adult Health Concerns Questionnaire: A psychiatric symptoms checklist. *Innovations in Clinical Practice: A Sourcebook, 7,* 289–297.
Steinberg, R., & Carter G., (1983). *Case management and the elderly.* Lexington, MA: Lexington Books.

Sullivan, W. P., & Fisher, B. J. (1994). Intervening for success: Strengths-based case management and successful aging. *Journal of Gerontological Social Work, 22*(1/2), 61–74.

Templer, D. I., LaVoie, M., Chalgujian, H., & Thomas-Dobson, S. (1990). The measurement of death depression. *Journal of Clinical Psychology, 46*, 834–839.

Vincenzi, H., & Grabosky, F. (1987). Measuring the emotional/social aspects of loneliness and isolation. *Journal of Social Behavior and Personality, 2*, 257–270.

Watson, D., & Friend, R. (1969). Measurement of social-evaluation anxiety. *Journal of Consulting and Clinical Psychology, 33*, 448–457.

Weil, M., & Karls, J. M. (1985). *Case management in human service practice.* San Francisco: Jossey-Bass.

White, M. (1987). Case management. In *The encyclopedia of aging* (pp. 92–96). New York: Springer.

White, M., Goldis, L., & Cebula, D. (1989). Implementing the care plan: Challenges of case management. In *Concepts in case management.* Unpublished manuscript, University of Minnesota, Long-Term Care Decisions Resource Center, Minneapolis.

Wood, J. B., & Estes, C. L. (1988). Medicalization of community services for the elderly. *Health & Social Work, 13*, 35–42.

Yesavage, J. A., Brink, T. L., Rose, T. L., & Leirer, V. O. (1983). Development and validation of a geriatric depression screening scale: A preliminary report. *Journal of Psychiatric Research, 17*, 37–49.

Zarit, S. H., Reever, K. E., & Bach-Peterson, J. (1980). Relatives of the impaired elderly: Correlates of feelings of burden. *Gerontologist, 20*, 649–655.

Zarit, S. H., & Zarit, J. M. (1985). *The hidden victim of Alzheimer's disease: Families under stress.* New York: New York University Press.

Zimet, G. D., Dahlem, N. W., Zimet, S. G., & Farley, G. K. (1988). The multidimensional scale of perceived social support. *Journal of Personality Assessment, 52*, 30–41.

7 Working with Traditional and Nontraditional Families of Elderly People

Carol R. Odell and Florence Safford

In recent years, there has been a growing awareness of the significance of the family to older clients, as well as recognition of the impact of increasing numbers of the very old on the family as a whole. Nowhere is this more pertinent than in the field of health, which is floundering under the burden of the high cost of care. In part because of these high costs, the viability of the family is often put to the test when the family must provide care to an elderly member at a time of acute medical need or for a chronic physical or mental disability.

To work effectively with these challenged families, practitioners must understand the nature of relationships in the older family, in terms of the family's capacity to provide both the basic human needs for affiliation, affection, and self-esteem to its elderly and whatever concrete, instrumental services are needed. To fully understand the dynamics of all generations, practitioners must first examine their own attitudes and beliefs about what family members owe one another.

Many practitioners working with elderly people express the belief that contemporary families do not care for their elders the way they did in "the old days" when many caring relatives were available, under one roof, to provide care if needed. This is a romantic vision of a past golden age from which modern man has fallen, the "world we have lost" syndrome (Laslett, 1965). Historians have shown this widely held belief to be an ideal that was never characteristic of American society (Hess, 1979).

Concerned about another widely held belief, the notion that elderly people are alienated from their families, sociologists have been studying relationships in older families for the past few decades, examining visiting and helping patterns. They have demonstrated that elderly people are involved in their family networks, living near enough to at least one family member to be in regular contact, and that they both receive and give help as needed (Brody, 1985; Shanas, 1979b; Sussman, 1976). Despite this evidence, the "alienation myth" has persisted, leading to ongoing discourse in the literature as to the true status of elderly people in the family system (Shanas, 1979a; Silverstone & Hyman, 1989). Scholarly opinion has now shifted to an equally generalized concept of elderly people as embedded in a supportive, caring network, which provides 80 percent of all home care services.

What is really known about the status of elderly people in their family networks? What is known about the quality and meaning of their relationships? What do we really know about the experience of caregiving as it is provided by what is euphemistically called "the informal support system"?

QUALITY OF FAMILY RELATIONSHIPS

Let us first examine the issue of the status of elderly people in the family in the context of their intergenerational relations. Traditionally, elders have been accorded respect and authority (not necessarily affection) by virtue of their age and presumed wisdom. Many family studies have pointed out that authority and respect, and indeed even family solidarity, have been affected as much by economic necessity as by loyalty and affection (Bengston & Treas, 1980).

The preference for independence between generations is the predominant cultural norm in western societies. One of the earliest characterizations of this preference of older people and their children, often quoted, is "intimacy at a distance." This phrase describes the wish to live separately and autonomously but near enough for intimacy (Rosenmayr & Kockeis, 1963).

One of the social functions remaining with the modern family after so many have been taken over by formal organizations is the provision of emotional support and intimacy. The family serves as a refuge or haven from the impersonal pressures of large bureaucratic systems, the place where a sense of personal control and intimacy can be found (Laslett, 1978).

How valid is this concept for the majority of older women who are widowed? Or for those elders who become isolated by physical or mental frailty? Are their needs for intimacy really met within the family? There are indicators that lead to the conclusion that many older people refrain from expressing their disappointment in their children to preserve family stability. They try to minimize differences (Bengston & Treas, 1980).

What has been described as "intimacy at a distance" may be "pseudo-intimacy," according to Blau (1973), a facade of family solidarity that obscures the loneliness of the elderly parent. Blau pointed out that parents and children have a mutual interest in preserving the fiction that parents are "insiders" and not "outsiders." Blau noted that although most children feel obligation and guilt toward aging parents, they do not necessarily provide a needed loving relationship.

Troll (1982) implicated a generation gap between elderly people and their adult offspring as causing diminished intimacy. Differences in moral values and approaches to life exist between these two older cohorts, just as frequently as between the young and middle cohorts. These gaps do not always lead to confrontation and conflict, however. Family discussions tend to avoid touchy issues for the sake of family integration.

One of the most reliable surveys of a large, cross-sectional sample, conducted by Harris and Associates (1975), found that only 25 percent of the 55- to 65-year-old population, and 43 percent of the over-80 population, felt close enough to their children to talk to them about "things that really bothered them."

Cicirelli (1983) also found that offspring are less likely to share intimate details of their lives and important decisions with older parents. He stated that they might avoid conflict by limiting the relationship to less intimate and important aspects of their personal lives. Despite this evidence of lack of intimacy, parents often report feeling closer to offspring than vice versa (Bengston & Black, 1973).

Ethnic families have been viewed as providing strong emotional support to their elders as well as mutual aid as a means of compensating for discrimination and prejudice. Researchers have reported that these assumptions are unfounded with respect to the capacity of modern ethnic families. Although the following studies are not comparable, and some results have been contradictory, there is clear evidence of the need for a closer look at assumptions about the strength of supports available for elders.

Regarding Hispanic elders, there is a tendency among practitioners and the public to romanticize, distort, and stereotype critical elements of family interaction. But a picture is emerging in which, despite a continuing ideal of intense intergenerational family concern and the actual availability of large kin networks, obligations and expectations of kin support are declining rapidly (Applewhite, 1988; Valle & Mendoza, 1978). Hispanic elders in San Diego, for example, were found to be less likely than whites to turn to their extended family in time of need, preferring to "suffer in silence" (Weeks & Cuellar, 1981). As a result of these disparities between the cultural expectations and the actual behaviors, high levels of alienation and a high degree of psychological problems have been found, particularly among elderly Hispanic women, whose disappointment with children and family is related to unmet needs dictated by traditional ethnic expectations (Sokolovsky, 1985).

Studies of other racial and ethnic groups have also brought into question the stereotyped view of the family support system as a resource for elderly people. They have alerted us to the cultural variations in norms of filial obligation and degrees of familism and have shown that support levels may be predicted more accurately by socioeconomic levels than ethnicity. They have found that high levels of family assistance in black populations, for example, are not apparent when social class is controlled as a variable, indicating that ethnic family support may also be forced by economic need at times (Gratton & Wilson, 1988; Rosenthal, 1986). Therefore, relying solely on family members for support and assistance may not meet the needs of families of color who are challenged to meet the cultural expectations of family bondedness while they struggle with the competing expectations of their occupational responsibilities.

These findings support Litwak's "shared function" theory, which identified the need for formal, agency-based services to complement the efforts of the family (1985).

CHALLENGE OF CAREGIVING

Not only is the older generation vulnerable when it looks to the family for affection and closeness, but the family is vulnerable as well when it assumes the challenge of caregiving to meet the needs of its dependent elderly (Zarit & Toseland, 1989).

Caregiving is a term coined and popularized in the past 25 years as the needs of the increasingly aged population emerged as a social problem. So many families are now confronted by this developmental crisis that parent care is now considered normative (Brody, 1985). Caregivers are now providing care to elderly parents for an average of 18 years, in contrast to 17 years for dependent children (U.S. House of Representatives Select Committee on Aging, 1987). Furthermore, the majority of these caregivers are employed outside of the home, and managing these conflicting responsibilities causes increased strain. Studies estimate that approximately 20 percent of workers in the United States have some type of caregiving responsibility, including executives as well as laborers (Lechner, 1991).

Hundreds of research reports have explored the stresses of caregiving and studied various interventions to ease the burdens, arriving at contradictory conclusions (Barer & Johnson, 1990; Biegel & Blum, 1990; Pearlin, Mullan, Semple, & Skaff, 1990).

There is an unbelievable lack of attention in the caregiving research, however, to the specifics of the tasks, leading to a total lack of comparability of the many studies. The term *caregiving* is used to describe such easy services as shopping, light housekeeping, and helping with finances, as well as an array of difficult services including personal care, managing incontinence, and total supervision of a severely impaired older person (Raveis, Siegel, & Sudit, 1988–1989; Zarit & Toseland, 1989).

Families are universally praised by practitioners and public commentators for maintaining their elderly in the community without knowledge of the nature of the care provided, whether it is based on economic necessity, or family solidarity and affection, or both. Home care is lauded by health care providers and policy analysts without concern as to whether the caregiver is too sacrificial, possibly demanding submission in exchange, and without attention as to whether the care is adequate or the caregiver competent to fulfill the physical and psychological needs of the older relative. There is also a lack of attention in the caregiving literature to the issue of whether the care required is short term or long term, or whether there is any respite available.

Who is the caregiver? It is generally assumed to be a middle-aged female in the family. The term *sandwich generation* has become popular to describe the middle-aged women who are sandwiched between responsibilities for elderly parents and responsibilities for college-aged or newly married but still dependent children (Miller, 1981). They constitute 77 percent of the adult children caring for frail and impaired elders (Abel, 1987). However, although growing numbers of working women are feeling burdened by the needs of their elderly parents, they continue to accept the caregiver role. They do so in part because of the typical assumptions that it is a moral duty for the family to care for its elders and that within the family it is primarily the responsibility of the women to fulfill this role. Feminist theorists have shown that women's identity includes a greater internalization of an injunction to care (Graham, 1984) and that they often judge themselves according to an ethic of responsibility to others (Gilligan, 1982). Thus, caregiving, which affects the entire family, is disproportionately accepted as a woman's burden.

Research findings indicate that the most overlooked caregivers are elderly spouses, who often need help with finances and respite (Zarit, Todd, & Zarit, 1986). Other studies have indicated that caregiver stress and capability are extremely varied, depending on both objective measures of burden and the subjective response to the demands (George, 1994; Kramer, 1997; Stuckey , Neundorfer, & Smyth, 1996). There is clearly a need to carefully assess each caregiving situation individually, recognizing the complex social and emotional forces that influence the giving and receiving of help. Practitioners can provide immeasurable aid to overwhelmed caregivers by helping them recognize the impact of traditional rules for behavior on the structure of modern families and by encouraging an appropriate balance of tasks with services from formal organizations.

An important resource to help in educating and counseling caregivers is a 12-part video series produced by the Dade County, Florida, Department of Human Services. It covers areas such as family relations, caregiver stress, leisure activities for the elderly, medication issues, and finances, as well as practical aspects of nursing and home care (available through Dade County Elderly Services Division, [305] 375-5335).

FAMILIES OF HOSPITALIZED AGED PEOPLE

Health care professionals, particularly in acute care settings, often find themselves spending as much or more time with the families of their elderly patients as they do with the patients themselves. The reasons for this are many: some of the patients are unable to assist in their own discharge planning, so family members are called upon to assist; family members seek help to deal with their feelings, the hospital system, and the community social services system; the hospital staff is called upon not just to discharge the patient, but to "do something" about family members who present patient care dilemmas, who ask challenging questions, who visit too often or not often enough, who seem to make the patient unhappy, or who are not really "family."

Who are these families, and how do we determine who is included? First, it is necessary to look at who is affected by events in the life of the elder. For whom does his or her illness, incapacitation, or reduced functioning make a difference? Who is touched by reverberations within the system considered significant to the patient?

Some of the traditional family members with whom practitioners work are the spouse, the children, the siblings, the cousins, and even the grandchildren. In this era of increasing longevity, sometimes the family of the old patient includes the still older, or oldest-old, generation.

Many elderly patients, however, are not fortunate enough to have members of their families living locally—they may have retired to the Sunbelt, leaving working members of their family in other states; they may be immigrants from any number of countries who now populate the cities, but have no relatives in the United States; they may have a long history of estrangement from their family; or they may simply have outlived all their relatives. They may be among those elderly people whose local relatives have left large urban areas because of high crime rates, changing demographics, and high cost of living. Often the elderly person declines to leave with the family because he or she is accustomed to the familiar neighborhood.

Without the availability of traditional family members, many resourceful elderly people have established pseudofamilies. Senior centers and adult day care facilities provide opportunities for the development of meaningful surrogate family relations. In a group discussion about family relations at a senior day care program, members whose next of kin lived far away often repeated the theme, "this is my family" or "you all are my family" (May & Flanagan, 1990).

Some elderly people have never had a family, and so for the most part friends have met their needs for affection and attention. Included in this group are homosexual elderly people and, to a somewhat lesser extent, those elderly people who have led isolated lives until physical or mental deterioration pushed them to turn to others, or others to reach out to them. Included in this latter group are those elderly people who have had a lifetime substance abuse problem or who are chronically and seriously mentally ill (Rathbone-McCuan & Hashimi, 1982).

Boundaries for older families are more difficult to identify than those for younger families. Older families sometimes include friends and exclude blood relatives. Friends and neighbors often function as families for elderly people—they share holidays with them, take them shopping and to the doctor, help them manage their banking, fill out their insurance forms, and assist with or arrange for housekeeping and yard help. Sometimes the significant other will be a postman, store owner, or employee of a business well known to the elderly individual. Sometimes the family is a homosexual partner or an "unlikely" heterosexual partner—someone "too" young or otherwise related, like a former sister-in-law.

Therefore when reaching out to the family for assistance, it is important for the practitioner to determine who it is who matters to the older patient and to whom the older patient matters. The more accepting the practitioner can be about the kind of family the patient needs, wants, and has accepted, the more effective he or she will be.

Some special considerations apply to the older homosexual man or woman. They are less likely to acknowledge their sexual orientation than are younger people (Berger, 1984; Berger & Kelly, 1986). Because of this reluctance, they may need to minimize the "friendship" of a partner or even give misleading information about a former spouse and children. Practitioners who are open to the patient's lifestyle differences and sensitive to his or her need to play a "straight" role can better facilitate the participation of the friend and the patient in significant planning. The professional's "buying into" the fabrication can make both friend and patient feel freer to participate in the planning process.

The past decade, however, has seen a shift in awareness and acceptance of homosexuality, even among elderly people (Kimmel, 1992; Quam & Whitford, 1992). Where family ties are lacking, surrogate families are sometimes developed through support groups (Slusher, Mayer, & Dunkle, 1996). Professionals should recognize the particularly varied forms of ties that are available for this population.

Another segment of the aging family population that may be overlooked consists of the old-old survivors of the Holocaust and their now young-old children. The unspeakable pain and anguish of these survivors continue to be documented, and many family and individual problems are being identified as resulting from posttraumatic stress (Bergmann, 1982; Kinsler, 1988). Practitioners can prepare for dealing with some of these issues by reading some of the growing body of literature related to this often repressed historical experience (Kestenberg, 1982; Laub & Auerhahn, 1985; Rosenbloom, 1983; Safford, 1995; Steinitz, 1982).

INTERVENTIONS WITH ELDERS AND THEIR FAMILIES

Tolstoy observed at the beginning of *Anna Karenina* that happy families are all alike—but each unhappy family is unhappy in its own way. This timeless wisdom can help practitioners remember to follow the basic principles of individualizing assessment of the troubled elderly client and his or her family, after casting away their own counterproductive assumptions and myths.

One of the basic areas in which older families need help is in recognizing the excess value placed on independence, which denies the reality of social interdependence. This value, along with the cherished norm of reciprocity, is so strongly internalized that most elderly people resist accepting help, even when their frailty is obvious. The "fear of becoming a burden" is one of the most common fears in late life (Harris and Associates, 1975).

Practitioners working with aging families should assist the generations in the area of communication to facilitate the expression of feelings about giving and receiving aid. Family members generally feel concern and responsibility when their elders become dependent. These feelings are related to the indebtedness they feel to their parents, the reciprocal duty to pay back in late life what was given earlier. These family members are frequently stressed by the unfamiliar role of assuming responsibility, which has been described as the developmental task of filial maturity (Blenkner, 1965). This task can be accomplished only with the cooperation of the elders, who must be willing to accept the assistance of their children. The task can be facilitated when reframed as a function of loyalty and justice over the generations, that is, in terms of the concept of generational ledgers in which the love, support, and concrete services provided over a lifetime are credited and "banked," available to be drawn upon for support and care when needed later in life (Boszormenyi-Nagy & Spark, 1973). This concept can ease the giving and receiving of help.

This model for ethical family behavior can help put into perspective the conflicts experienced by family members as their personal choices and individual needs become limited by the competing needs of frail or dependent elders.

A cautionary note is indicated, however, with respect to reciprocity and generational ledgers, when the balance sheet shows debits instead of credits. Reciprocity sometimes calls for "getting even," or "paying back," for ancient hurts and unmet psychological or instrumental needs. Families may need help in learning to forgive in order to accept protective and caring roles.

Another caution is urged when counseling middle generations to accept and meet the dependency needs of very elderly parents. The amount of help that is required may be beyond the capacity of the "aging children" and may cause excess stress for all generations.

Families should be helped to recognize the growing role of social services, home health services, congregate housing, and, when appropriate, institutional services to complement their efforts for their elders (Brody, 1985). These formal supports can often meet the needs of elderly people, including emotional and self-esteem needs, more satisfactorily than the families. Families and formal organizations can function optimally as an interdependent partnership in sharing care of the dependent elderly (Dobrof & Litwak, 1977).

Many researchers have addressed the issue of dependable behavior and competing responsibilities (Hess & Waring, 1983; Safford, 1987; Schlesinger, Tobin, & Kulys, 1980; Silverstone & Hyman, 1989). Silverstone and Hyman pointed out that even caring and responsible family members may not necessarily want to be intimate with one another. Their book, *You and Your Aging Parent*, can guide families to balanced behavior by making them aware of the normal variations in family conflicts and the range of options they can choose to meet their unique needs.

Schlesinger et al. (1980) studied the relationship between parental morale and the behavior of the offspring who were designated the "responsible child." They found that although there was not a high degree of interaction between the generations, the parents' well-being was associated with their perception of the children as aware of what their wishes would be in a crisis and their children's knowledge of community resources. The parents were satisfied with the expectation of future responsible care management by their designated child. These findings were supported by more recent research on expectations of filial responsibility (Hamon & Blieszner, 1990).

A common response to a parent's increasing dependence is concern or "worried watchfulness." This is becoming a prevalent bond between the generations (Marshall, Rosenthal, & Synge, 1983). This watchful concern is related to lack of knowledge and skills in assessing when help is needed, how much to offer, and how to provide it, in addition to lack of skills in communication of needs within the family. This is another area where practitioners can help by facilitating communication between generations.

This need for knowledge and skills was addressed in an early training program (in 1975) for families of impaired elderly people. The program provided knowledge about the aging process, guidance for the assumption of new roles, and psychological support, leading to one of the first support programs of families of the mentally impaired aged (Safford, 1980). Families can now be referred to similar support programs throughout the country through the Alzheimer's Association (telephone: [800] 621-0379). Family education programs and support group interventions are offered through many public and voluntary agencies that serve elderly people. Information for referrals is generally available through the local agency on aging.

Still another approach to helping families meet the needs of their elders when they are challenged by apparently overwhelming demands is offered in several empathic guide books, which provide insights, knowledge, and principles for problem solving (Bumagin & Hirn, 1979; Eisdorfer & Cohen, 1986; Safford, 1987; Shelley, 1988; Silverstone & Hyman, 1989).

Family efforts to balance competing responsibilities are supported by the responses of social institutions to supplement family care with home health care and, when appropriate, nursing home care. Family relationships can be enhanced if the excess stress due to idealized expectations is reduced through the use of these community resources that still permit a role for the family (Bengston & Smith, 1979; Dobrof & Litwak, 1977). Litwak's theory of shared function between primary groups and formal organizations, in which each complements the other's goals, is another useful framework to reduce the conflicts in family members who believe they have to provide all the care themselves (Litwak & Meyer, 1966).

There are many other examples of programs offering concrete services and emotional support to encourage maximum family involvement in the lives of their elders, such as senior centers, adult day care, Meals-on-Wheels, and friendly visiting, to cite a few (Lowy, 1980; Monk, 1985). Many have been in existence for decades, and others continue to emerge as innovative models, such as various forms of respite care to relieve caregivers. To provide services for families that live at a distance from their frail elders, geriatric case managers have emerged as private practitioners. Some agencies have developed case management services for long-distance caregivers such as "Family Lifeline" of the Jewish Family Services (Ehrlich & Frank, 1988).

Finally, it must be acknowledged that there are no simple solutions to the complexities of relationships in the aging family. Several texts are now available with varied models of interventive techniques. A selected bibliography appears at the end of this chapter. In addition, Volume 17 of *Generations*, "A New Look at Families and Aging" (1992), provides a stimulating update on the diverse families in late life and the complex issues that challenge them today.

Kuypers and Bengston (1983) caution wisely that improving family relations may not be the right goal for all members of the family. The notion that more interaction is better, or that "closer equals happier," must be avoided. In "Toward Competence in the Older Family," they suggest the following steps to assess the capacity of the older family to meet its needs for support and to help it provide the support necessary to avoid social breakdown:

- clarify nature of crisis event
- suggest roles of short-term involvement
- examine family resources, expectations, and conflicts
- examine moralisms and guilt
- describe and mobilize external supports
- delimit reasonable involvements
- identify feasible goals
- foster realistic view of future
- mobilize strengths; avoid old issues
- program quick success
- follow up on and develop external supports.

Although not labeled as such, it is a framework through which practitioners can join an elderly family in a nonjudgmental and accepting manner to help them help themselves in the context of their own value systems and family system. This highly recommended crisis approach offers a model for communicating with the vulnerable family that can lead to a rapid understanding of the expectations and resources of the family.

REFERENCES

A new look at families and aging. (1992, Summer). *Generations, 17*(3).

Abel, E. K. (1987). *Love is not enough: Family care of the elderly*. Washington, DC: American Public Health Association.

Applewhite, S. (1988). *Hispanic elderly in transition*. New York: Greenwood Press.

Barer, B., & Johnson, C. (1990). A critique of the caregiving literature. *Gerontologist, 30*, 26–29.

Bengston, V., & Black, K. (1973). Intergenerational relations and continuities in socialization. In P. Bales & K. Schaie (Eds.), *Life-span developmental psychology* (pp. 207–234). New York: Academic Press.

Bengston, V., & Smith, K. (1979). Positive consequences of institutionalization: Solidarity between elderly parents and their middle-aged children. *Gerontologist, 19*, 438–447.

Bengston, V., & Treas, J. (1980). The changing family context of mental health and aging. In J. Birren & K. Schaie (Eds.), *Handbook of mental health* (pp. 400–428). Englewood Cliffs, NJ: Prentice Hall.

Berger, R. (1984). Realities of gay and lesbian aging. *Social Work, 29*, 57–62.

Berger, R., & Kelly, J. (1986). Working with homosexuals of the older population. *Social Casework, 67*, 203–210.

Bergmann, M. (1982). Recurrent problems in the treatment of survivors and their children. In M. Bergmann & M. Jocovy (Eds.), *Generations of the Holocaust* (pp. 247–266). New York: Columbia University Press.

Biegel, D. E., & Blum, A. (Eds.). (1990). *Aging and caregiving: Theory, research and policy.* Newbury Park, CA: Sage Publications.

Blau, Z. (1973). *Old age in a changing society.* New York: Watts.

Blenkner, M. (1965). Social work and family relationships in later life with some thoughts on filial maturity. In E. Shanas & G. Streib (Eds.), *Social structure and the family* (pp. 46–59). Englewood Cliffs, NJ: Prentice Hall.

Boszormenyi-Nagy, I., & Spark, G. (1973). *Invisible loyalties.* New York: Harper & Row.

Brody, E. (1985). Parent care as normative stress. *Gerontologist, 25*, 19–29.

Bumagin, V., & Hirn, K. (1979). *Aging is a family affair.* New York: Crowell.

Cicirelli, V. (1983). Adult children and their elderly parents. In T. Brubaker (Ed.), *Family relationships in later life* (pp. 31–46). Beverly Hills, CA: Sage Publications.

Dobrof, R., & Litwak, E. (1977). *Maintenance of family ties in long-term care.* Washington, DC: U.S. Department of Health, Education, and Welfare.

Ehrlich, P., & Frank, T. (1988). Family lifeline: Bridging the miles. *Gerontologist, 28*, 108–111.

Eisdorfer, C., & Cohen, D. (1986). *Loss of self.* New York: W. W. Norton.

George, L. K. (1994). Caregiver burden and well-being: An elusive distinction. *Gerontologist, 34*, 6–7.

Gilligan, C. (1982). *In a different voice: Psychological theory and women's development*. Cambridge, MA: Harvard University Press.

Graham, H. (1984). Caring: A labour of love. In J. Finch & D. Groves (Eds.), *A labour of love: Women, work and caring* (pp. 13–30). London: Routledge & Kegan Paul.

Gratton, B., & Wilson, V. (1988). Family support systems and the minority elderly: A cautionary analysis. *Journal of Gerontological Social Work, 13*(1/2), 81–94.

Hamon, R., & Blieszner, R. (1990). Filial responsibility expectations among adult-child older parents pairs. *Journal of Gerontology, 45*(3), 110–112.

Harris, L., and Associates. (1975). *The myths and realities of aging in America.* Washington, DC: National Council on Aging.

Hess, B. (1979, January 9). Family myths. *New York Times,* Op-Ed page.

Hess, B., & Waring, J. (1983). Family relationships of older women. In E. Markson (Ed.), *Older women* (pp. 227–251). Lexington, MA: Lexington Books.

Kestenberg, J. (1982). Survivor parents and their children. In M. Bergmann & M. Jocovy (Eds.), *Generations of the Holocaust* (pp. 83–102). New York: Columbia University Press.

Kimmel, D. C. (1992). The families of older gay men and lesbians. *Generations, 17*(3), 37–38.

Kinsler, F. (1988). The loneliness of the Holocaust survivor. *Journal of Psychology and Judaism, 12*(3), 156–177.

Kramer, B. J. (1997). Gain in the caregiver experience: Where are we? What next? *Gerontologist, 37*, 218–232.

Kuypers, J., & Bengston, V. (1983). Toward competence in the older family. In T. Brubaker (Ed.), *Family relationships in later life* (pp. 211–228). Beverly Hills, CA: Sage Publications.

Laslett, B. (1978). Family membership, past and present. *Social Problems, 25*(5), 476–490.

Laslett, P. (1965). *The world we have lost.* London: Methuen.

Laub, D., & Auerhahn, N. (1985). Knowing and not knowing the Holocaust [Special issue]. *Psychoanalytic Inquiry, 5*(1).

Lechner, V. M. (1991). Predicting future commitment to care for frail parents among employed caregivers. *Journal of Gerontological Social Work, 18*(1/2), 69–84.

Litwak, E. (1985). *Helping the elderly: The complementary roles of informal networks and formal systems.* New York: Guilford Press.

Litwak, E., & Meyer, H. (1966). A balance theory of coordination between bureaucratic organizations and community primary groups. *Administrative Science Quarterly, 11*, 35.

Lowy, L. (1980). *Social policies and programs on aging.* Lexington, MA: Lexington Books.

Marshall, V., Rosenthal, C., & Synge, J. (1983). Concerns about parental health. In E. Markson (Ed.), *Older women* (pp. 253–273). Lexington, MA: Lexington Books.
May, A., & Flanagan, M. (1990). Satisfaction with intergenerational relations. Unpublished manuscript, N. E. Focal Center Adult Day Care Program, Deerfield Beach, FL.
Miller, D. A. (1981). The "sandwich" generation: Adult children of the aging. *Social Work, 26*, 419–423.
Monk, A. (Ed.). (1985). *Handbook of gerontological services*. New York: Van Nostrand Reinhold.
Pearlin, L. I., Mullan, J. T., Semple, S. J., & Skaff, M. M. (1990). Caregiving and the stress process: An overview of concepts and their measures. *Gerontologist, 30*, 583–594.
Quam, J., & Whitford, G. (1992). Adaptations and age-related expectations of older gay and lesbian adults. *Gerontologist, 32*, 367–374.
Rathbone-McCuan, E., & Hashimi, J. (1982). *Isolated elders*. Rockville, MD: Aspen.
Raveis, V., Siegel, K., & Sudit, M. (1988–1989). Psychological impact of caregiving on the care provider: A critical review of extant research. *Journal of Applied Social Sciences, 13*, 40–79.
Rosenbloom, M. (1983). Implications of the Holocaust for social work. *Social Casework, 64*, 204–213.
Rosenmayr, L., & Kockeis, E. (1963). Propositions for a sociological theory of aging and the family. *International Social Science Journal, 15*, 410–426.
Rosenthal, C. (1986). Family supports in later life: Does ethnicity make a difference? *Gerontologist, 26*, 19–24.
Safford, F. (1980). A training program for families of the mentally impaired elderly. *Gerontologist, 20*, 656–660.
Safford, F. (1987). *Caring for the mentally impaired elderly: A family guide*. New York: Henry Holt.
Safford, F. (1995). Aging stressors for Holocaust survivors and their families. *Journal of Gerontological Social Work, 24*(1/2), 131–153.
Schlesinger, M., Tobin, S., & Kulys, R. (1980). The responsible child and parental well-being. *Journal of Gerontological Social Work, 3*(2), 3–16.
Shanas, E. (1979a). Social myth as hypothesis: The case of family relations of old people. *Gerontologist, 19*, 3–9.
Shanas, E. (1979b). The family as a social support system in old age. *Gerontologist, 19*, 169–174.
Shelley, F. (1988). *When your parents grow old* (2nd ed.). New York: Harper & Row.

Silverstone, B., & Hyman, H. (1989). *You and your aging parent* (3rd ed.). New York: Pantheon.

Slusher, M. P., Mayer, C. J., & Dunkle, R. E. (1996). Gays and lesbians older and wiser (GLOW): A support group for older gay people. *Gerontologist, 36,* 118–123.

Sokolovsky, J. (1985). Ethnicity, culture and aging: Do differences really make a difference? *Journal of Applied Gerontology, 4*(1), 6–17.

Steinitz, L. (1982). Psychosocial effects of the Holocaust on aging survivors and their families. *Journal of Gerontological Social Work, 4*(3/4), 145–152.

Stuckey, J. C., Neundorfer, M. M., & Smyth, K. A. (1996). Burden and well-being: The same coin or related currency? *Gerontologist, 36,* 686–693.

Sussman, M. (1976). The family life of old people. In R. Binstock & E. Shanas (Eds.), *Handbook of aging and the social sciences* (pp. 415–449). New York: Van Nostrand Reinhold.

Troll, L. (1982). Family life in middle and old age: The generation gap. *Annals of the American Academy of Political and Social Science, 464,* 38–46.

U.S. House of Representatives Select Committee on Aging. (1987). *Exploring the myths: Caregiving in America.* Washington, DC: U.S. Government Printing Office.

Valle, R., & Mendoza, L. (1978). *The elderly Latino.* San Diego, CA: Campanile Press.

Weeks, J., & Cuellar, J. (1981). The role of family members in the helping networks of older people. *Gerontologist, 21,* 388–394.

Zarit, S., Todd, P., & Zarit, J. (1986). Subjective burden of husbands and wives as caregivers: Longitudinal study. *Gerontologist, 26,* 260–266.

Zarit, S., & Toseland, R. (1989). Current and future directions in family caregiver research. *Gerontologist, 29,* 481–483.

SUGGESTED READINGS

Biegel, D., Shore, B., & Gordon, E. (1984). *Building support networks for the elderly: Theory and applications.* Newbury Park, CA: Sage Publications.

Burnside, I., & Schmidt, M. G. (1994). *Working with the elderly: Group process and techniques* (3rd ed.). Boston: Jones and Bartlett.

Eyde, D. R., & Rich, J. A. (1983). *Psychological distress in aging: A family management model.* Rockville, MD: Aspen.

Greene, R. (1986). *Social work with the aged and their families.* New York: Aldine de Gruyter.

Hartman, A., & Laird, J. (1983). *Family centered social work practice.* New York: Free Press.

Lustbader, W., & Hooyman, N. (1994). *Taking care of aging family members: A practical guide.* New York: Free Press.

Silverstone, B., & Burack-Weiss, A. (1983). *Social work practice with the frail elderly and their families.* Springfield, IL: Charles C Thomas.

Springer, D., & Brubaker, T. H. (1984). *Family caregivers and dependent elderly.* Newbury Park, CA: Sage Publications.

8 Ethnic Issues in Health Care Delivery to Elderly People: Specific Focus on Black Americans and Hispanics

Terry Conward and Gema G. Hernandez

In planning the delivery of health care services, there is a tendency to consider "minorities" as one group. This lumping together ignores the between-group and within-group variations that exist. There are within-group variations in class mores, values, beliefs, practices, and socialization patterns among ethnic groups. Sometimes there are as many within-group variations as there are variations between groups.

The misconception about the within-group homogeneity of ethnic groups is borne out in the fact that much of the research conducted about blacks has been done with lower-class subjects and the findings have then been generalized to the entire black population. These generalized findings become the norm for all blacks and are measured against the norm for whites that was established with middle-class subjects. Comparative studies use these same sample populations, ignoring important class differences that translate into differences in values, beliefs, practices, and socialization patterns.

This chapter addresses issues that affect the delivery of health care services to ethnic groups. Specifically, it focuses on cultural values and beliefs, culturally influenced health care practices, and the role of family and caregivers among blacks and Hispanics. Finally, a psychosocial model for culturally sensitive services delivery is presented.

Terry Conward provided the general information on ethnic issues and the specific focus on black Americans, and Gema G. Hernandez provided the focus on Hispanics.

THE PROBLEM OF GENERALIZATIONS

Whenever we address ethnic issues, we run the risk of making generalizations with which some may take issue. In generalizing, or attempting to derive or induce an overriding concept from particulars, it is understood that the process necessarily neglects certain bits of information. That is, it is understood that generalizations about a group do not and cannot apply to every member of the group. Nevertheless, generalizations have their place. It is useful, and indeed necessary, for the practitioner to take into account certain relevant cultural differences in working with an ethnic patient. However, it is a mistake to apply social work knowledge, principles, and techniques to all patients as if these differences do not exist.

One of the major barriers to culturally sensitive practice is a fear of appearing racist when using these generalizations. Often we are fearful of expressing opinions because we do not want to be accused of being biased. Therefore, we pretend that we have no prejudices. The truth is that everyone has prejudices. We often unconsciously act on those prejudices when delivering services to ethnic groups, without recognizing and confronting these prejudices, getting beyond them, and understanding the cultures of those we are trying to serve. We must begin to focus more on cultural and ethnic differences, preferences, and strengths as we intervene in people's lives at such a critical point as hospitalization or chronic illness with lasting disability. If the cultural and ethnic differences that make each group special are ignored, the intervention will be ineffective.

PLIGHT OF ELDERLY PEOPLE OF COLOR

Many factors have affected the economic and social plight of elderly people of color. The lack of equity in educational opportunities hindered upward mobility and participation in social security and retirement benefits. Even today, de facto segregation across this country acts to limit educational opportunities for young adults from oppressed racial and ethnic groups, creating a situation in which there is never parity. Even when the educational variable is addressed, men of color are still more likely to be unemployed or underemployed, with little opportunity to significantly affect their economic future (Taylor & Chatters, 1988).

Women, blacks, and Hispanics are more likely than white males to be concentrated on the edges of the labor market, with lower wages, minimal fringe benefits, and high vulnerability to economic fluctuations. This segmentation of the market has direct consequences for lifetime earnings and the availability of private pension plans. Lifelong disadvantages in the marketplace become disproportionate impoverishment in old age.

The plight of elderly people of color has been characterized as one of "double jeopardy" or multiple hazards (Jackson, 1980). Unlike other older people, these men and women bear the additional economic, social, and psychological burdens of living in a society in which racial equality remains more myth than social policy.

When the double jeopardy hypothesis was initially postulated by the National Urban League in 1964, the focus of concern was in the areas of income and health. These remain the major problems confronting elderly people. The data presented by Taylor and Taylor (1982) indicated that the black elderly population had lower incomes, less education, lower occupational status, less adequate housing, and poorer health than did the white elderly population.

Some historical perspectives may help to explain why many black aged individuals have inadequate income despite pension or old age assistance. Historically, blacks living in or migrating to urban areas to attempt to build a life of security found themselves inadequately equipped, whether by general education, job training, or experience, to qualify for the better-paying, usually more secure jobs. Today, therefore, these blacks who have survived to age 65 or older have generally accrued little if any retirement benefits. Because the early social security program did not include domestic servants and farm laborers, the majority of blacks were excluded from this benefit (Ehrlich, 1975).

Today, although the overwhelming majority of elderly black families, whether headed by men or women, receive social security income, poverty still characterizes the black elderly disproportionately to the white elderly (Hill, 1978; Jackson, 1988).

The majority of the black elderly represent a population too old to work or too undereducated to qualify for work. During their productive years, they were at the bottom of the economic ladder. As a result, their retirement benefits are inadequate and often must be supplemented by supplemental security income (SSI). The black elderly, despite marked increase in their standard of living since 1965, with the advent of SSI, still remain the poorest of the poor and are 10 times more likely to be on welfare than any other ethnic population (U.S. Department of Health and Human Services, 1980). According to the most recent census information, the poorest of all elderly people are unmarried black women, 60 percent of whom had incomes below the poverty level in 1990 (U.S. Bureau of the Census, 1991).

HEALTH AND HEALTH PRACTICES AMONG BLACK AMERICANS

There is general agreement among investigators that health is a crucial problem for most black elders (Jackson, 1988; Morrison, 1983). Data indicate that one-fourth of all aged blacks have health problems. Surprisingly, blacks in all socioeconomic levels experience similar problems related to health and use of health-related resources. This situation is attributed to the fact that, among the very old, even those who were financially successful, blacks were subjected to discriminatory practices that resulted in unequal access to physicians and mistrust of hospitals. As a consequence, they tended to rely on folk health beliefs.

The literature on black elderly people points to diversity in lifestyles, socioeconomic status, living arrangements, education, and life satisfaction. However, a general profile depicts the black elderly person as someone who is living alone, single, poor, undereducated, and in poor health (Williams, 1980). The black frail elderly tend to be sicker and more likely to be confined to their homes than any other ethnic group. The literature points to discrimination in health care, underuse of health services, sharing of medications, and use of folk remedies as epidemiological explanations as to why this population is sicker at the point of entry into health care systems and tends to remain so (Jackson, 1978; Wolf, Breslau, Ford, Ziegler, & Ward, 1983).

The most pressing problems involve access to health care, patient education, and the prevention of morbidity and mortality associated with diseases for which blacks are at high risk (Carter, 1988). The black elderly are at risk and disproportionately suffer from hypertension, diabetes, and heart disease, along with the problems of vision and hearing loss suffered by all aged regardless of race (Jackson, 1978). Obtaining satisfactory medical care is difficult for poor aged blacks who are dependent on government health care from the county or through Medicaid. Many elderly people are required to make multiple appointments to correct a problem that could have been taken care of in one visit, so that doctors can get adequate reimbursement from Medicaid by billing for each visit (Jackson, 1978).

Black Americans tend to underutilize traditional health care systems because of economic issues. Many resort to home remedies passed down by family tradition. There is a tradition of folk medicine practice, which varies among groups. The vast majority do not frequent folk healers or "root doctors." Those who do tend to alternate between the root doctor and traditional medicine, but do not use both at the same time.

Among people from The Bahamas living in Miami, seeking treatment through folk medicine is common practice. Their proximity to their homeland makes for easy access to a well-organized folk healing system. There is constant travel between The Bahamas and Miami. They also make use of American root doctors. They tend to use orthodox health systems only for crises and, therefore, are chronically in poor health.

People from Haiti living in Miami, on the other hand, use orthodox health systems as much as possible. They make frequent use of emergency rooms, even for routine medical problems. They prefer Haitian doctors and tend to be lifelong patients of the same doctor. Generalizations regarding Haitian health practices are difficult to make because many are illegal aliens whose lack of status as U.S. citizens leads to a strong sense of community and mutual aid. If one person in the community has a health card that provides care in a clinic, others will use the same card to obtain care, a situation that leads to confusion in health records.

HEALTH AND HEALTH PRACTICES AMONG HISPANICS

Specific information about the cultural values and beliefs of elderly Hispanics and their caregivers, and how these values and beliefs affect their health and health practices is scarce. Before what is known can be discussed, however, it is necessary to define and delineate the many subgroups that make up the Hispanic population.

Who Are the Hispanics?

Hispanics are considered by many to be a homogeneous group, but in reality they are one of the most heterogeneous ethnic groups. As a group, Hispanics share a unique cultural and social heritage and a remote historical past. The recent historical experience of Hispanics living in the United States reflects a wide range of intragroup variation. This intragroup variation exists among Cuban, Puerto Rican, and Mexican Americans.

Cuban Americans migrated from an island whose political history and geographic location created a fusion of elements that gave Cubans their sense of uniqueness (Hernandez, 1991a). The Puerto Ricans are by birth U.S. citizens, but their country of origin does not enjoy full statehood status. Mexican Americans comprise two distinct populations. One group, the majority, has lived for generations in territory that once belonged to Mexico but now belongs to the United States. Mexican ancestral territory comprises what is today the states of California, New Mexico, Arizona, Texas, and Utah (Lopez & Aguilar, 1990). As a result of this loss, Mexico was forced to create a man-made border. Across this artificially created border has come the second population, the Mexican Americans who constitute the biggest influx to this country of undocumented Hispanics.

The term *Hispanic* does not convey unique racial or facial characteristics. Hispanics belong to the three major races. White Hispanics are direct descendants of English and Spanish colonists (Saruski & Mosquera, 1979). Brown Hispanics can trace their roots to the Aztecs, Maya, and other indigenous groups and are of the Mongoloid race. Finally, there are a number of Hispanics whose ancestors came from Africa at the time of slavery, and they are black (Ortiz, 1979). In addition, just like in any other group, interracial relations have produced a mixture of the three races.

Hispanics have a common language, Spanish, although this is not true when we include Brazilians, who speak Portuguese, or Paraguayans and Guatemalans, who speak Guarani and Quechua, respectively.

A great number of Hispanics are Roman Catholics, but Hispanics also practice Judaism, Protestantism, and Santeria and attend Jehovah's Witness and Mormon churches (Pedraza, 1990).

Not all Hispanics living in the United States are foreign born. On the contrary, 71 percent of these Hispanics were born in the

United States. The others were born primarily in Mexico, Cuba, or a Central American country (Delgado, 1991).

The degree of acculturation present among Hispanics varies from full acculturation to the host culture, as with some Mexican American elderly whose families have lived in the Southwest for generations, to no acculturation because of age or recent migration. Even though the Cuban Americans were the last group of Hispanics to come to this country in large numbers with a sense of peoplehood, their rate of acculturation exceeds that of any other ethnic group in the history of the United States (Hernandez, 1991a). The de-Cubanization (Gonzales-Reigosa, 1976) of the first generation of Cuban Americans was an important phenomenon that caused great distress to their elderly parents, who observed the disappearance of the cultural values and beliefs of their homeland.

The median age of the Cubans at the time of their political migration was 58 years (Carbonell, 1991). The Cuban Americans are the oldest Hispanic group living in the United States today, as well as one of the oldest groups among the general non-Hispanic population. In 1990, the median age of Cuban Americans was 41.4 years, and the median age for the non-Hispanic population was 34.9 years (Delgado, 1991). The median age of Hispanics as a group, including Cuban Americans, was 25.9 years (Lopez & Aguilar, 1990). This makes Hispanics as a group the group with the youngest population in the United States. If the Cuban group is taken from this calculation, the median age of the Hispanic group drops by almost 10 years. Of all Hispanics, only Cuban Americans have a percentage of elders (17 percent) similar to or higher than the percentage of elders among the general population, that is, 12 percent (Delgado, 1991).

Because of this diversity of racial characteristics, countries of origin, languages, socioeconomic factors, and religious affiliations, to classify someone as Hispanic, we must rely on his or her self-identification. Hispanics cannot be easily identified unless they identify themselves by showing their cultural pride.

Profile of the Elderly Hispanic

According to the National Coalition of Hispanic Health and Human Services Organizations in their National Hispanic Healthy People 2000 Conference (1991), Hispanics as a group are the fastest-growing population in the United States today. They also have the fastest-growing elderly population in this country, growing at a rate seven times higher than the rest of the elderly groups.

The most important problems facing Hispanic elders today are the lack of financial resources, limited transportation, lack of adequate and affordable housing, no access or limited access to health care facilities, and underutilization of public services in general and in-home services in particular (Hernandez, 1991b). As a group, they are less likely to have a pension, and they tend to live in poverty or near the poverty threshold. The median income for Hispanic elderly people was $6,642, compared with $6,069 in the non-Hispanic black population and $10,048 in the non-Hispanic white population (Delgado, 1991).

Hispanic elderly people are geographically concentrated in the southern and western parts of the United States, particularly in California, Florida, and Texas. Eight of 10 Hispanic elderly men and women live in four states—California (25.8 percent), Texas (21.2 percent), Arizona (18.8 percent), and Florida (13.5 percent) (Lopez & Aguilar, 1990). As of March 1989, 47.6 percent of Hispanic elderly were Mexican Americans, 18.8 percent Cuban Americans, 10.9 percent Puerto Ricans, and 8.4 percent from Central America; 15 percent were classified as other (Delgado, 1991). As with the non-Hispanic population, the majority of the elderly Hispanics are female (Lopez & Aguilar, 1990).

Health Characteristics of Hispanic Elderly People

As mentioned above, as a group Hispanics are more likely to be poor and underserved, and they suffer disproportionately more from illness and disability (Delgado, 1991). They have a lower rate of Medigap insurance (medical insurance to cover the portion Medicare does not cover) (Lopez & Aguilar, 1990) and a general distrust of the health care system. They are more likely to be undiagnosed for cervical cancer or untreated for tuberculosis or to suffer unknowingly from uncontrolled diabetes or hypertension (Delgado, 1991).

Cuban Americans have a higher rate of health insurance coverage than any other Hispanic group, and Puerto Ricans are more likely to be covered by Medicaid (Lopez & Aguilar, 1990). This coverage may be why Puerto Ricans use public health care facilities, such as hospitals, outpatient clinics, and emergency rooms, more than any other Hispanic group (Delgado, 1991). Because these data include Puerto Ricans living on their island, they may reflect the lack of linguistic and cultural barriers present in the health care system in Puerto Rico. On the other hand, Mexican Americans are less likely to use such services. Specifically, Mexican Americans do not have routine medical checkups or preventive dental and eye examinations (Lopez & Aguilar, 1990).

Other intergroup differences exist as well. Cuban Americans have the highest rate of Medicare insurance and Mexican Americans the lowest (Espino, 1991). The Cuban American mortality rate is similar to that of the non-Hispanic white population (Espino, 1991). Mexican Americans and Puerto Ricans have the highest death rate among Hispanics (Espino, 1991) and one of the highest among the general non-Hispanic population.

Elderly Hispanics tend to weigh more than non-Hispanic elderly. Cultural factors appear to play a role in the greater acceptance of weight among Hispanics. The high consumption of fat in the native diet, the lack of exercise, and a genetic predisposition to a lower metabolic rate contribute to the propensity for being overweight. Diabetes is three times more common among the Puerto Ricans (26.1 percent) than in the general population (Delgado, 1991), and the rate of diabetes is much lower among the Cuban Americans (15.9 percent) and somewhat lower in the Mexican American population (23.9 percent). It is still a serious problem for Hispanics in general. One hypothesis that is being tested is that whatever is predisposing Hispanics to diabetes is also preventing them from getting heart attacks. Researchers are currently looking for that variable.

In general, Hispanics have a high rate of cervical, gallbladder, liver, and stomach cancer. This is attributed to the lack of preventive care exhibited by the group. In addition, Hispanic elderly people exhibit multiple chronicities as a result of a number of diseases, leaving devastating effects because they were not treated properly or were treated too late. In the National Coalition of Hispanic Health and Human Services Organizations report, access to medical care was correlated with sociodemographic factors for Mexican Americans, Puerto Ricans, and Cuban Americans. The overall access shows a positive correlation of degree of medical care they received with education, annual income, and age of the participants (Delgado, 1991).

In general, Hispanic elderly men and women tend to seek medical help only when they are ill. Preventive examinations are not part of their behavioral repertoire. Hispanics' concept of well-being represents a balance of the social, emotional, and physical needs of the individual elderly, and yet health care providers unfamiliar with the Hispanic culture are not addressing the well-being of their elderly Hispanic patients in a holistic fashion. This failure contributes to the low utilization rate. If a patient lacks the *confianza* and trust in a health care provider, the patient is less likely to go to him or her again or is less likely to follow his or her advice. It is estimated that medication noncompliance among elderly Hispanic people is as high as 63 percent, compared with 33 percent noncompliance for non-Hispanics (Espino, 1991). Hispanic elderly depend instead on culturally competent healers, pharmacists, and friends to cure their acute and chronic conditions. This may be why they exhibit more functional impairments than the non-Hispanic populations.

If the system continues to ignore the cultural values and beliefs of the Hispanic elderly population, these men and women will continue to avoid contact with the hostile environment, regardless of whether or not the services are being provided free of charge. The elderly Hispanic patient should participate in his or her own recovery process. Practitioners, therefore, must engage the patient by respecting the patient's beliefs and value systems.

Mental Health Issues among Hispanic Elderly People

Illness behavior is governed by rules that define the acceptable way of being ill, acceptable illnesses, and the mode of expressing those illnesses (McGoldrick, Pearce, & Giordano, 1982). These rules differ from culture to culture. In dealing with mental health issues, it is important for the social worker, psychologist, and other health professional to realize that he or she may be looking at behavior that has not been recognized as illness behavior by the subject's culture (Hernandez, 1991b). In dealing with mental illness, the cultural definitions of mental well-being and mental illness are extremely important because mental health, mental illness, and the concept of well-being are culturally defined and culturally determined.

Practitioners who are not culturally competent have been imposing their symptom labels and illness definitions on all Hispanic patients. But cultural differences exist in the way a patient expresses depression, anxiety, and suspicion. Once the practitioner becomes culturally competent, he or she will be able to distinguish the differences between culturally prescribed behavior and mental illness. Cultural expectations about pain and suffering are correlated with the type of behavior and emotions patients will display in public. Knowing these cultural expectations allows the practitioner to effectively intervene in the process.

The fact that the elderly Hispanic people live in a society that does not support their cultural view of the world and their belief system acts as a stressor and makes them highly susceptible to what the non-Hispanic culture classifies as depression and anxiety. Hispanic elderly men and women, especially Cuban American elders, are people in transition. This transition brings despair, irritability, anxiety, and helplessness. If viewed within their cultural and historical context, these feelings are quite understandable, considering the situation.

The biggest stressor faced by an elderly Hispanic is the degree of acculturation experienced by his or her own family. Familism is an important characteristic of Hispanics (Bernal & Flores, 1982). The family is the most important social unit. The bond of loyalty Hispanics have for the nuclear, as well as the extended, family represents the most important support available for practitioners to build on in dealing with mental health issues (Sandoval, 1984). On the other hand, this familism also represents the biggest emotional burden if an individual is not able, or is unwilling, to fulfill his or her culturally prescribed role within the family (Hernandez, 1991a). The family's degree of bilingualism will, in itself, tell the mental health specialist a great deal about potential family conflicts among the children, parents, and grandparents (Hernandez, 1991a). The inability of the grandparents to understand the cultural values and beliefs of the new culture leads to isolation of the elderly family member within his or her own family.

Substance abuse appears to be a serious problem for Hispanic males of all ages. This phenomenon is due to a wide variety of factors, such as the lack of an appropriately defined role for alcohol in the Hispanic culture, the alcohol and tobacco industries' intensive targeting of the Hispanic market, and the use of chemical substances as tools to cope with the demands of a culturally insensitive world.

Even though it has been reported that depression and anxiety are the major mental health problems facing elderly Hispanics today, the results of such findings are questionable because the instruments used to identify depression, mental illness, and anxiety are culturally biased and data obtained from a non–culturally sensitive instrument that are then analyzed or interpreted using different cultural contexts further compromise the results of the survey. A significant and urgent challenge for the practitioner in gerontology is to recognize this gap in knowledge and to develop culturally accurate instruments that can provide meaningful data for research and practice.

The underrepresentation of elderly Hispanic clients in the Mental Health and Health Care Program of the Older Americans Act is mainly due to the fact that the practitioners and service providers are evaluating, providing treatment for, and delivering services to the Hispanic elderly in a manner that violates their cultural identity and dignity.

CAREGIVING AMONG ELDERLY PEOPLE OF COLOR

As increasing numbers of ethnic elders are surviving to very old age, families are confronted with the need to provide care for frail elderly people with multiple chronic impairments.

Archbold (1983) identified two caregiving roles—care provision and care management. Care provision entails identifying the services needed and providing them directly. Care management involves identifying the services needed and arranging for them to be provided by someone else. Socioeconomic status is a primary determinant of whether one is a care provider or a care manager. Care providers are more likely to live in intergenerational households.

Cultural and ethnic differences in socialization account for differences in response patterns to behavioral expectations in later life. For example, some Jewish mothers tend to raise their children for independence. The home and children are the most important values in the mother's life. Men are expected to be successful and provide well for their families. Women are expected to be good wives and mothers. The role of the mother is a sacrificial one, with little expectation that the children will return anything to her except to make her proud by being successful in their respective roles. This generalization is contrasted with the frequently cited problem of guilt in children induced by their failure to repay the sacrifices with dutiful visits, frequent phone calls, and assumption of the caregiver role, when necessary.

For black and Hispanic families, the role of the mother is the same in terms of being good wives and mothers. However, according to a widely cited generalization, the children are reared to be successful so that they will be able to take care of their parents. The parents expect the children to provide for them in their old age. (But see chapter 7 for discussion of misconceptions about Hispanic family relationships.)

The task of caring for a frail elderly relative is usually a progressive, all-consuming activity that cannot be incorporated into a person's life without having a significant impact on his or her sense of self, time, freedom, career, and relationships (Archbold, 1983). This role becomes even more difficult when conflicting demands of other responsibilities related to the family, job, or social obligations compete for scarce resources.

It has been commonly thought that black elderly people have more family members to share in providing care than other groups. However, there has been a downward trend in the average household size of blacks. In 1890, the average household size was 5.32 people; in 1975, 3.27 people; and as of 1992 there was an average of 2.4 children in African American families (U.S. Bureau of the Census, 1979, 1992).

The black elderly are likely to have been married but are not likely to enter old age still married. They run greater risks of separation, divorce, and early widowhood (Jackson, 1980; Wolf et al., 1983). Therefore, in the declining years of life, many end up alone. Thus, solitary life may be neither the elderly person's desire nor by his or her own design.

There is also a perception that black families do not place their elders in nursing homes. Data indicate, however, that many black elderly men and women live alone and, in increasing numbers and despite the cost, are being placed in nursing homes (Carter, 1988; Wolf et al., 1983). Hispanics and blacks want the best available care for their family members. If they have to make a choice between placing an elderly parent in what they consider an inferior institution and making the sacrifice to maintain a parent at home, they will often select home care (Morrison, 1983). Home care decisions may be related to a variety of factors. Among these are the cost of adequate nursing home care, the guilt associated with the cultural expectation that children should not "put their parents away," and the perception that people go to nursing homes to die (Dickerson, 1983; Morrison, 1983).

McAdoo (1978) pointed out that one of the strongest black cultural patterns has been that of extensive kin-helping systems. Kin and nonrelatives have taken responsibility for the young and old through informal adoption and other creative alternative living arrangements and helping patterns to overcome the negative effects of racism and poverty. The family's effective environment consists of a social network of relatives, friends, and neighbors, which acts to provide emotional and monetary support, as well as protection of the family's integrity from assault from outside forces. McAdoo found that this helping pattern persisted regardless of socioeconomic status, even among upwardly mobile families. However, the declining family size and economic reality may have an impact on this pattern of kin help.

Babchuk (1978) made a distinction between the networks of close kin and very close friends. The importance of family support for elderly people has been examined from the perspective of the obligation of family members to provide assistance and the types of assistance provided. There is overwhelming agreement among researchers that as people become aged and ill, the family is the major source of help and support. When health begins to deteriorate, the family consistently emerges as the major provider of needed services to elders. For minorities, augmented families may include unrelated individuals and a friend network that is accepted as family.

In the hospital setting, the mere fact that patients receive a large number of visits from relatives and friends often leads discharge planners to assume that this will translate into support and care arrangements upon discharge. This is not always the case. This assumption may lead to inappropriate or premature discharge without the appropriate support systems, resulting in increased readmissions and institutionalization.

PSYCHOSOCIAL MODEL FOR DELIVERY OF HEALTH CARE SERVICES

In working with elderly people of color, a family development systems model including the family, friends, and social networks can be used to ensure that comprehensive support is employed. The importance of cultural traditions influencing the decision-making process should be recognized and used as a part of the services model. The practitioner should facilitate rather than direct, providing information regarding alternatives that would promote a more individualized decision-making process.

Both black and Hispanic cultures are steeped in religious practices and customs. Religious traditions may influence decisions to a greater extent among these groups than in the majority culture. Therefore it is most important to look at the church as a source of support and assistance.

There are several roles for practitioners in identifying and using informal supports and community resources for hospitalized elderly people. Because this is often the entry point for the old person into the health care system, it is crucial for the practitioner to be successful at this stage:

1. The practitioner should become familiar with the ethnic and cultural beliefs and practices of the client population. Efforts must be directed at recognizing and confronting one's own cultural biases to prevent them from interfering with the helping relationship.
2. The culturally sensitive practitioner should help the family and patient cope with the illness and facilitate full participation in the treatment decision-making process as informed by current knowledge of cultural practices.
3. The practitioner should help the family members to become involved in the recuperation process. The family should be included as a major component of the discharge planning process. It may be necessary to use interpreters or collateral contacts to facilitate communication.
4. The practitioner should maintain a resource file for identifying and accessing culturally relevant formal and informal

services to make the discharge easier and promote optimal recuperation.

There are some obstacles that must be overcome to be effective in this process:

1. There is a shortage of facilities and financial resources to meet the needs of patients of color ready for discharge. Workers must become political advocates for these patients for improved government programs. They must advocate for resources to meet unmet needs. They must also advocate to ensure that programs are accessible and appropriate.
2. There are cultural and racial barriers to effective planning. Communication patterns and language are common barriers. Many blacks and Hispanics are protective of family information, especially relating to finances. Their reluctance to share information may relate to cultural mores or to distrust of how the information will be used. There is a tendency for blacks to give "yes" and "no" responses without further clarification, whereas Hispanics may diffuse information with irrelevant detail.
3. Many families of color see health professionals and social workers as "welfare" workers and are reluctant to share information that they think may have an impact on their benefits. They have little or no idea of what services social workers offer. There is a great need to promote an understanding of the role of a medical social worker.
4. Patients and families may not understand or agree with the physician's diagnosis. However, minorities tend not to question the physician or ask for a second opinion. They either follow blindly or refuse to follow through the treatment plan.
5. Recuperation plans may be hindered by a cultural tradition that dictates doing *for* the sick and elderly. Although rehabilitation plans may call for the patient to do as much as possible for himself or herself, the family may be unable to cope with watching him or her struggle. Recuperation in an institution may not be a viable alternative because of cost and the tradition of keeping the family member in the home.

6. Another major barrier to family participation is transportation. Many black and Hispanic aged lack transportation. For many, public transportation is not easily accessible, and private transportation is too expensive. The majority of family members may work and be unable to take time away from jobs to keep scheduled appointments.
7. The inaccessibility of family members at the time of assessment sometimes results in the family's being left out of the planning process. The practitioner should make sure to follow up with the family to pull them into the process. Oftentimes the ratio of patients to workers presents a barrier to planned follow-through, but sensitivity to the particular needs of families of color should lead to appropriate prioritization.

These principles for interventions with elderly people of color and their families at the time of discharge from acute hospital settings are applicable to working with those families on a long-term basis as well. Once a relationship has been established that demonstrates cultural understanding and concern, and an up-to-date knowledge of resources, the practitioner becomes the pivotal source of future help and support, which is predictably needed by the frail elderly.

REFERENCES

Archbold, P. (1983). Impact of parent caring on women. *Family Relations, 32*(1), 39–47.

Babchuk, N. (1978). Aging and primary relations. *International Journal of Aging and Human Development, 9*(2), 137–151.

Bernal, G., & Flores, O. P. (1982). Latino family in therapy engagement and evaluation. *Journal of Marital and Family Therapy, 8*, 357–365.

Carbonell, J. (1991, March). *Profile of the clients of Little Havana Activities and Nutritional Centers.* Paper presented to the Public Health Department, Miami.

Carter, J. (1988). Health attitudes/promotions/preventions: The black elderly. In J. S. Jackson (Ed.), *The black American elderly* (pp. 292–303). New York: Springer.

Delgado, J. (1991, May). *Health status of Hispanics.* Paper presented at the National Hispanic Healthy People 2000 Conference, Washington, DC.

Dickerson, M. F. W. (1983). Problems of black high risk elderly. *Journal of Black Studies, 14*, 251–260.
Ehrlich, I. F. (1975). The aged black in America: The forgotten person. *Journal of Negro Education, 44*(1), 12–23.
Espino, D. (1991, March). *Ethnogeriatric medicine: Hispanic health status.* Paper presented at the Thirty-Fifth Conference of the American Gerontological Society, New Orleans.
Gonzales-Reigosa, F. (1976). Las culturas del exilio. *Boletin del Instituto de Estudios Cubanos, 89*, 90.
Hernandez, G. G. (1991a). In T. Brink (Ed.), The family and its aged members: The Cuban experience [Special issue]. *Clinical Gerontologist.*
Hernandez, G. G. (1991b). Not so benign neglect: Researchers ignore ethnicity in defining family caregiver burden and recommending service [Letter to the editor]. *Gerontologist, 31*, 271–272.
Hill, R. (1978). A demographic profile of the black elderly. *Aging, 287*(8), 2–9.
Jackson, J. J. (1978). Special health problems of aged blacks. *Aging, 287*, 15–20.
Jackson, J. J. (1980). The economic well-being and financial security of black elderly families. *Journal of Minority Aging, 5*, 306–317.
Jackson, J. S. (Ed.). (1988). *The black American elderly.* New York: Springer.
Lopez, C., & Aguilar, E. (1990). *On the sidelines: Hispanic elderly and the continuum of care.* Washington, DC: National Council of La Raza.
McAdoo, H. P. (1978). Factors related to stability in upwardly mobile black families. *Journal of Marriage and the Family, 40*(4), 761–776.
McGoldrick, M., Pearce, K., & Giordano, J. (Eds.). (1982). Introduction. In *Ethnicity and family therapy.* New York: Guilford Press.
Morrison, B. J. (1983). Sociocultural dimensions: Nursing homes and the minority aged. *Journal of Gerontological Social Work, 6*, 127–145.
Ortiz, F. (1979). *Los negros brujos.* Havana: Colección Ebano y Canela.
Pedraza, T. (1990, August). *Cuban culture.* Paper presented at the Dade County Mental Health Association, Miami.
Sandoval, M. (1984, April). *Cuban health and mental health practices.* Presentation to community nurses, South Miami Hospital.
Saruski, J., & Mosquera, G. (1979). *The cultural policy of Cuba.* New York: United Nations Educational, Scientific, and Cultural Publications.
Taylor, R. J., & Chatters, L. M. (1988). Correlates of education, income and poverty among aged blacks. *Gerontologist, 28*, 435–441.
Taylor, R. J., & Taylor, W. H. (1982). The social and economic status of the black elderly. *Phylon, 43*(4), 295–306.

U.S. Bureau of the Census. (1979). *Population reports.* Washington, DC: U.S. Government Printing Office.

U.S. Bureau of the Census. (1991). *Poverty in the United States: 1990 current population reports* (Series P-60, No. 175). Washington, DC: U.S. Government Printing Office.

U.S. Bureau of the Census. (1992). *Current population reports* (Series P-23, No. 182). Washington, DC: U.S. Government Printing Office.

U.S. Department of Health and Human Services. (1980). *Characteristics of the black elderly.* Washington, DC: U.S. Government Printing Office.

Williams, B. S. (1980). *Characteristics of the black elderly.* Washington, DC: U.S. Government Printing Office.

Wolf, J. H., Breslau, N., Ford, A. B., Ziegler, H. D., & Ward, A. (1983). Access of the black urban elderly to medical care. *Journal of the National Medical Association, 75*(1), 41–46.

9 Hidden Problem of Elder Abuse: Clues and Strategies for Health Care Workers

Jordan I. Kosberg

Those working in the health care field are often at vantage points to identify elderly people who are victimized by the abusive behavior of others. Whether in the emergency room, health clinic, hospital, professional's office, or patient's home, health care workers should be sensitive to the possibility of elder abuse problems among their geriatric patients. Some workers (such as visiting nurses or home health workers) often are the only non–family members permitted to visit the home of an elderly person. Whether in a private dwelling or within a long-term care facility, they are often able to view the care of elderly people during both daytime and nighttime, weekday and weekend (whether a member of the institution's staff or visiting a facility).

This chapter presents an overview of the problem of elder abuse. Those who function as health care workers can play vital roles in the detection, assessment, and prevention of, and intervention into the problem of elder abuse—a problem that can occur in the home and within long-term care facilities. It is hoped that this overview will both educate and sensitize individuals in the overall "battle" against what can be considered one of society's most serious and invisible problems.

MANY FACES OF ELDER ABUSE

The existence of elder abuse as a social problem was first discussed by Baker (1975) in an article on "granny battering" that appeared in a British medical journal. Starting in the latter part of the 1970s, American writers began to focus on the problem.

Over the years, there has been a plethora of articles and books on the topic and the creation of a periodical, the *Journal of Elder Abuse and Neglect,* which is solely devoted to the topic. The National Committee for the Prevention of Elder Abuse has been created as a vehicle to organize individuals and to encourage the study of the problem and dissemination of research and program efforts.

Over the years there has been little agreement on the definition of elder abuse. Different researchers have used their own definitions and measurements of the problem. Academic researchers have had different views of the problem than have those working in programs and services at community or state levels. For example, researchers have tended to measure elder abuse as the consequence of acts of omission or commission by an abuser against an elderly person. On the other hand, protective services workers and many health care workers include self-neglect (adversities not involving others) in their definition of the problem and to be included for professional action.

Kosberg (1990) discussed elder abuse as including several specific types of adversities against older people: First is *passive neglect,* which is characterized by a situation in which the elderly person is left alone, isolated, or forgotten. *Active neglect,* on the other hand, is a type of abuse characterized as the intentional withholding of items necessary for daily living, such as medicine, companionship, and toileting assistance. Third, *psychological abuse* is characterized by verbal or emotional intimidation brought on by situations in which the older person is infantilized, frightened, humiliated, or threatened. Fourth is *physical abuse,* which occurs when an older person is hit, slapped, bruised, sexually molested, cut, burned, or physically restrained. Fifth is, by any other name, *theft* involving material or financial misappropriation or misuse when not being used for the benefit, or with the approval, of the elderly person. Sixth, *violation of rights* occurs when an older person is denied those rights given to any competent adult to make decisions for oneself. For example, such abuse can result from efforts to force an elderly person from his or her dwelling or to force the person into another setting without any forewarning, explanation, opportunity for input, or against the older person's wishes. Seventh, and finally, *self-abuse* is a form of elder abuse that can necessitate intervention by those in the helping professions. This problem can become neglectful behavior when the self-abuse is known by others (that is, family, friends, aides, health workers) who do not seek to either prevent or intervene in the situation. Indeed, it is possible that the formal or informal caregiver might assist in the self-abuse (that is, buying alcohol or medication which is being abused). As has been indicated, elder abuse has been defined differently by others.

The intentionality of the abuser will differ. This is to suggest that some types of abuse are done out of caregiving ignorance or the caregiver's incompetence to understand the meaning of acts of omission or commission and their adverse consequences on the older person. Passive neglect and self-abuse are two such examples. Other forms of abuse are conscious, deliberate, and premeditated. Theft and physical abuse are two examples. As will be discussed, it is important to diagnose the motivations of the abuser to better understand the dynamics for prevention and intervention.

Although the motivations of the abuser will vary, the consequences for the older abused person will remain similar. These results, which will vary from situation to situation and person to person, can range from minimal social, economic, and psychological damage to adversely affecting the quality of the person's life, to—at its worse—death. The severity of abuse, too, varies by individual. For example, the loss of a familiar object such as a wedding ring may be more tumultuous to a widowed elderly person than would be psychological abuse. Some older people come from backgrounds in which interactions are demonstrative and physical; thus, an observer might misinterpret such behavior as abusive when, in fact, it is not perceived by the older person as such. Accordingly, it is necessary to verify suspected abuse by questioning the older person.

The abuse of an elderly person varies not only by the type of abuse, but also by the different types of abuse occurring together. For example, the physical abuse of an elderly relative may be accompanied by the denial of rights. The theft of personal possessions by a nursing home aide may be accompanied by a hostile attitude toward the resident (that is, psychological abuse). In addition, elder abuse will vary by the duration of the abuse from a relatively short period to over a lengthy period of time. Abuse will vary by the frequency in which it occurs, from just one time (perhaps as a result of a major emotional event) to frequently or ongoing. Some abuse occurs in an unpredictable way (an unanticipated "burst" of frustration); other types of abuse occur in a predictable way (that is, when the older person receives a pension check or when the son becomes intoxicated).

EXTENT OF INVISIBILITY PROBLEM

According to an American Association of Retired Persons study, each year in the United States 1 million to 2 million elderly men and women are victims of elder abuse in all types of settings (Simon, 1992). The U.S. House of Representatives Select Committee on Aging reported, in 1990, that 1.5 million elder people are victims of abuse or neglect every year. The National Aging Resource Center on Elder Abuse estimated that there were 735,000 domestic elder abuse victims in 1991. An estimate in 1994 by the National Center on Elder Abuse projected the number of elder abuse victims annually at approximately 1.84 million (cited by Baron & Welty, 1996).

In 1981, and in one of the first official examinations of the problem of elder abuse by the government, the U.S. House of Representatives Select Committee on Aging published "Elder Abuse: An Examination of a Hidden Problem." The committee concluded, after hearing expert testimonies and reading research findings, that "some 4 percent of the nation's elderly may be victims of some sort of abuse from moderate to severe. In other words, one out of every 25 older Americans, or roughly one million elder Americans, may be victims of such abuse each year" (p. 4).

As Baron and Welty (1996) stated: "Professionals believe that the number of cases of elder abuse is underestimated in all studies" (p. 37). These authors listed the reasons for such unreliable figures as being a result of the methodological limitations of the studies, the lack of a federal definition of elder abuse, and the failure to include abuse occurring each year to residents within the nation's long-term care facilities. Additionally, formal reports of abuse and neglect are perceived to be only a rough (and under-representative) sample of the actual number of elder abuse cases.

There are many possible explanations for the under-reporting of elder abuse. First, elder abuse is often not detected. It can occur within the home and may not be seen by outsiders—neighbors or professionals alike. Indeed, as opposed to children whose abuse can be detected by teachers, health care workers, or neighbors, the physical condition of some elderly people living in the community may preclude their leaving the house (or, indeed, their bed) to be seen by outsiders. And elder abuse within long-term care facilities may also be out of sight and undetected. Kosberg (1973) called institutionalized elder populations among the most dependent, voiceless, invisible, and powerless groups in society.

Elder abuse is often a result of adverse treatment by relatives, whether in the community or in institutional settings. Nonrelatives and professionals alike are often reluctant to intervene in situations which are perceived to be "family affairs." In fact, the abused older person and the abusing person both may deny the existence of a problem in the family to outsiders. As a poignant example of such "conspiracies" of family silence between the abused and abuser, a book by Pizzy on spouse abuse is titled "Scream Quietly or the Neighbors Will Hear."

An additional reason for the lack of knowledge about the extent of the problem pertains to the fact that abused elderly people are unlikely to report their adversities. Simply put, they can be embarrassed by the actions of a relative (for example, "Who would admit that a daughter is hitting her mother?") or by their own gullibility with a stranger (for example, "No, I didn't ask to see his identification as a bank official wanting access to my account"). In addition, some abused older people accept their poor treatment and believe it to be a result of getting "paid back" (as they had been a child or spouse abuser). Some elderly people who are abused do not report the abuse to others because they fear retaliation by the abuser, especially if the abuser is the caregiver. Aides and orderlies or family members who care for dependent older people (who cannot perform their own activities of daily living) are especially vulnerable to such apprehension about the retribution resulting from reporting abuse. Relatedly, should the demands needed by an older person be perceived to be the cause of the abuse (resulting, for example, from caregiving burden and frustration), the older person may be reluctant to blame the caregiver. There might also be the fear that legal or criminal action will be taken against the abusing family member (such as a son or daughter).

Another explanation for the lack of abuse reporting results from the older person's fear that the solution to the problem will be worse than the problem; that is, removal from the home and placement into an institutional setting. It may be the case that an abused older person may think that no one will believe his or her abuse, or that the elderly individual will not know to whom to report the abuse. In a recent study of one long-term care facility, it was found that the great majority of both residents and their family members did not know about the ombudsmen program to be used in reporting abuse and maltreatment (Payne & Cikovic, 1995).

There is little reliable research on abuse within long-term care settings. Authors of one study of elder abuse in institutions (Pillemer & Moore, 1989) admitted that their study probably suffered from an under-reporting of abuse. It is suspected that many older people in the community are unaware of Protective Services or other elder abuse hotlines. In a recent publication, Kosberg and Bowie (1997) wrote about elderly men under-reporting victimization. Whether victims of crime on the street by strangers, or abuse within the home by family members, or maltreatment within long-term care facilities, there is suggestion that older men have often been socialized to avoid admitting the existence of a problem and are less likely to verbalize their concerns and apprehensions to others.

Taken together, abuse of elderly people is an under-reported and invisible social problem in society. As such, there are special challenges for the detection of such adversities by health care workers, among others.

EXPLANATIONS FOR ELDER ABUSE

Aside from a general curiosity about why one would abuse an elderly person, the explanations of elder abuse have ramifications for better understanding the dynamics of the problem and for the prevention and treatment of elder abuse. What follows is a brief overview of the more predominant explanations of the problem of elder abuse.

Ansello (1996) addressed the causes of elder abuse and discussed the psychopathology of the abuser, who has personality or psychological disorders that result in abusive behavior. In addition, he suggested that there can be the transmission of violence within a family. Deviant behavior and lifestyle, too, is associated with intrafamily abuse. Certainly, if there is any one factor which has been consistently found to be related to elder abuse, it is substance abuse (alcohol and drugs) by the abuser (Hwalek, Neale, Goodrich, & Quinn, 1996).

Kosberg (1990) also discussed sociological explanations, such as unwanted caregiving responsibilities or the perception of excessive caregiving costs. A social exchange explanation describes abuse as resulting from the inability of the elderly person to maintain the normal reciprocal relationship with another person and the anger resulting from the increasing disequilibrium.

Holmes and Rahe (1967) developed a Life Crisis explanation for adversity within families. According to this view, elder abuse can occur when the caregiver experiences an excessive number of life-changing events (that is, responsibilities, economic pressures, illnesses, and so forth) that result in a state of emotional overload. In discussing the factors highly or moderately associated with self-neglect among elderly people, Longres (1995) identified living arrangements, mental illness, drug or alcohol problems, and dementia.

A poor relationship between parent and adult child will not necessarily lessen with the passing of years. In fact, given the increasing dependence of an elderly parent on the child, the relationship might well worsen. Such a notion of intergenerational conflict has long been discussed. Almost 30 years ago, Cavan (1969) wrote that conflict between older and younger generations resulted, in part, from a lack of normative definition of the rights and responsibilities of middle-aged children with regard to their elderly parents. It is believed such ambiguity continues to exist, and differences in expectations between generations may produce the potential for and the reality of maltreatment and neglect.

There are several explanations for the causes of abuse within long-term care facilities by members of the staff. Certainly the failure to screen out unsuitable employees is one important reason to explain some forms of abuse by staff (that is, theft and violence). Economic misappropriation by owners and administrators of long-term care facilities may result from efforts to gain from theft of residents' funds and possessions or from efforts to commit fraud against the government (that is, Medicaid and Medicare benefits).

Kosberg (1988) suggested that there may be two groups of potential victims within long-term care facilities: the elderly residents and lower-echelon staff. Those in the latter group often perform rather unpleasant tasks (that is, toileting, bathing) for elderly residents who may be uncooperative, condescending, and prejudicial. This makes caregiving more difficult (whether within institutions or in private dwellings in the community). Such conditions, along with low pay, a lack of career ladders, and working for unsympathetic and unappreciative supervisors and administrators, set the scene for staff frustration and anger directed toward the potential cause of the problem and a victim unable to defend himself or herself: the elderly person.

HIGH RISK FACTORS RELATED TO ELDER ABUSE

Recently, there has been increased attention to the identification of those who are likely to be abused or to be abusing. As Ansello (1996) suggested: "Over time, . . . risk factors have come to serve as embryonic theories through an inductive process of theory building" (p. 14).

Kosberg and Nahmiash (1996) developed a conceptual model of the dynamics associated with elder abuse. Their conceptualization included attention to the characteristics of the elderly victim, the abuser, the social context, and the cultural milieu. Table 9.1 presents an overview of the model (revision of Kosberg & Nahmiash, p. 35). Inasmuch as the risks of elder abuse involve a multidimensional assessment of issues, Kosberg and Nahmiash concluded: "In addition to being able to assess the characteristics of victims and abusers, social workers and health care workers should understand the contributions made by the social and cultural dynamics that influence attitudes and behavior to mistreatment and abuse" (p. 45). Because health care providers are often the reporters of suspected cases of elder abuse to adult protective services programs (Hwalek et al., 1996) or to others, hopefully the high risk factors will be helpful in such actions.

TABLE 9.1

Framework for Conceptualizing Elder Abuse

Characteristics of Elderly Victim	Elder Abuser
Gender	Substance abuser
Marital status	Mental/emotional illness
Health condition	Lack of caregiving experience
Chronological age	Reluctance to give care
Substance abuse	History of abuse
Living arrangements	Dependency
Psychological issues	Dementia
Problem behavior	Personality traits
Dependence	Lack of family supports
Isolation	
Social Context	**Cultural Milieu**
Financial problems	Ageism
Family violence	Sexism
Lack of social support/encouragement	Attitudes toward violence
Family disharmony	Reactions to abuse
Living arrangements	Attitudes toward people with disabilities
	Family caregiving imperatives

DETECTION AND ASSESSMENT

Given the invisibility of the problem of elder abuse, the lack of reporting of the problem by elderly people and what is known about the causes and risk factors, health care workers need to consider the detection of the problem and assessment of the abused and the abusers. As Kosberg and Nahmiash (1996) stated: "Health care providers often function in settings (for example, clinics, emergency rooms, private dwellings, long-term care facilities) in which the abuse and neglect of elderly people can be identified. Care providers must be able to recognize the specific characteristics of actual or potential abuse victims and their abusers" (p. 31).

The consequences of certain types of abuse are obvious, if proper assessment is undertaken. Certainly physical symptoms can be detected (such as burns, injuries, and bruises). But health care workers need to be sensitive to the more subtle behavioral signs of abuse and neglect, which include depression, fear, confusion, withdrawal, and anger, among others. In a recent article, Rosenblatt (1996) urged the proper documentation of possible abuse both as a mechanism by which to begin a systematic investigation and a method by which to avoid a possible lawsuit. Such documentation involves the collection of demographic, psychosocial, and caregiver data, information on the medical history and environmental characteristics, patient-client observations, and laboratory tests.

Screening protocols have been developed to identify such physical and behavioral systems of elder abuse (Quinn & Tomita, 1986; Sengstock & Hwalek, 1985). Kosberg (1988) developed a High-Risk Assessment Index to be used in discharge placement decisions from health care settings. As opposed to the conceptual framework of abuse developed by Kosberg and Nahmiash (1996), the High-Risk Assessment Index had been created as a case management tool to be used in the screening of those elderly people who were being placed in community settings (perhaps as a result of hospital discharge or an inability to remain living independently) and those who would provide the care. The purpose of the index is to help those from social and health services systems to identify "markers" that might individually and collectively suggest the possibility of a high-risk placement decision. The four-part index assesses the characteristics of the elderly person, the potential caregiver, the family care system, and the congruity of perceptions of relationship between the elderly person and the caregiver and the preferred placement plan, and is summarized in Table 9.2 (revised from Kosberg, 1988, p. 48).

More recently, Ramsey-Klawsnik (1996) wrote about the detection and assessment of physical and sexual abuse in health care settings. She identified three different situations by which abuse can be identified: elderly patient discloses the abuse to the health care worker, no disclosure but there is physical evidence, and others seek assistance for the elderly person.

Fulmer and Gould (1996) discussed the presence and nature of elder neglect, the relationship between caregiver neglect and self-neglect, and provide an Elder Abuse Assessment Form. Although the virtues of such assessment protocols are stressed, the

TABLE 9.2

High-Risk Placement Index

Characteristics of Elderly Person	Characteristics of Caregiver
Female	Problem drinking
Advanced age	Medication/drug abuser
Dependence	Demented/confused
Problem drinking	Mental/emotional illness
Intergenerational conflict	Caregiving inexperience
Internalizer	Economically troubled
Excessive loyalty to family	Abused as child
Past abuse	Stressed
Stoicism	Unengaged outside the home
Isolation	Blamer
Impaired condition	Unsympathetic
Provocative behavior	Lacks understanding
	Unrealistic expectations
	Economically dependent
	Hypercritical
Characteristics of Family	**Congruity of Perceptions between Older Person and Caregiver**
Lack of family support	Quality of past relationship
Caregiving reluctance	Quality of present relationship
Overcrowded dwelling	Preferred placement decision of older person
Isolation	Preferred placement decision of potential caregiver
Marital conflict	
Economic pressures	
Intrafamily problems	
Desire for institutionalization	
Disharmony in shared responsibility	

authors do conclude "Ultimately clinicians must rely upon good clinical judgment" (p. 98). Sengstock and Steiner (1996) discussed the assessment of nonphysical abuse: psychological abuse and exploitation.

James O'Brien (1996), a physician, wrote: "It is unfortunate that many health care practitioners are ill-equipped to respond when confronted with elder abuse or neglect" (p. 51). It is hoped that increasingly, long-term care facilities, clinics, hospitals, and other settings in the health care continuum will have established procedures and utilize protocols for the systematic screening of older clients who may be abused. Obviously, the first step in such a process is the recognition of the possible existence of the problem and refusal to necessarily accept—at face value—explanations given for the condition of a elderly person brought into an emergency room or seen by private practitioner. Additionally, within long-term care facilities, there is the need to establish a mechanism for ensuring the adequacy of care and protection of elderly residents and their possessions and for reporting suspected cases of abuse and maltreatment of older people. Such adversity can be the result of the actions of staff or volunteers, family members, or other residents in the facility.

Detection and assessment necessitates the honest and open communication with those from the health care field. Health care workers in contact with elderly people who might be thought to be victims of abuse should be able to communicate with them in a quiet and private location. Emphasis should be placed on assistance and support, not the possibility of criminal charges against anyone, confrontation between the older person and possible abuser, or discussion of alternatives to the present situation (unless there is apparent imminent danger to the older person). The alleged abuser should be questioned separately, and explanations for potential abuse compared between the suspected abused person and the possible abuser. Those involved with the detection of abuse should be especially sensitive to the identical explanations of what might have happened, which could reflect a fabricated story by which the abuse is disguised.

Within an institutional setting or within a private dwelling, differences in the perceptions of the situation between a member of the staff or formal caregiver (that is, home health worker, homemaker) and the older person (or family member who suspects abuse is taking place) will need to be explored in depth. It may be the policy of an agency, or institutional facility, that all suspected cases of elder abuse are turned over to either an Adult Protective Service worker or reported to an Elder Abuse hotline. However, often agencies or institutions prefer to handle internally alleged cases of abuse by assessing the merits of the complaint, rather than to "go public" with the case and face possible adverse publicity with state departments or the mass media.

Indeed, such "informal" efforts may circumvent established policies that mandate the reporting of suspected cases of elder abuse.

It is known that not all cases of suspected or reported abuse are verified by fact-finding efforts. Some charges of abuse result from an elderly person's desire for attention or from a confused or demented condition. Other cases of unsubstantiated charges of abuse result from anger at a facility (or particular member of the staff) by an elderly person, a family member, or a former or present employee. Thus, the need to verify alleged abuse is imperative before action takes place.

INTERVENTIONS

Interventions to assist elderly people include both prevention before and treatment after abuse has occurred. There are many activities which can take place and include direct, programmatic, and policy efforts. The following represent a sample of interventions for use within the health care system.

Prevention, obviously, pertains to keeping an older person "out of harm's way." At one level this refers to making proper placement decisions when an older person will be discharged from a hospital or otherwise moved from the present location elsewhere. As Nerenberg and Haikalis (1996) stated: "Discharge planners play a pivotal role in reducing the risk of abuse to victims once they leave the protected hospital environment" (p. 207). Although they are, in part, referring to the discharged planning for people who have been abused, their concerns are more generally applicable to the placement of any older person; for the wrong placement, in the care of the wrong person or persons, may well result in abuse of the discharged geriatric patient. These authors describe the need for possible counseling of older people, for referrals to community resources to protect the older person (such as Adult Protective Services workers, long-term care ombudsman, or domestic violence programs), and for assistance for those caring for the older person (that is, family and caregiver support groups, respite care, financial management).

Kosberg (1988), too, was concerned about health care workers making effective placement decisions, and he developed the Consequences of Care Index (CCI) to be used with those who are or might become the caregivers of impaired or vulnerable elderly people. This case management instrument is used in screening caregivers by assessing the degree to which they either anticipate or actually experience the following problems: social disruptions to themselves and their families, psychological and psychosomatic disturbances, economic costs, low value to the caregiving experience, and the perception of the elderly person as a provocative individual. While on one hand the CCI permits the detection of a problem area seen by a caregiver (or potential caregiver) which can lead to counseling, education, and mobilization of community caregiving support, on the other hand the CCI has identified either present caregiving situations or potential ones which are viewed to be questionable (and possibly leading to ineffective care or, worse, to elder abuse).

Within an institutional setting, careful staff screening and ongoing staff supervision can be helpful in preventing the occurrence (and continuation) of abuse. Ombudsmen programs (which exist in every state) can be a mechanism for the detection of possible abuse, and there are over 200 private nursing home resident advocacy organizations in the country (Kosberg & Mullins, 1985). These organizations provide surveillance not only over nursing home care, but also over the public and quasi-public Ombudsmen programs, and they advocate for the upgrading of staff characteristics and needed state policies and national legislation. Collectively, these efforts contribute to improved quality of care provided within long-term care facilities and to the reduction of the probability of institutional abuse of elderly residents.

Once abuse occurs, or is detected, a quick determination of the immediate danger of the situation to the older person within a home or long-term care facility is necessary. As mentioned, in some states there are mandatory reporting laws with a reporting mechanism (such as a toll-free hot line). Among other agencies or departments to be contacted are a family services agency, area agency on aging, adult protective services, or a legal services agency. In less threatening situations, the older person and family members should be encouraged to seek "relief" from the problematic situation that is resulting in abuse or maltreatment, whether this entails counseling or relocation of the elder.

Again, relocation of the older person should be the last resort, rather than the first (except in life-threatening situations). Ideally, psychological intervention might be appropriate for the older person. Booth, Bruno, and Marin (1996) discussed the use of therapy with abused and neglected patients in the community and within institutional settings and provided helpful suggestions for the psychological treatment of such victims. Additionally, they provided useful information for the intervention of abusers as well, and discussed primary, secondary, and tertiary forms of assistance. Such forms of treatment can include not only individual counseling but family and marital counseling and support groups as well (for both abused and abusing individuals).

Supporting community services are also necessary. Especially for those caregivers without informal support systems, for whom there are not others to share caregiving responsibilities, formal supporting services are vital to relieve family members from the often constant and demanding care of a dependent elderly relative. Such needed services can include adult day care, day hospitals, friendly visitors, respite care, homemaker and home health aides, and chore services.

CONCLUSION

Should social or psychological interventions or programs not resolve the cause of the problems resulting in abusive behavior, legal action should be taken, whether within private dwellings in the community or within the confines of long-term care facilities. And as Kosberg (1986) stated: "It is hoped that, as a result of the publicity given to the existence and causes of elder abuse, those caring for the dependent elderly will voluntarily seek professional guidance to deal with their feelings or the consequences of excessive demands upon them before an eruption of abusive behavior" (p. 125). This refers to the importance of public education which, at once, familiarizes all to the existence of elder abuse in diverse settings and sensitizes them to the potential causes of such abuse. Hopefully, such awareness will reduce the placement of vulnerable older people into the care of those unsuited for such responsibilities and will lead to greater programmatic attention to the preventive and interventive efforts in the community and within institutional settings.

Abuse of elderly people is a potential problem affecting those from all strata of society; no racial, ethnic, religious, or socioeconomic group is spared. It is realized that this chapter on elder abuse has not discussed the importance of cultural diversity with regard to causes, assessment, and interventions. The major reason for this omission is that there is still little known about the dynamics of elder abuse that occurs in different cultural groups, as a result of a lack of systematic research in this area. The situation should improve in the future, though, and the first national conference on Understanding and Combating Elder Abuse in Minority Populations is planned, sponsored by the American Public Welfare Association and the National Center on Elder Abuse, and which will focus on the abuse in African American, Hispanic, Asian/Pacific Islander, and American Indian communities, as well as among lesbian and gay and developmentally disabled populations.

As was discussed earlier, those in the health care field are in key positions to identify the existence of elder abuse and to report the existence of such adversities. However, it is also possible that these health care workers, themselves, might be especially vulnerable to some of the forces that make individuals abuse and maltreat older people (that is, they are unappreciated, overworked, underpaid, care for a provocative individual, or face outside sources of stress). Accordingly, the responsibilities for health care workers are formidable, indeed, and pertain to surveillance over the care of elderly people, over one's peers and fellow workers, and to themselves as well.

As the population in the United States ages, there will be more impaired elderly people who will be dependent on others. Thus, the potential problem of elder abuse and maltreatment will grow, necessitating the awareness and concern of all citizens and requiring special attention by those in the health care field.

REFERENCES

Ansello, E. F. (1996). Causes and theories. In L. A. Baumhover & S. C. Beall (Eds.), *Abuse, neglect, and exploitation of older persons* (pp. 9–29). Baltimore: Health Professions Press.

Baker, A. A. (1975). Granny battering. *Modern Geriatrics, 5*(8), 20–24.

Baron, S., & Welty, A. (1996). Elder abuse. *Journal of Gerontological Social Work, 25*(1/2), 33–57.

Booth, B. K., Bruno, A. A., & Marin, R. (1996). Psychological therapy with abused and neglected patients. In L. A. Baumhover & S. C.

Beall (Eds.), *Abuse, neglect, and exploitation of older persons* (pp. 185–203). Baltimore: Health Professions Press.

Cavan, R. (1969). *The American family* (4th ed.). New York: Crowell.

Fulmer, T. T., & Gould, E. S. (1996). Assessing neglect. In L. A. Baumhover & S. C. Beall (Eds.), *Abuse, neglect, and exploitation of older persons* (pp. 89–103). Baltimore: Health Professions Press.

Homes, T. H., & Rahe, R. H. (1967). The social readjustment rating scale. *Journal of Psychosomatic Research, 11*(2), 213–218.

Hwalek, M. A., Neale, A. V., Goodrich, C. S., & Quinn, K. (1996). The association of elder abuse and substance abuse in the Illinois elder abuse system. *Gerontologist, 36*, 694–700.

Kosberg, J. I. (1973). The nursing home: A social work paradox. *Social Work, 18*, 104–110.

Kosberg, J. I. (1986). Understanding elder abuse: An overview for primary care physicians. In R. J. Ham (Ed.), *Geriatric medicine annual 1986* (pp. 115–127). Oradell, NJ: Medical Economics Books.

Kosberg, J. I. (1988). Preventing elder abuse: Identification of high risk factors prior to placement decisions. *Gerontologist, 28*, 43–49.

Kosberg, J. I. (1990). Assistance to victims of crime and abuse. In A. Monk (Ed.), *Handbook of gerontological services* (2nd ed., pp. 450–473). New York: Columbia University Press.

Kosberg, J. I., & Bowie, S. L. (1997). The victimization of elderly men. In J. I. Kosberg & L. W. Kaye (Eds.), *Elderly men: Special problems and professional responsibilities* (pp. 216–229). New York: Springer Press.

Kosberg, J. I., & Mullins, L. C. (1985). Advocacy organizations for nursing home residents: Variations in activities and objectives. In *The social welfare forum* (part II, pp. 242–249). Washington, DC: National Conference on Social Welfare.

Kosberg, J. I., & Nahmiash, D. (1996). Characteristics of victims and perpetrators and milieus of abuse and neglect. In L. A. Baumhover & S. C. Beall (Eds.), *Abuse, neglect, and exploitation of older persons* (pp. 31–49). Baltimore: Health Professions Press.

Longres, J. F. (1995). Self-neglect among the elderly. *Journal of Elder Abuse and Neglect, 7*(1), 69–86.

Nerenberg, L., & Haikalis, S. W. (1996). Discharge planning. In L. A. Baumhover & S. C. Beall (Eds.), *Abuse, neglect, and exploitation of older persons* (pp. 207–220). Baltimore: Health Professions Press.

O'Brien, J. G. (1996). Screening: A primary care clinician's perspective. In L. A. Baumhover & S. C. Beall (Eds.), *Abuse, neglect, and exploitation of older persons* (pp. 51–64). Baltimore: Health Professions Press.

Payne, B. K., & Cikovic, R. (1995). An empirical examination of the characteristics, consequences, and causes of elder abuse in nursing homes. *Journal of Elder Abuse and Neglect, 7*(4), 61–74.

Pillemer, K. A., & Moore, D. W. (1989). Abuse of patients in nursing homes: Findings from a survey of staff. *Gerontologist, 29,* 314–320.
Quinn, M. J., & Tomita, S. U. (1986). *Elder abuse and neglect: Causes, diagnosis and intervention strategies.* New York: Springer Press.
Ramsey-Klawsnik, H. (1996). Assessing physical and sexual abuse in health care settings. In L. A. Baumhover & S. C. Beall (Eds.), *Abuse, neglect, and exploitation of older persons* (pp. 67–87). Baltimore: Health Professions Press.
Rosenblatt, D. E. (1996). Documentation. In L. A. Baumhover & S. C. Beall (Eds.), *Abuse, neglect, and exploitation of older persons* (pp. 143–161). Baltimore: Health Professions Press.
Sengstock, M. C., & Hwalek, M. (1985). *Comprehensive index of elder abuse.* Detroit, MI: Wayne State University Press.
Sengstock, M. C., & Steiner, S. C. (1996). Assessing nonphysical abuse. In L. A. Baumhover & S. C. Beall (Eds.), *Abuse, neglect, and exploitation of older persons* (pp. 105–122). Baltimore: Health Professions Press.
Simon, M. L. (1992). *An exploratory study of adult protective services programs' report elder abuse clients.* Washington, DC: American Association of Retired Persons.
U.S. House of Representatives Select Committee on Aging. (1981). *Elder abuse: An examination of a hidden problem* (Committee Publication No. 97-277). Washington, DC: U.S. Government Printing Office.

10 Tools for Ethical Reasoning in Long-Term Care Management

Martha Pelaez

Mrs. Victoria is an 87-year-old widow who has been living in an apartment hotel for the last 12 years. Four years ago, at the request of a neighbor, she was assessed by the case manager of a social services agency. She was found to be alert and oriented but physically weak and in need of assistance with all her activities of daily living. The case manager arranged for a homemaker and for a nurse to visit on a regular basis to help monitor her multiple health problems.

After four years of working with Mrs. Victoria, the case manager believes her condition is so rapidly deteriorating that she can no longer stay in the apartment hotel without additional hours of service or without an around-the-clock companion. Mrs. Victoria has no relatives in the city. The program cannot provide her with as much help as she needs, nor can Mrs. Victoria afford to pay for it. The case manager knows that the time has come to place Mrs. Victoria in a more protective environment—in this case, a nursing home. Mrs. Victoria, still alert and with full knowledge of the consequences of her decision, refuses to move to a nursing home.

Consider these questions:

- Does Mrs. Victoria have the right to determine how and where she is going to spend the remainder of her life?
- Should Mrs. Victoria continue to receive full support from the program even though this support is insufficient and is helping her remain in an inappropriate environment?
- Is there a duty to respect Mrs. Victoria's wishes regardless of the consequences?

Serving some of Mrs. Victoria's needs puts a strain on the budget of the program, and therefore others who could be more adequately served by these services are still on the waiting list. Is there an obligation to allocate resources in terms of benefits and risks to the majority of the clients?

Doing the right thing is not always a matter of knowing the professional standard of conduct for a specific role or knowing the legal basis for choosing a course of action. An increasing number of people working within the long-term care system find themselves guided by a variety of professional identities and personal values.

Mrs. Victoria's case manager may confront ethical conflicts as a gatekeeper for the social services agency providing care when the demands of her different roles and identities clash. For example, her own personal values and what she considers her professional role as a social worker may differ from the policies and values of the social services agency employing her.

Ethical dilemmas are those that pit value against value or one ethical principle against another. In these circumstances, if the case manager acts in accordance with one set of values or principles—for example, if she chooses to protect Mrs. Victoria's right to self-determination rather than choosing to protect her from physical harm or self-neglect—she is choosing one apparent good over another, without having conclusive justification for this choice. Ethical dilemmas frequently create ethical distress. A study of ethical reasoning will help the practitioner understand the process of ethical deliberation and moral justification and will assist him or her in coping with the increasing challenge of "doing the right thing" in an imperfect and often complex system of health and social services delivery.

Judgments about particular actions are justified by rules, which are justified by principles and in turn by ethical theories. Let us say that Mrs. Victoria's case manager accepted the wishes of her client who, although severely disabled, is alert and knows the consequences of her decision to remain in her apartment rather than moving to a nursing home. The case manager may feel that it is morally wrong to act against Mrs. Victoria's wishes, even if her client's decision could prove unsafe. When questioned by her supervisor, the case manager may justify her action by appealing to an agency rule that requires case managers to "always obtain consent for intervention." In addition, the case manager may appeal to the principle of autonomy and even express a belief in an ethical theory of respect for people as fundamental to all her decisions. This reasoning provides her with an overall justification for the action taken.

In reality, cases are seldom simple. Often they are complicated by questions of fluctuating or borderline client decision-making capacity, by conflicting rights of client and family caregivers, and by limited resources available to the case managers. A review of ethical theories and principles will help the practitioner analyze the ethical dimension of many practice conflicts.

WHAT ARE ETHICAL THEORIES?

A theory is defined by the *Oxford American Dictionary* as a statement of the principles on which a subject is based. An ethical theory is a statement of the principles on which the "ought" of human conduct is based. Ethical reasoning is often based on two distinct ethical theories: utilitarian (teleological) and duty-based (deontological) theories.

Utilitarianism employs only one ethical principle in deliberating the rightness or wrongness of an action: the principle of utility. This principle asserts that "in all circumstances, we ought to produce the greatest possible balance of value over disvalue for all persons affected or the least possible balance of disvalue if only bad results can be brought about" (Beauchamp & Childress, 1983, p. 20).

Here is an example of utilitarian thinking: even though it is agreed that health and social services providers ought to respect their client's autonomy, consideration of autonomy should not completely override considerations of available resources, costs, or competing obligations. The case manager applying the principle of utility to Mrs. Victoria's situation may not honor her refusal to move to a nursing home if a more economical and efficient alternative to a protective environment offering 24-hour companionship is unavailable. The case manager may decide the limited agency resources and funding would benefit more clients who require less assistance. According to this principle, the overall benefit to the greatest number of people should be weighed against the overall (collective) harm or (individual client) risks. In deciding a particular course of action in Mrs. Victoria's situation, the principle of utility would require the case manager to consider and weigh the overall benefit to everyone involved against the overall harm or risks. The course of action that maximizes the benefits to everyone is the course of action that is ethically justified. The principle of utility may also require that in developing rules of actions, these rules be judged by whether or not they maximize benefits to society as a whole. In summary, a utilitarian theory measures the rightness or wrongness of an action (or rule) by its consequences.

On the other hand, a deontological theory is based on the belief that there are certain moral duties that are so fundamental that they ought to determine the rightness or wrongness of an action regardless of the consequences. Here is an example of deontological reasoning: health professionals have a duty to save lives, regardless of whether or not a particular life may be worth saving, and regardless of whether or not a particular person wants to be saved. Beauchamp and Childress characterize a deontologist as one who holds that "at least some acts are wrong and others right, independent of their consequences" (1983, p. 33). In Mrs. Victoria's situation, the case manager would respect the principle of self-determination as so fundamental that it would absolutely determine the right course of action without regard to the consequences. The moral duty to respect Mrs. Victoria's autonomy and choice would be fundamental in planning her care plan and living situation.

For some deontologists, like W. D. Ross, moral duties are always binding unless there is a conflict between two or more duties. Moral duties may be expressed in terms of fundamental ethical principles, such as respect for autonomy, beneficence, and justice. In situations in which respecting autonomy conflicts with the principle of beneficence, Ross (1963) maintains that one's actual duty is determined by examining the respective weights of the two competing moral duties and doing that which brings the greatest balance of right over wrong to that situation. In other words, moral duties are prima facie universal, but in fact each situation requires a balancing or weighing of a variety of moral duties. Ross presents a model of ethical reasoning that incorporates elements of both a deontological and a utilitarian approach. In the case of Mrs. Victoria, the case manager needs to consider at least three moral duties: (1) the duty to honor Mrs. Victoria's autonomy, (2) the duty to benefit Mrs. Victoria, and (3) the duty to allocate limited resources fairly. The case manager must then decide by weighing the competing moral duties. If it is determined that the greatest benefit to the client, as defined by the client's system of values, is to stay at home, then the case manager needs to negotiate a care plan for the client that accommodates the client's wishes and best interests as well as uses limited resources fairly. When each and every value cannot be successfully accommodated with creative use of formal and informal resources, then a systematic review of priorities based on the client's system of values needs to be made.

In practice, case managers need to learn how to apply a pattern of moral reasoning that combines elements of both the deontological and the utilitarian approach. That is, the case manager needs to understand the meaning of ethical principles such as autonomy and beneficence, as well as to be able to accommodate conflicting values and interests in such a way as to bring about the greatest amount of benefits over burdens.

PRINCIPLES OF AUTONOMY AND BENEFICENCE

What Is the Principle of Autonomy?

Although the etymological root of autonomy suggests the definition "self-rule" *(autonomos),* the conceptual content of such a definition defies easy interpretation. Collopy (1988) summarized the many meanings of autonomy as follows: "In its most general terms, autonomy signifies *control* of decision-making and other activity by the individual" (p. 10). Agich (1988) added that autonomy must not be restricted to a concept of independence and noninterference but must recognize that an action is free if the individual agent can identify with the elements from which this action flows.

All long-term care management (that is, the management of long-term health care, usually by a social worker or case manager) implements values, personal and societal. Case managers act on value premises about what constitutes a long life, what role health and safety play in a hierarchy of goals, and how much effort and resources are worth spending for prolonging or improving quality of life. However, health, physical impairments, safety, and risks have different meanings and values for different individuals. The principle of autonomy claims that the competent individual has the right to act according to the individual's set of values even when these values are in conflict with the values of the case manager and even if they contradict generally accepted societal values.

Autonomy becomes problematic in long-term care management when it is invoked to justify the right to make foolish choices based on personal idiosyncratic values. Collopy (1988) observed that "autonomy remains a dormant issue as long as the human agent adheres to conventional norms and does not test communal tolerances for 'error' or 'wrongdoing.' But when an individual compromises his own best interest or works against the collective will, autonomy becomes a highly charged issue" (p. 10). In the example, Mrs. Victoria's decision to remain in her own apartment is more important to her than compromising her safety. As a competent individual, she has chosen what she wants to do based on her values with full knowledge of potential consequences. To deny her free choice is the same as denying her autonomy. Autonomy in long-term care emphasizes that older people are subjects, not objects, and have the right to control their destinies.

Therefore, an examination of the principle of autonomy as it relates to specific care management situations should include discussion of the meaning of autonomy from the perspective of the language of rights. What does it mean to say that an older person has a moral right to autonomy? There are two types of rights: negative rights are claims to noninterference, and positive rights are claims of entitlement (Beauchamp & Childress, 1983). Within long-term care management, positive notions of autonomy involve serious considerations of how individuals should be empowered to achieve goals in accordance with their own values and how they should be supported in their autonomous choices. A notion of negative autonomy would simply forbid interference with an individual's self-determination.

In the case of Mrs. Victoria, the dilemma would be to develop a balance between positive and negative notions of autonomy. The case manager would try to uphold the client's negative rights by noninterference with Mrs. Victoria's intense desire to remain out of a nursing home; however, she would also try to enhance Mrs. Victoria's autonomy by offering strength and support. The case manager would not condone the impending risks of Mrs. Victoria's choice; rather she would try to draw out and enlarge Mrs. Victoria's perspective of the potential danger in her current living arrangements and would bring whatever additional formal or informal resources that may be needed to enable Mrs. Victoria to stay home.

Collopy (1988) explored four additional polarities within the concept of autonomy. A review of these polarities is helpful in understanding the complex nature of ethical dilemmas faced by case managers practicing in a long-term care setting.

Decisional autonomy versus autonomy of execution. In the best of circumstances, autonomy should be both decisional and executional. For example, Mrs. Victoria should be able to decide where she wants to live, what food to eat, and what clothing to wear and then should be able to manage her living environment and activities of daily living without help. However, lacking the physical ability to manage by herself does not mean that she lacks the ability to choose what she wants to do. Clearly, lacking the ability to execute an action does not mean that the person also lacks the ability to decide what he or she wants in relation to that action.

As a person grows older, the fear of physical dependency is usually compounded by the fear of having one's case manager take over all decisions regarding one's personal life. In Mrs. Victoria's case, the social services case manager should negotiate with her to reach what the client considers a meaningful choice for an acceptable living arrangement. Knowing the client's values and preferences in order of importance leads to open communication. The case manager's concern for Mrs. Victoria's safety may have more than one solution, although the situation involves agency limitations of staffing and funding. For the case manager to negotiate a workable solution, she should know why the client refuses to move to a nursing home. If Mrs. Victoria's most important value is to remain autonomous and she equates a move to a nursing home with losing her independence, then the case manager has offered a meaningless choice. Fears of dependency or of leaving familiar surroundings may be nonnegotiable values. Alternatives other than moving to a nursing home may not appear to the client as a sign of losing her independence and therefore become meaningful choices.

Direct versus delegated autonomy. Direct autonomy is immediate control of one's decisions, choices, and actions. Delegated autonomy is power freely given to others to make decisions for oneself. Both types of autonomy are important. For example, a person may delegate to his or her accountant many decisions concerning the way his or her money is to be invested. Delegation is different from surrender because the person maintains responsibility for what is delegated. In addition, the individual is responsible for selecting, instructing, and firing, if necessary, the person to whom he or she has delegated these powers.

The client in a long-term care setting delegates to the case manager, based on the assumption of the case manager's professional knowledge, the choice of appropriate interventions for a given outcome. However, seldom is the client perceived as being really involved in setting goals and outcomes or as maintaining responsibility for part of the care-planning process. Therefore, delegated autonomy may be mistaken for total surrender. In surrendering, one gives up power to control as well as responsibility for outcome. In negotiating a living arrangement for Mrs. Victoria, it is important to involve her in selecting meaningful choices. As long as she is a part of the care-planning process, her feelings of autonomy will remain intact.

Competent versus incapacitated autonomy. One of the most frequent challenges to maintaining autonomy within the long-term care context involves the determination of competency or decision-making capacity. The feasibility of respecting autonomy in geriatric practice is often seriously limited by the mental capacity of the frail older person. Is Mrs. Victoria capable of making decisions about how and where she lives and dies?

The President's Commission for the Study of Ethical Problems in Medicine and Biomedical and Behavioral Research (1982) views competency as consisting of three elements:

- Possession of a set of values and goals. Values give a framework for comparing options. Autonomy protects the individual's right to choose his or her own values. Therefore, it is a contradiction in terms to judge a person's capacity to make autonomous choices by whether his or her values correspond with professional judgment.

- Ability to communicate and understand information. Older adults with multiple chronic medical conditions requiring multiple medications may also have diminished vision and hearing or impaired cognitive functions. The requirements of informed consent emphasize that the health care provider should communicate with the patient or client using language that the client can understand.
- Ability to reason and to deliberate about one's choices. Reasoning includes the ability to compare the impacts of alternative outcomes on personal goals and life plans. Are the commonly used tests actually appropriate for assessing an older person's capacity to make choices? One test commonly used is the following: "As long as the client agrees with me, I will not question the client's capacity." Another frequently used test is the mental status examination. This offers questionable evidence regarding reliability and validity as a test of competence to make some choices.

Therefore a consensus has developed among practitioners and ethicists that the actual measurement of capacity should avoid labeling a person "competent" or "incompetent" with a blanket definition; reasonably and judgmentally coherent choices and actions should be respected; and those who are not capable of making decisions should be protected by a surrogate decision maker who will act on behalf of the incapacitated, making choices that the individual would have made had he or she been able to choose.

Immediate vs. long-range autonomy. Immediate autonomy refers to present choice, and long-range autonomy refers to future freedom. For example, if a depressed stroke patient refuses rehabilitation, he is giving up any potential for recovery of functions in the future. Is the case manager justified in interfering with the wishes of the patient to safeguard the patient's future autonomy?

To the extent that the case manager is committed only to long-term goals, it is easy to justify many paternalistic interventions in the present. On the other hand, to the extent that the case manager is committed to short-range goals, he or she may find it simple to abandon the client and justify this action in the name of autonomy. A clear tension should be preserved, and no simple solutions should be accepted without struggling with the ethical tension created by the conflict between short- and long-range goals (Collopy, 1988).

In Mrs. Victoria's case, the case manager feels the client is currently in an unsafe living arrangement and suggests a different living situation—a nursing home. The client refuses. If the case manager intervenes and goes against Mrs. Victoria's wishes for the good of her safety and long-range autonomy, then her immediate wishes are deferred. Mrs. Victoria conversely equates her autonomy with her short-range goals of not moving into a nursing home. The tension between long-range and short-range goals centers on the ultimate good Mrs. Victoria will derive. If Mrs. Victoria's choice is upheld and by that choice the client remains in an unsafe environment, incurring injury or death, then immediate autonomy has thwarted long-range autonomy. However, if the case manager chooses for Mrs. Victoria a long-range goal of autonomy, this intervention would have an impact on her immediate autonomy and current choice.

What Is the Principle of Beneficence?

The literal meaning of *beneficence* is "to benefit." The dictionary defines it as simply an act of kindness. The earliest expression of this principle in health care is found in the Hippocratic Oath, in which the physician is mandated to act in all matters to benefit the patient. In long-term care the principle of beneficence has played an important role in supporting arguments in favor of social and health care programs to benefit the frail older and disabled adult.

The principle of beneficence argues for an ethic of care management that is based on responsibility for and commitment to the well-being of the care recipient. It is in this context that the principle of beneficence sometimes enters into conflict with the principle of autonomy. For example, when the wishes of an individual are contrary to his or her welfare, the case manager may confront a series of dilemmas: Should the client's right to self-determination be subordinated to his or her welfare? Or, when is a case manager justified in overriding the principle of autonomy for the client's own good? Or, whose values are relevant for determining what constitutes the client's own good?

Feinberg (1983) justified paternalistic intervention, that is, action overriding a client's autonomy for his or her own good only when the client's action is considered to be "substantially nonvoluntary or when temporary intervention is necessary to establish whether it is voluntary or not" (p. 11). Paternalism is, therefore, supported by the principle of beneficence in those cases in which the client lacks decision-making capacity or is acting under undue coercion. In these cases, there is no substantial conflict of principles between autonomy and paternalism.

Mill (1977) was not willing to go along with beneficent actions interfering with an individual's liberty. For Mill, no adult individual was warranted in saying to other adults that they shall not do with their life for their own benefit what they choose to do with it. Cases of paternalism involving violation of autonomy for the client's own good, even though the client is capable of making decisions, are in direct conflict with both the principle of autonomy and the principle of beneficence. In these cases, the definition of "benefit" is made without regard to the values and priorities of the person to be benefited.

In the context of long-term care practice, paternalism is often problematic for the following reasons: (1) the tools available for assessing the decision-making capacity of chronically ill and frail older persons are limited, and clinical judgment is not always well informed; (2) older persons in long-term care settings are vulnerable to coercion and subtle manipulation; and (3) the stereotypes attached to aged people by society often influence the decision makers.

The tension between autonomy and paternalism is, therefore, made clear in the long-term care setting. The core of autonomy consists of the "intellectual/volitional capacities and operations which constitute human self-determination" (Collopy, 1988, p. 10). And the basis for paternalism is that those who are incapable of understanding what they choose, or who choose under coercion, should be protected from their own harmful choices. The challenge for the practitioner is to examine his or her actions against the full meaning of autonomy, with particular attention to the contextual nature of decision-making capacity and to the prejudices, stereotypes, and situations in long-term care that make older persons particularly susceptible to the premature and often unnecessary interventions of paternalism.

DEVELOPING A MORAL ACTION GUIDE

Ethical decisions in long-term care settings come in many flavors, shapes, and sizes, and no single formula can ensure success in resolving all ethical issues. Moody (1988) proposed a procedural standard for ethical conduct in long-term care that is summarized as the "three Cs": communication, clarification, and consensus-building. Other authors (Beauchamp & Childress, 1983; Purtillo & Cassel, 1981) have suggested a rational, systematic method to be applied to solving practical moral dilemmas. In this method, one identifies the problems, analyzes the situation, identifies alternative solutions, weighs competing alternatives, and finally makes a decision.

Combining a systematic and rational approach to decision making with Moody's three Cs would provide the practitioner with a moral action guide that is responsive to the complex situations of long-term care.

The following steps are useful as ethical reasoning guidelines:

1. *Identify the real problem:* The problem arises often from a conflict among well-accepted values, such as the inability to reach the most desirable client goal without challenging well-established professional or societal norms. However, on many occasions the real problem is a clear identification of these values that are important to everyone involved in the decision-making process.
2. *Analyze the situation:* Inspect all available data and understand the situation before jumping to solutions. Make a list of all relevant facts relating to the situation. Examine these facts from the perspective of the client or patient and family caregivers or significant others. Open channels of communication, if necessary, to enable each party to talk about their values and perceptions.
3. *Identify alternative solutions:* The most obvious solution is not always the best one. List all alternative courses of action that could be used to address the stated problem. Elicit from the client or patient, family, and significant others the ways in which each of their values relate to each of the alternative solutions or care options.
4. *Weigh competing alternatives:* Continue the negotiating process by searching for a consensus in alternative care options

or solutions reflecting the multiple interested parties' values and ethical concerns. Focus on agreement about values and options and then on disagreements. Ask all parties to discuss why and how they see their preferences as agreeing or conflicting. Weigh competing alternatives for care, listing in order of importance the reasons for options and degree of risk or benefit for patient or client. In negotiated consent, Moody (1988) argued that "what is called for is not an ethics of individual decisions, either patients' rights or professional virtues, but a social ethics, a communicative ethics based on deliberation and negotiation" (p. 69).

5. *Make a choice and justify the decision:* Complex and difficult situations may not always provide all interested parties with all the necessary information or with unlimited time to make the perfect decision. However, when a decision is made, it is important that those involved in the decision-making process be able to communicate the reasons and values underlying their decisions. Justifying a decision is accomplished by relating the decision to values and accepted moral principles. Finally, one must be ready to revise a particular choice or decision on the basis of reflection and exposure to other similar situations.

REFERENCES

Agich, G. J. (1988). *Autonomy in long term care.* Unpublished manuscript, Southern Illinois University, Carbondale.

Beauchamp, L. T., & Childress, J. F. (1983). *Principles of biomedical ethics.* New York: Oxford University Press.

Collopy, B. J. (1988). Autonomy in long term care: Some crucial distinctions. *Gerontologist, 28* (Suppl.), 10.

Feinberg, J. (1983). Legal paternalism. In R. Sartorius (Ed.), *Paternalism* (pp. 3–18). Minneapolis: University of Minnesota Press.

Mill, J. S. (1977). *On liberty, collected works of John Stuart Mill.* Toronto: University of Toronto Press.

Moody, H. R. (1988). From informed consent to negotiated consent. *Gerontologist, 28* (Suppl.), 64.

President's Commission for the Study of Ethical Problems in Medicine and Biomedical and Behavioral Research. (1982). Washington, DC: U.S. Government Printing Office.

Purtillo, R. B., & Cassel, C. K. (1981). *Ethical dimensions in the health professions*. Philadelphia: W. B. Saunders.

Ross, W. D. (1963). *Foundation of ethics*. Oxford, England: Oxford University Press.

11 HIV/AIDS and the Elderly

James H. Riley

An elderly patient was admitted to a nursing home in Florida for intravenous antibiotic rehabilitation of pneumonia and then discharged to return home. During a review of the patient's medical chart the social worker found that the patient had been diagnosed with HIV. A review of the patient's medication record revealed no use of typical HIV/AIDS medications or protocols. When the patient's daughter was queried, she admitted being aware of her mother's diagnosis and added that "Mom is not aware that she has AIDS; we did not tell her because we were afraid she would just give up." When asked about treating the HIV infection, the patient's attending physician concurred with the daughter and said, "What's the point? She is probably not going to live much longer anyway." As far as the social worker could determine, the patient was unaware of her HIV status. During the social services assessment, the patient described various opportunistic infections associated with HIV but was unaware of their origin.

This scenario raises many questions and issues. By Florida state law, the patient must be furnished with an HIV pre- and posttest counseling session, and the patient must sign a written consent to be tested for HIV. Was this done? If so, why was the patient not informed of her HIV status? Why was the patient not treated with antiviral or prophylactic protocols? Most important, why was the power of self-determination taken from her by a family member and a physician? If this were a person in her 30s or 40s, would she not have been informed so that she might make plans for the future and put her affairs in order? Was this an act of ageism?

EPIDEMIOLOGIC DATA

Many studies conducted concerning HIV/AIDS and the elderly generally define this population as anyone 50 years of age and older: "We live in an aging society, with over one-fourth of the population of the United States over the age of 50" (Nazon & Levine-Perkell, 1996, p. 21). The Centers for Disease Control has collected AIDS data since the early 1980s and has reported that since then, 10 percent of all newly diagnosed cases have been in the 50-year-old and older group (Nazon & Levine-Perkell, 1996; Rosenzweig & Fillit, 1992; Schmidt & Kenen, 1989). Although it appears that the 10 percent ratio remained steady from 1989 to 1996, it should be noted that the elder group reported 10,492 new cases of AIDS in 1989 (Schmidt & Kenen, 1989) and 38,151 new cases of AIDS in 1993 (Linsk, 1994), an increase of approximately 28,000 new cases in just four years. These figures do not include those infected with HIV who have not yet developed AIDS.

It is estimated that for each reported case of AIDS, there are 3.5 to 4.3 unreported HIV cases (Douglas & Pinsky, 1996). Using 3.9 as an average, it can be calculated that approximately 40,918 people, 50 years or older, had contracted HIV in 1989 and by 1993 approximately 148,789 had contracted HIV. Today, many people are living longer with HIV/AIDS than during the 1980s. This is in part due to earlier testing and detection of the virus and in part due to earlier treatment of HIV, associated opportunistic infections, and preventative treatment and care. In 1994 Linsk reported that approximately 79,986 people age 40 to 49, were diagnosed with AIDS. Using the ratio of 3.9 HIV cases per 1 AIDS case, it is conceivable that an additional 312,000 50-plus-year-olds will be diagnosed with AIDS within six years. Presently, the 40-to-49-year-old group represents 21 percent of all reported AIDS cases. It is easy to see that the 50-plus-year-old group could represent 25 percent to 30 percent of all AIDS cases. Further, one could speculate that those infected with HIV who are in their late 40s and early 50s will live into their 60s.

BIOLOGICAL ASPECTS OF AIDS AND AGING

As the name indicates, AIDS attacks the immune system, reducing the body's ability to resist microorganisms that cause infections that can ultimately result in death. Symptoms of HIV are often nonspecific, such as fatigue, chronic pain, loss of appetite, weight loss, and decreased physical and mental functioning (Linsk, 1994). These same symptoms are often mistakenly assumed to be part of the aging process.

When the immune system is compromised, the person with HIV is vulnerable to opportunistic infections and malignancies, the most common of which are associated with elderly AIDS patients: *Pneumocystis carinii* pneumonia, tuberculosis, *Mycobacterium avium* complex, herpes zoster, and cytomegalovirus (Wallace, Paauw, & Spach, 1993). Malignancies such as Kaposi's sarcoma and non-Hodgkin's lymphoma have been prevalent in elderly lesbians and gay men with AIDS. Neurological damage related to affected brain cells is also common, as are the terminal symptoms of AIDS-related dementia, which can be mistaken for Alzheimer's disease (Crisologo, Campbell, & Forte, 1996).

Because the immune system becomes less efficient as part of normal aging, the elderly are in great danger when exposed to HIV. Geriatric AIDS has only recently been recognized as a significant social problem, competing for resources in our complex social and health care systems. Social workers and other health professionals are required to broaden their concepts of AIDS to understand the effect of AIDS on the elderly and their families as well as on the geriatric institutions that serve them (Gutheil & Chichin, 1991).

WORKING WITH ELDERLY PEOPLE WITH HIV/AIDS

There are several issues for the practitioner to be aware of when working with the elderly men and women who are at risk for or have been diagnosed with HIV/AIDS. Some of these issues are transmission, prevention, assessment, psychosocial factors, AIDS and dementia, care and treatment, and death and dying issues.

Transmission

HIV is contracted through sexual activity, intravenous drug use (needle sharing), and blood transfusions or organ transplants. The virus is sexually transmitted through direct contact with infected blood, semen, and vaginal secretions (Talashek, Tichy, & Epping, 1990). In 1994, Linsk reported that 62 percent of those over 50 contracted HIV in 1992 through gay or bisexual sexual activities (down from 90 percent in 1982) and 6 percent of those over 50 contracted HIV in 1992 through heterosexual sexual activities (up from 0 percent in 1982). The decline in gay-bisexual transmission of HIV may be explained by the belief that as gay males age they are involved in fewer sexual activities, maintain longer single-partner relationships, and have fewer random sexual relationships (Talashek et al., 1990). The trend of the elderly to remain in monogamous relationships, however, is declining.

HIV is also transmitted through heterosexual activity among the elderly. Rosenzweig and Fillit (1992) studied an 88-year-old woman who contracted HIV through a heterosexual partner. It was speculated, after questioning family members, that this woman's spouse was an intravenous drug user. It is probable that through the spouse's needle sharing, he contracted HIV and then transmitted it to his spouse. Contrary to popular belief, frequency of sexual activity among the elderly heterosexual population may decline, but it does not halt.

Fowler (1997), age 60-plus, a former feature writer and reporter for the *Kansas City Star* and writer for *Bon Appetite* magazine, educates elderly people about HIV/AIDS because of her personal experience in becoming infected. She reports that following her divorce in the early 1980s, she dated a man she had known all her adult life. Fowler is honest in reporting that she knew little about AIDS except that it seemed to affect only those in the gay community. She believed that engaging in sex with her long-time friend would present little risk for her; approximately six years later she was diagnosed with HIV.

Leigh, Temple, and Trocki (1993) reported that 82 percent (321) of those over 50 ($n = 392$) stated that they had intercourse at least one time per month during the previous year. This compares with 84 percent (905) of those aged 18 to 49 ($n = 1078$) who also reported having intercourse at least once per month. Of those aged 50 and older, 71 percent reported having intercourse at least two times per month compared with 76 percent of those aged 18 to 49, and 43 percent reported having intercourse at least one time per week compared with 59 percent of those aged 18 to 49 (Leigh et al., 1993). It is obvious from these figures that the frequency of sexual intercourse for those aged 50 and over and those younger than 50 is very similar. When assessing the elderly person who presents with HIV/AIDS symptoms, the practitioner must avoid ageism by not ruling out sexual history simply because of the client's age.

Sexual transmission is not the only method of contracting HIV. Blood transfusions and intravenous drug use account for some HIV transmissions as well. Transmission of HIV through blood transfusion rose from 0 percent in 1982 to 17 percent in 1988 and fell to 8 percent in 1992 (Linsk, 1994). Blood screening began in 1985 and may explain the decline from 1988 to 1992. Because of the natural aging process, the elderly are more susceptible to medical declines requiring blood transfusions. Elderly people are more likely to contract HIV through blood transfusions than through sexual transmission or intravenous drug use (Talashek et al., 1990). Further, those who contracted HIV through transfusion may infect others through sexual activities (Catania et al., 1989). Finally, intravenous drug use among the elderly may be more prevalent than previously believed. A minimal number of elderly people reported using intravenous drugs in 1982; by 1988, 8 percent reported using intravenous drugs, and by 1992, 11 percent reported using intravenous drugs (Linsk, 1994). Indeed, it would appear that the use of intravenous drugs among the elderly is increasing.

Prevention

For the practitioner, education seems to be the major prevention strategy against HIV infection. Many education programs have been designed to address the younger-than-50 population, with most aimed at adolescents and young adults. Little is known about elderly sexual behavior and consequently few HIV education programs have been directed toward the elderly population (Fooken, 1994; House & Walker, 1993; Linsk, 1994).

Talashek et al. (1990) suggested that education about safe sex practices is most important and recommended some specific areas of education: avoiding multiple partners, unidentified partners, or prostitutes. Further, they warned against having sex with someone who is experiencing genital discharge, warts, herpes, or other suspicious lesions. It is recommended that latex condoms and diaphragms be used in combination with a spermicide.

As previously discussed, it is clear that the belief that the elderly do not participate in sexual activities is more myth than reality (Whipple & Scura, 1989). It would be advantageous for the practitioner to view the elderly as sexually active and provide appropriate safer sex education to this population. It is important to educate the elderly about sexuality, risky sexual behavior, and pertinent protective methods (Visser & Ketting, 1994).

An AIDS Prevention for Seniors program was offered at the Little Havana Senior Center in Miami and was enthusiastically received by the many elderly members who attended. Many of these participants were single, through divorce or widowhood, and still engaged, or interested in, sexual activity. The use of condoms and other methods of safe sex were not familiar to many in this population, which may also mirror the experience of other groups of seniors. Their receptiveness to education about AIDS prevention might serve as a reminder for health care professionals to offer similar programs in a variety of congregate settings: public housing, condominiums, places of worship, community health centers, continuing education centers, retiree programs, and so forth. The opportunities are endless and the potential for successful outcomes is promising.

California, New York, and some other states have established elder AIDS prevention units (Lade, 1997). Florida has followed suit with the Senior HIV Intervention Program, which began in May 1997, serving primarily Palm Beach, Broward, and Dade counties in southeast Florida (Lade, 1997). The program is a joint venture between the Florida State Department of Health and the Florida Department of Elder Affairs. In addition to educating the elderly population, the program will also provide support groups for elderly people with HIV and for their children, grandchildren, and friends. Lade stated this program is needed because AIDS among elderly residents of Florida rose 13 percent (from 1,030 to 1,160) between June 1, 1996, and April 30, 1997.

Another training program available for practitioners who wish to present educational workshops is offered by Rita Strombeck, director of Health Care Education Associates of Palm Springs, California. She has produced a video about AIDS and older people, titled *The Forgotten Tenth*. This video can be used as the basis for a discussion of attitudes and behaviors. The video is part of a package that includes a leader's guide and a participant's workbook. The package costs $95, and additional workbooks can be purchased for $5 each. For more information or to order the materials, call (760) 323-4032. This program has received national attention through the intensive summer training series of the American Society of Aging in San Francisco.

Assessment

Because of the type of risky behavior that leads to being HIV positive, it is difficult for many health care professionals to imagine someone's grandmother or elderly parent HIV positive. This form of stereotyping is another example of ageism (Lavick, 1994; Lloyd, 1989; Nazon & Levine-Perkell, 1996). The elderly deserve the same careful assessment, or screening, for presenting HIV symptoms as those younger than 50 years of age, and in fact they are very familiar with the process of being assessed (Schmidt & Kenen, 1989).

What is of primary concern to the practitioner is the method of performing the assessment. A general medical history should be solicited from the client, with particular attention paid to organ transplants and blood transfusions and dates. When asking the client about the possibility of intravenous drug use, the practitioner must remain nonjudgmental and nonreactive if the response is in the affirmative. It is equally important to ascertain a detailed sexual history from the elderly client, and again, it is important to remain nonjudgmental (Lavick, 1994). Because of the possible embarrassment this may cause the client, it is imperative to proceed with "sensitivity in communication and attentive listening" (Talashek et al., 1990, p. 35). These are particularly useful skills because of the personal nature of the types of questions asked of the client. It should be understood that there is the potential for "significant emotional responses, particularly when age, language, gender, or cultural differences exist between the client and practitioner."

If the assessment uncovers a positive diagnosis, the practitioner needs to inform the client not to make any drastic life decisions, particularly if the diagnosis is made in the early stages of the HIV/AIDS continuum. As one 51-year-old client stated, "When I learned of my diagnosis I quit my lucrative job, sold every thing, and spent all my life savings. Now it is eight years later and I have nothing. I have to depend on Medicaid for medical attention and friends for day-to-day living expenses and support. I was just sure I would be dead in two weeks."

Psychosocial Factors

The practitioner should be aware of the psychosocial factors affecting the elderly with HIV/AIDS. Some of these factors include ageism and stigmatization, life stage, community support systems, adult children, and the affected elderly (elderly parent as caregiver of HIV-positive child).

Ageism and stigmatization. Some elderly people with HIV/AIDS must contend with double societal bigotry: ageism and HIV-related stigmatization. The practitioner must be aware that simply because a person is over 50 does not preclude him or her from being HIV positive. Despite being over 50, many elderly people are at risk for contracting HIV through unprotected heterosexual, homosexual, or bisexual intercourse or intravenous drug use (Lavick, 1994; Lloyd, 1989; Nazon & Levine-Perkell, 1996). However, many Americans choose to believe that elderly people are not involved in these risky behaviors solely based on the person's age. Further, the elderly are also stigmatized by virtue of being HIV positive (Lloyd, 1989; Nazon & Levine-Perkell, 1996; Schmidt & Kenen, 1989). The practitioner needs to be aware of these impacting prejudices that could prevent the elderly from using resources to which they are entitled.

Life stage. Lavick (1994) addressed the issue of the elderly's life stage from the perspective of Erik Erikson's theory of eight stages of life. In stage seven, generativity versus stagnation (ages 24 to 54), the task is to resist stagnation and begin to contribute to the quality of life of future generations (Barker, 1991). Obviously this task will be difficult to successfully complete for the HIV-positive older adult who is faced with a life-threatening disease. In the eighth stage, integrity versus despair (older than 54), the individual may develop a unique integration with mankind or develop a sense of regret of how his or her life was experienced (Barker, 1991). Knowing that the elder with HIV may be overwhelmed with regret and issues of death, the practitioner might suggest individual or group psychotherapeutic interventions, with the goal of achieving a sense of integrity through transcending a preoccupation with loss and working toward leaving some form of legacy for family or community (Lavick, 1994).

Community supports. As with HIV education, which is primarily focused at the younger population, many HIV community support systems do not accommodate the older population

(Piette, Wachtel, Mor, & Mayer, 1995). Programs such as support groups, special housing, and substance abuse treatment are not geared to seniors. This phenomenon may be due, in part, to limited resources. Compounding the problem is the fact that more elderly are being diagnosed with HIV at a time when the American health care system is overburdened and managed health care is in effect (Crystal, 1989; Schmidt & Kenen, 1989). Schmidt and Kenen warned of the ethical issues of providing services to the younger HIV patient, based on age, in light of the constraints on the U.S. health care budget. The practitioner can more efficiently use an individual's health care benefits by referring the older HIV patient to a physician who specializes in infectious diseases rather than to a general medicine practitioner. This approach could allow the individual better use of his or her benefits and not waste crucial health care dollars on ineffective treatments.

Adult children. Many elderly HIV-positive clients have adult children for whom family counseling may be effective (Crisologo et al., 1996) in disclosing one's HIV status, although it is an individual decision. Some choose not to disclose their status in order not to burden their children (Lavick, 1994). According to Lavick, some other people decide to disclose their status "to their adult children so that they may take an active role in financial planning or in issues of wills, trusts, or durable powers of attorney" (p. 128). The practitioner must be aware that this issue is often not simply a matter of whether to disclose or not. Many times, disclosing HIV status may also mean the older person has to disclose his or her sexual orientation or practice or intravenous drug use (Lavick, 1994).

Elder caregivers. Finally, not all HIV issues have to do with the older person being infected but rather *affected* by HIV. Of concern for many older people is the issue of caregiving for a child who is HIV positive. It is posited that the elderly parent caregiver of one who is HIV positive may represent a significantly large group of those affected by HIV (Brabant, 1994). The elder parent faces issues of caregiver burden, economic strain, AIDS-related stigma, isolation, and knowledge of the progression of the disease in his or her child (Brabant, 1994). It is paramount that the practitioner involve the older parent in HIV education, support groups, and respite care where appropriate.

AIDS and Dementia

In addition to the practitioner being familiar with HIV transmission, prevention, assessment, and psychosocial issues, he or she must also be alert to misdiagnoses of dementia and other psychiatric conditions (Garvey, 1994). In 1989 Weiler reported that HIV had previously been discovered in the spinal cord, spinal fluid, and brain of some patients. In other words, HIV directly infects the central nervous system and causes dementia (Navia, Jordan, & Price, 1986). By 1994 more had been learned about the effects of HIV on the central nervous system. It is now clear that HIV can cause dementia, as well as "symptoms of mania, psychosis, major depression, and even obsessive–compulsive disorder" (Buckley, 1994, p. 586). This information is particularly useful to the practitioner confronted with the "young" elderly person who appears to present with dementia prematurely or with elders who present with symptoms of psychiatric disorders when no previous history exists.

Care and Treatment

Any person with HIV/AIDS will require increased, more frequent, and intensified medical services as the disease progresses. The elderly typically experience age-related illnesses with time, and this situation is compounded when their health status has been compromised by HIV (Whipple & Scura, 1989). When this appears to be the case, the practitioner must anticipate the next level of care for his or her client. The least restrictive environment, at home, is the preferable setting in which the elderly patient can receive medical care. Based on this approach, the home health care industry is the fastest-growing section of the U.S. health care system (Garvey, 1994).

It is imperative that the practitioner also pay attention to the elderly caregiver of the elderly person with HIV, as noted earlier. Caregivers may be fearful of contracting the disease at the same time they are experiencing the grieving process for their loved one (Crisologo et al., 1996). The practitioner may intervene with HIV education, a referral to an appropriate support group, and provision of respite care.

At some point in the progression of the HIV disease, the elderly person may require inpatient acute hospital care because of multiple medical diagnoses (Fillit, 1994). Eventually this patient may require long-term care in a skilled nursing facility (SNF).

Many people believe that hospitalization is too expensive and that lengths of stay are too long (Benjamin, 1988; Fillit, 1994). Medicare's hospital prospective payment system oriented around diagnosis-related groups is designed to reduce hospital costs and lengths of stay (Benjamin, 1988; Fillit, 1994). One alternative to caring for the elderly with HIV/AIDS is the nursing home, after the patient has been medically stabilized in the hospital. AIDS, previously viewed as a terminal disease, is now often seen as a chronic condition, requiring occasional hospital acute care, subacute care, SNF long-term care, and home health care (Gentry, Fogarty, & Lehrman, 1993). The practitioner needs to be aware, however, that an elderly person with HIV/AIDS may not be allowed admission to an SNF if the facility is already overburdened, or that the person may receive a lower level of care because of the stigma attached to the disease (Crisologo et al., 1996). Again, practitioners should advocate for the least-restrictive and preferred level of care for their clients.

Medical social workers and independent geriatric case managers can assist the elderly patient in linking to community-based services (Garvey, 1994). Social workers can monitor the course of the illness and advocate or mediate on behalf of the elderly client for community services, health care services, AIDS services organization assistance, and psychosocial support services (Crisologo et al., 1996). Social workers, mental health counselors, and psychologists can provide individual and family counseling services to assist with family reactions, conflicts, and death and dying issues.

In addition to medical services, many community agencies can provide Meals on Wheels, transportation, day care activities, social activities, respite care, support groups, assistance with housing, access to medications, and alternative treatments. Many larger communities have federally funded (Ryan White Grant) case management agencies to assist the AIDS patient in accessing services at no cost to the patient. If these agencies exist in your area, your local county health department should be able to provide the local phone number.

Douglas and Pinsky (1996) provided many resource phone numbers; among them are those included below.

National AIDS Information Hot Line

English, (800) 342-2437
Español, (800) 344-7432
Hearing-Impaired/TDD, (800) 243-7889

Treatment Guides

AIDS/HIV Treatment Directory (American Foundation for AIDS Research), (800) 458-5231
AIDS Treatment News (John James, editor), (415) 255-0588, (415) 255-4659 (fax)
Treatment Issues (Gay Men's Health Crisis [GMHC]), (212) 367-1040

Financial Assistance for HIV Drugs

Call your local county department of health.
Federal—Health Resources and Services Administration, AIDS Drug Reimbursement Program, (301) 443-4170

Treatment Information Hot Lines

Available clinical trials in your area, sponsored by the Centers for Disease Control (CDC), (800) 874-2572 (9 A.M.–7 P.M. EST)
National Institutes of Health (NIH), (800) 243-7644

International Travelers

CDC International Travelers Hot Line provides up-to-date information about current world areas of infectious diseases and vaccination requirements for host countries, (404) 332-4555

Death and Dying

Perhaps one of the more difficult aspects for the client and practitioner to cope with is the grief and bereavement inherent in the progression of the HIV/AIDS disease. This phenomenon, in large part, is due to the reminder that we too are mortal (O'Neil, 1989). There are at least two points along the HIV/AIDS disease continuum at which death may become an issue.

The first point of concern for the practitioner is "the time shortly after the diagnosis of HIV infection is made," when there is the greatest risk for suicide (Conwell, 1994, p. 64). Conwell suggested that the practitioner assess the patient for possible pre-existing psychiatric conditions that may lead to suicidal ideation. This is particularly important in light of the fact that many elderly people already are struggling with a comorbid medical condition affecting the client's ability to complete previously simple activities of daily living. Assisting the client to move beyond this point is crucial. Some clients have actually talked about a new "lease on life." One client said, "As strange as this sounds, this is possibly the best thing that has ever happened to me. I have stopped using alcohol, gotten closer to my family, and I spend my time volunteering to help others. In a way, my life has never been better, it was like a wake-up call."

The second point of concern is the actual dying process at the end stage of the disease. When death is relatively imminent, of primary concern to the practitioner is the management of pain, easing of suffering, and acceptance of the inevitable for his or her client. Hospice services, offering comfort care, can be used in the home, nursing home setting, and hospital environment. Again, the key element, in addition to client self-determination, is the less restrictive the environment, the better. This is a time when many people may visit the client, and visitation should be accomplished with as few restrictions as possible.

Garvey (1994) suggested the use of an interdisciplinary team to assist the client. She described a hospice model developed by the Visiting Nurses Hospice of San Francisco, working in conjunction with the Department of Public Health, to provide services at home for the elderly man or woman with AIDS. This is an approach that seems plausible in virtually all geographic locations. Garvey stated that the care team consists of "a registered nurse (case manager, social worker, counselor(s), therapist(s), nutritionist, home care aide, medical director, chaplain, volunteer(s), and an on-call system" (p. 119). The care team works in collaboration with the caregiver and significant others to provide support to them as well as the client (Garvey, 1994).

In addition to hospice services, the practitioner can offer direct comfort to the client who is experiencing the end stages of the disease. One of the techniques at the disposal of the practitioner is the use of life review through reminiscence. Working with the dying elderly client can be accomplished by helping the client work through unresolved conflicts, maintain dignity and self-esteem, and integrate past experiences (Beaver & Miller, 1985; Carlson, 1984). It is important that the practitioner be aware that the elderly client is beginning to mourn his or her own death. Carlson (1984) stated that "reminiscing aids the elderly individual in dealing with issues of separation and loss and is a form of working through what parallels a normal mourning process" (p. 82).

Lest we practitioners allow the idea of HIV and the elderly to spell only doom and gloom, we can always think of the example of Sandra Baker. Baker contracted HIV through intravenous drug use. She has been free of drugs for two years and, now age 60, she lives in Harlem and hopes to educate and inspire other elderly people, as Magic Johnson has done for younger people (Gross, 1997). Or Sue Saunders, age 64, who contracted AIDS by having unprotected sex but now devotes her time to teaching seniors about the dangers of this incurable disease. She is the volunteer coordinator of the new Florida AIDS initiative for seniors (Lade, 1997).

As we recognize that people are living longer with HIV/AIDS, in part as a result of new medical treatments, it may be time to view this illness as a manageable chronic disease with many courageous elders modeling the way. As many clients have proclaimed to this writer in personal conversations, "I am not dying from this virus; I am learning to live with it."

Resources

There are local agencies that can provide various services for the person who is infected with HIV. Douglas and Pinsky (1996) compiled the following list of national phone numbers as points of contact.

HIV-2 Testing

Anonymous testing, have physician contact: Centers for Disease Control AIDS Program, (404) 639-3174 or your local health department

Legal Matters

American Civil Liberties Union–Lesbian and Gay Rights Project, (212) 549-2500

National Lawyers Guild AIDS Network, (415) 285-5067 (office), (415) 285-5066 (fax)

Intergovernmental Health Policy Project-AIDS Policy Center (George Washington University) (202) 624-5400

Military

Military Law Task Force (National Military Project on AIDS), (619) 233-1701

G.I. Rights Network, (415) 474-3002

Immigration

The Center for Immigrants' Rights, (212) 505-6890

National Network for Immigrants' and Refugee Rights, (510) 465-1984

Sexual Minorities (gay men and lesbians)

Lambda Legal Defense and Education Fund, (212) 809-8585

National Gay and Lesbian Task Force, (202) 332-6483

Human Rights Campaign, (202) 628-4160

Women

Women's AIDS Network (San Francisco AIDS Foundation), (415) 487-3000, (415) 487-8000

Planned Parenthood, (212) 541-7800, (415) 441-7858

Ethnic and Racial Minorities

IMPACT, (301) 931-8331 (answering machine and recorded message only)

National Council of La Raza–AIDS Project, (202) 785-1670

Midwest Hispanic AIDS Coalition, (773) 772-8195

National Coalition of Hispanic Health and Human Services Organizations (COSSMHO), (202) 387-5000

People of Color Against AIDS Network, (206) 322-7061

Substance Users (narcotics, alcohol, etc.)

ADAPT-Association for Drug Abuse Prevention and Treatment, (212) 289-1957

People with Hemophilia

National Hemophilia Foundation, (212) 219-8180

Informational Pamphlets

HIV, AIDS, and Older Adults, *Age Page*, National Institute on Aging, U.S. Department of Health and Human Services, Public Health Service, 1994, (800) 222-2225

AIDS: A Multigenerational Crisis, and Women's Initiative Fact Sheet, American Association of Retired Persons, Social Outreach and Support Programs Division, 601 E Street, NW, Washington, DC 20049, (800) 424-3410 for members

REFERENCES

Barker, R. L. (Ed.). (1991). *The social work dictionary* (2nd ed.). Silver Spring, MD: National Association of Social Workers.

Beaver, M. L., & Miller, D. (1985). *Clinical social work practice with the elderly.* Homewood, IL: Dorsey Press.

Benjamin, A. E. (1988). Long term care and AIDS: Perspectives from experience with the elderly. *Milbank Quarterly, 66*(3), 415–443.

Brabant, S. (1994). An overlooked AIDS affected population: The elderly parent as care giver. *Journal of Gerontological Social Work, 22*(1/2), 131–145.

Buckley, R. A. (1994). Differentiating medical and psychiatric illness. *Psychiatric Annals, 24*(11), 584–591.

Carlson, C. (1984). Reminiscing: Toward achieving ego integrity in old age. *Social Casework, 61*(4), 81–89.

Catania, J. A., Turner, H., Kegeles, S. M., Stall, R., Pollack, L., & Coates, T. J. (1989). Older Americans and AIDS: Transmission risks and primary prevention research needs. *Gerontological Society of America, 29*(3), 373– 381.

Conwell, Y. (1994). Suicide and terminal illness: Lessons from the HIV pandemic. *Crisis, 15*(2), 57–58, 64.

Crisologo, S. A., Campbell, M. H., & Forte, J. A. (1996). Social Work, AIDS and the elderly: Current knowledge and practice. *Journal of Gerontological Social Work, 26*(1/2), 49–70.

Crystal, S. (1989). New demands and economic consequences. *Generations, 13*(4), 23–27.

Douglas, P. H., & Pinsky, L. (1996). *The essential AIDS fact book.* New York: Simon & Schuster.

Fillit, H. (1994). Challenges for acute care geriatric inpatient units under the present Medicare prospective payment system. *Journal of the American Geriatrics Society, 42*(5), 553–558.

Fooken, J. (1994). Sexuality in the later years: The impact of health and body-image in a sample of older women. *Patient Education Counseling, 23*, 227–233.

Fowler, J. (1997, March/April). Over 60, with HIV: One woman's story. *Aging Today*, 5.

Garvey, C. (1994, June). AIDS care for the elderly. *AIDS Patient Care,* 118–120.

Gentry, D., Fogarty, T. E., & Lehrman, S. (1993, June). Providing long-term care for persons with AIDS. *AIDS Patient Care,* 130–137.

Gross, J. (1997, March 16). Hoping to be inspiration for seniors. *New York Times,* p. A1.

Gutheil, I. A., & Chichin, E. R. (1991). AIDS, older people, and social work. *Health & Social Work, 16*, 237–241.

House, R. M., & Walker, C. M. (1993). Preventing AIDS via education. *Journal of Counseling and Development, 71*(3), 282–289.

Lade, D. C. (1997, May 20). AIDS cases rise among seniors. *Ft. Lauderdale Sun-Sentinel*, pp. A1, A4.

Lavick, J. (1994, June). Psychosocial considerations of HIV infection in the older adult. *AIDS Patient Care*, 127–129.

Leigh, B. C., Temple, M. T., & Trocki, K. F. (1993). The sexual behavior of U.S. adults: Results from a national survey. *American Journal of Public Health, 83*, 1400–1408.

Linsk, N. L. (1994). HIV and the elderly. *Families in Society, 75*, 362–372.

Lloyd, G. A. (1989). AIDS & elders: Advocacy, activism, & coalitions. *Generations, 13*(4), 32–35.

Navia, B. A., Jordan, B. D., & Price, R. W. (1986). The AIDS dementia complex. *Annals of Neurology, 19*, 517–524.

Nazon, M., & Levine-Perkell, J. (1996). AIDS and aging. *Journal of Gerontological Social Work, 25*(1/2), 21–31.

O'Neil, M. (1989). Grief & bereavement in AIDS & Aging. *Generations, 13*(4), 80–82.

Piette, J., Wachtel, T. J., Mor, V., & Mayer, K. (1995). The impact of age on the quality of life in persons with HIV infection. *Journal of Aging and Health, 7*(2), 163–178.

Rosenzweig, R., & Fillit, H. (1992). Probable heterosexual transmission of AIDS in an aged woman. *Journal of American Geriatrics Society, 40*, 1261–1264.

Schmidt, R. M., & Kenen, R. H. (1989). AIDS in an aging society: Ethical & psychosocial considerations. *Generations, 13*(4), 36–39.

Talashek, M. L., Tichy, A. M., & Epping, H. (1990). Sexually transmitted diseases in the elderly: Issues and recommendations. *Journal of Gerontological Nursing, 16*(4), 33–40.

Visser, A. P., & Ketting, E. (1994). Sexual health: Education and counseling perspectives on contraceptive use, HIV and sexuality. *Patient Education and Counseling, 23*, 141–145.

Wallace, J. I., Paauw, D. S., & Spach, D. H. (1993). HIV infection in older patients: When to suspect the unexpected. *Geriatrics, 48*(6), 61–70.

Whipple, B., & Scura, K. W. (1989). HIV and the older adult: Taking the necessary precautions. *Journal of Gerontological Nursing, 15*(9), 15–19.

12 Death, Bereavement, Loss, and Growth: Two Perspectives

Mary O'Donnell and Florence Safford

Providing services to people who are dying, or to the bereaved who are grieving, calls for the utmost sensitivity, strengthened by knowledge. This is an arena of human interaction in which emotions are most vulnerable, for the elderly client and his or her family, as well as for the practitioner. There are so many different forms of denial that are used as defenses against death anxiety that the compassionate practitioner must continuously monitor his or her readiness and openness to understand the pain or fears of the client.

The first part of this chapter was written by a health care professional and educator who is a pioneer in hospice care. The content is organized to guide the practitioner in learning about the needs of those suffering significant losses or impending losses, while developing an awareness of his or her own emotional responses to these needs. It is presented without direct reference to scholarly research, although it reflects extensive practice informed by the range of extant research.

The second part of this chapter presents a discussion of some of the research and literature that has expanded our recent knowledge of dying and death as biopsychosocial processes, particularly as relevant to gerontology.

A THEORETICAL AND PRACTICAL PERSPECTIVE

> No one knows with regard to death whether it is not really the greatest blessing that can happen to man;

The theoretical and practical perspective is provided by Mary O'Donnell, and the scholarly perspective is provided by Florence Safford.

> but people dread it as though they were certain that it is the greatest evil.
>
> — *Socrates, while on trial for his life*

In Western society, we have insidiously allowed the acknowledgment of death and grief to become so abbreviated that it hardly exists. In the workplace, an individual is rarely given more than three days off when a loved one dies; in acute care settings, everything is done to prolong life, sometimes regardless of the patient's expressed oral and written wishes; nursing homes still insist on maintaining broken, comatose, vegetative bodies with feeding tubes; and death itself is all too often cluttered with the personal agendas and cultural and religious ethics of health care professionals, politicians, clergy, and the community. How we, as individuals and as a society, react to death will fashion the path for the type of mourning and reconciliation that the bereaved will follow.

Working with people who are dying is similar to working with their survivors. It calls for an ability to understand the depths of their feelings without accepting them as our own feelings. It calls for the ability to lend strength through caring, while avoiding the surrogate mourner role. It calls for the acceptance of death, while affirming the gift of life, day by day.

Dynamics of Grief

Loss is a universal state that, from the time of leaving our mother's womb to the time of our own death, is a frequent and often unwanted companion. Loss occurs when there is an irreplaceable separation from anyone or anything that has profound meaning to us. Loss comes in smaller and greater dimensions, accompanied by a variety of reactions, responses, and feelings and is unique to each of us. There is no cookbook response or intervention for the grief that follows loss, and just when we think we have cried all of our tears we will hear a song, smell a perfume, see the gesture of a hand, or feel a fabric, and our heart swells, our throat shuts, and the sorrow of loss is upon our cheeks.

Smaller losses occur when we start off for kindergarten and leave Mom behind, when we suffer minor injuries, when we do not read the fine print on the insurance policies, when we lose articles of personal meaning, when people give us advice when we need reassurance, when normal stress becomes "overload," and when a string of similar losses occurs in a brief time frame. Larger losses occur when we are neglected, abused, or seriously ill; when we are unwanted or orphaned in childhood; when our first love decides that we are not the one; when war intervenes with our own agenda; when the happy marriage turns to acrimony and divorce; when a child of any age dies; when our friends die; and when we face our own death.

Losses may be perceived or real, or perceived and real. Whatever they are, they will, according to our personality, mold how we learn to cope with the normal challenges of life. Some suffer enough despair that major, chronic illness manifests itself, relationships suffer, and life has little significance. Others pick up the pieces, glue them back together, and carry on, and still others search for their own particular meaning, change their present style, and attack each day with appreciation and gusto.

Loss for the older person is not different from loss for people in other age groups, but it is more profoundly affected by the following possibilities:

- a chronic illness affecting the survivor
- few familial support systems
- a fixed and inadequate income
- physical impairment such as decreased vision, hearing, or reflexes
- self-enforced isolation in condominiums
- enforced immobility because of lack of transportation
- unplanned role changes (such as when a woman finds that she has to balance the checkbook and pay the bills or a man has to do the cooking and laundry, if they have been unaccustomed to doing these tasks)
- increased costs of Medicare
- a poorly educated health consumer
- loss of a spiritual identity
- increased crime against elderly people
- a loss of cultural or ethnic identity
- distance of health and day care facilities.

Grief is like a high-rise building—it stacks upon itself story by story—and unless there is a sound foundation or timely intervention, the person will collapse from the weight. Grief presents itself in a variety of ways. Physically, people may lose or gain weight, feel a tightness in the throat, develop migraine headaches, suffer from constant mild colds, feel short of breath, sleep poorly, or have nightmares and hallucinations, which add to their distress.

The psychological self often feels guilt, anger, betrayal, relief, isolation, sadness, disbelief, hostility, abandonment, and fear. Depression is almost always present. People often express feelings of going mad or crazy, which heightens their sense of lost control.

The cognizant self discovers an inability to concentrate, a desire to put off tasks, difficulty in making decisions, memory loss of the time before the death occurred, and difficulty in thinking clearly.

The behavioral self may weep endlessly; refuse to speak about the death; vent rage against the dead person, physicians, nurses, the church or synagogue, and so on; keep extremely busy; isolate oneself; refuse to eat; deny the death; function minimally, particularly while driving, shopping, banking, and cooking; talk constantly about the actual death; be relieved; or, while grieving, still continue to function at a moderate to good level.

People grieve differently, at different times, and in different ways. There is no one right way. It is, therefore, important that they are encouraged to mourn their loss in their way and that we recognize their way.

As older people live longer, it is now becoming less unusual not only to outlive one's peers but also to survive one's children. This circumstance can truly leave the frail elderly totally alone at a time when they most need other people.

Walk this path beside them. In older clients, it is imperative to remember that they may have lost a life partner of many years and that children and grandchildren may live at a distance and will arrive for the funeral and leave immediately afterward. If there was illness prior to the death, there may be few other social supports in place because their energy was devoted to the one who has died. If there is any history of dysfunction or overdependence, any current physical or mental illness, or a future that may see a drop in income followed by a forced change in lifestyle, it is important to allow them to recover from the immediate shock and then to assess their present and long-term needs while providing reassurance that life does continue.

Remember that the death of a spouse means the survivor's entire social support network is irrevocably changed. Widows and widowers often find themselves excluded from the sociability of couples, and they are at an age when friends and older relatives may also be dying. However, research does not necessarily conclude that this death and loss prevent the building of other social systems; indeed many widows seem to be more active than during the marriage. However, men, particularly in the U.S. culture, are often not well prepared for spousal loss, particularly if it follows shortly after retirement. The American male tends not to develop broad social networks during his working life—unlike Europeans, West Indians, and Central and South Americans—and spousal loss may be devastating to the point of suicide or may cause an early involvement in a new relationship and marriage at a time when thoughts and feelings are guided by loneliness and not reason. Conversely, widowed men up to the age of 75 are approximately 1½ times more likely to die than married men of the same age. On the other hand, friends may become more important than at any other time of their lives, and individuals may spread their wings and become increasingly independent.

Well do I remember the joy of a 73-year-old lady who had never driven, who learned to drive after her husband's death—not only did this enhance her freedom, but it certainly reinforced her self-esteem and confidence.

Be sensitive to the way in which death occurs. If it is a sudden, traumatic event, do remember that recovery is often more confused and slower. This is a time for professional intervention and follow-up.

The grief process starts whenever loss happens. Thus, when someone is told that he or she has a terminal disease and that nothing curative can be done, the individual will express a variety of emotions ranging from shock to extreme depression. Not only will the person suffer a variety of feelings, but so will the immediate family and close friends. These feelings may be expressed as guilt, anger, blame, fear, helplessness, hopelessness, yearning, and protestation.

When death occurs—whether from disease, sudden trauma, suicide, murder, or a gentle failing of all bodily systems—and there are family survivors, there will almost inevitably be pain and regret.

Practice Implications

The manifestations of grief travel a crooked path and broadly fall into three phases. However, it is best not to label people as being at any one phase, because individuals go backward and forward in response to the internal and external current events in their lives.

Phase one is denial, which includes numbness, shock, anger, repeatedly reliving the moment of death, yearning for the loved one to return, dreaming of the loved one, feelings of disorientation, and performing everyday tasks automatically. Decisions must be made, but this is a time when major changes in the individual's lifestyle should be avoided. The lives of individuals in this situation are usually in a state of confusion, and it is all too easy for well-meaning relatives and friends to persuade them to sell their home, change location, change jobs, and so on, which may cause severe regret later on.

Avoid giving undesired and inappropriate advice, but do encourage grieving clients to seek competent and reasonable legal advice, to seek resolution of insurance policies (which under normal circumstances are paid promptly and provide a source of cash income), to contact the local social security office to identify benefits and receive them, and to seek medical attention, both for a general physical examination and to resolve current ailments. Grieving people, particularly elderly people, tend to neglect themselves, and it is important to maintain as healthy a body as possible.

Avoid clichés, such as "I know just how you feel," "it's God's will," "time will heal," "no sense dwelling on the past," and so forth. Too often these meaningless phrases are used because we cannot think of anything else to say or we think that they are helpful. They are not, and not only may distress or outrage the recipients but also may prevent them from venting their own feelings and shedding healing tears.

The most important thing that we can do is to be there. We do not have to say anything. This is not a time to tell people "everything is going to be all right," "don't cry, you will make yourself ill," "you've got to be strong," or "I know just how you feel." None of us ever knows how the other one feels.

This is a time to attend the viewing or the funeral, to send a cheerful bouquet of flowers, to listen again and again and again to the repeated story, to allow the tears to flow, or to write a note remembering something special about the person who has died. We should be sure that there is someone to prepare a small, attractive meal two or three times a week; to drive the person to the bank, church, cemetery, supermarket, or beauty parlor; to do the grocery shopping; or to accompany him or her on a walk. Be available to take calls from the bereaved, but also phone them because they are often reluctant to reach out. Avoid taking sides in family arguments and staying too long. Remember that this is an exhausting time, when sleep patterns are often severely interrupted and deep fatigue can cause further physical and emotional distress. Encourage the person to treat himself or herself gently and to be open to help from others.

This phase may last several days or weeks. The reality of the death usually occurs between four and six weeks after family members and friends begin to withdraw their intensive support and return to their own lives. This is usually when the bereaved most need their help.

Phase two is a period of disorganization, which can manifest itself in a variety of ways, such as expressed feelings of anger and guilt, self-blame and blaming others, preoccupation with "if only's," desire to change places with the dead person, inability to remember the good times, difficulty in accomplishing small routine tasks, rebuffing friends, fear for own safety, nightmares, minor or major physical illness, self-isolation, withdrawal and despair, relief and awareness of a new life, suicide wishes, unusual behaviors, mild to severe depression, and lack of concentration.

We can encourage the bereaved to be with the pain, not to push it away; allow the ventilation of anger wherever it is focused; discourage the increased use of alcohol and prescription drugs; suggest a medical checkup; be there for them; help them organize their paperwork into small nonthreatening tasks so that they are not overwhelmed; help them to recognize that what they are feeling is extraordinarily painful but normal; remind them that while it seems the feelings will never go away, one day they will wake up feeling a little better; refuse to be rebuffed; recognize that the anger and reproach are not directed at you; encourage the reaffirmation of spiritual and religious beliefs; suggest a time each day to either exercise, meditate, or to be alone; remind them that grief is a series of progressions and regressions; discourage major decision making; be there or make sure someone is there on the really rough days, particularly anniversaries, birthdays, and religious and public holidays.

Phase two may last for weeks or months. Usually, however, a spouse needs at least 13 months before a true feeling of "being better" happens, partly because this period covers a year of first occasions alone: the wedding anniversary, important holidays, grandchildren's birthdays, waking up without the beloved, joining friends for dinner, and so on. Each event is a reminder of the loss and may trigger a small or large sadness.

Phase three is the move toward reconciliation and is manifested in the following ways: shedding fewer or no tears; getting through the day with fewer thoughts of the loved one; reaching out to new activities; reinvesting energies into a new focus, which may be a relationship, volunteering, role changing, or career; committing to others; improving physical health; remembering more realistically; adjusting to life alone; remembering the good memories and happy times; and recognizing that there is a future and making goals. We can encourage healthy living habits, nonjudgmentally accept new goals and activities, provide support during this time of growth and challenge, and encourage feelings of control and empowerment.

There are many variables that will influence the individual's ability to cope with death and his or her own road to recovery. They include an excessive burden of decision making if wills, living wills, and funeral arrangements were not made prior to death; a previous history of chronic depression; other significant losses or separations in the previous 12 months; relocation out of the area to a smaller home, nursing home, adult congregate living facility, apartment, or condominium; lack of support systems; reduction of financial resources because of prolonged, uninsured, or inadequately insured illness and the cessation of the partner's income; concurrent life crises such as chronic illness or the loss of an adult child; institutionalization; previous dysfunction because of physical or mental impairment or excessive alcohol or medication use; the loss of home, feared or actually caused by this death; and a history of poor coping skills and family dysfunction that would affect grief resolution. A person or family whose situation includes one or more of these variables needs careful assessment and referral to a trained bereavement counselor or skilled mental health professional.

If anyone mentions suicide, listen very seriously. Suicide may seem the only viable option when one is alone, frail, and with few monetary or community supports. Find out if your community has a crisis intervention program, and do your best to get the bereaved person into it. Find out if the family physician will intervene, or if there is a counselor who can help immediately. Remember that people do take their own lives, and sometimes suicide is not preventable no matter how much intervention is attempted.

Grief work can be enhanced by encouraging people to do the following:

- join bereavement groups
- go for individual counseling
- learn and practice daily meditation
- improve health styles
- write a diary about the loved one's life
- write down the "if only's" and recognize that one did one's best
- take 15 minutes to mourn every day
- make donations to favorite charities in memory of special days
- create photo albums, scrapbooks, videos, and audiotapes about the loved one
- make one's own funeral arrangements and will
- make a living will
- let other people know where important documents are
- keep life current with significant others
- do one task at a time to prevent becoming overwhelmed
- do not give things away too soon—wait until it feels comfortable
- develop skills that were there but never used.

One of the most useful tools for the therapist working with older clients is reminiscence therapy. The technique is to take the individual back to earlier times and to encourage him or her to remember and talk about particular years in the past.

To trigger memories, talk about such things as significant dates; hobbies and interests; holidays and vacations; political changes; social and technical changes; the saddest, happiest, and favorite times; photograph albums, toys, and clothing; food, smells, and sounds; occupation and schooling; and famous events.

The benefits are numerous and include a quick method to release feelings, change concentration, recall other times of sorrow and thus normalize the present, reinforce happy times, bring thoughts of the dead person up close, refute idealization, share the person's life, value the past, and help to establish the future. Reminiscence therapy allows people to laugh and cry and, most of all, to share—something that we all love to do and that almost always gives a sense of well-being, however fleeting.

The ultimate goal of grief work is to reconcile with the past and to reinvest energies into the present and the future. Life has irrevocably changed, but that does not mean that it will not be full of joy and hope again.

> The hour of departure has arrived, and we go to our ways—I to die and you to live. Which is the better, God only knows.
>
> — *Socrates*

A SCHOLARLY PERSPECTIVE

Although the amount of literature on death, dying, and bereavement that has accumulated in the past two decades is formidable, much of the information is impressionistic or based on small, nonrepresentative samples. Research with vulnerable populations is difficult, in part because of the ethical concern not to intrude during times of extreme sorrow. Observations of behaviors, statements of needs, and feelings may be easily distorted by the intensity of the emotions elicited or by the reactions of the researcher or practitioner. Nevertheless, the substantial body of research available provides a basis for assessing and administering to the needs of the dying and the bereaved ("Death and Bereavement," 1987; Hansson, Stroebe, & Stroebe, 1988b).

This review is a selective discussion of some issues and practice implications identified in the literature. It addresses issues related to working with the dying—psychosocial aspects of death in old age, interventions with terminally ill elders, hospice care, right-to-die concerns, and living wills and other advance directives—as well as issues related to working with the bereaved—loss and grief in old age, assessment of risk of becoming ill or suicidal, and interventions with the bereaved. Impacts on practitioners and research issues are also covered.

Working with Dying People

Psychosocial aspects of death in old age. One of the earliest contributions to understanding the psychological responses to dying was made in the 1960s by Elisabeth Kübler-Ross, a Swiss psychiatrist who was dedicated to humanizing the experience. Her work grew from recognition of the universality of denial of dying and the typical avoidance of the patient by professional caregivers. As family support networks diminished and the place of death moved from the home to the hospital, she identified the need for new supports. Through training personnel about the dynamics of the dying process, Kübler-Ross was most influential in improving treatment of the dying.

Kübler-Ross's work was based on systematic observations of the death process, which led to her formulation of a "stage" theory of dying. She describes five stages of adjustment to knowledge of impending death: (1) shock and denial—"no, not me; it can't be true"; (2) anger and resentment—"why me?" (3) bargaining—"if you'll only give me. . . , then I'll. . . "; (4) depression—"what's the use?"; and (5) acceptance—withdrawal and a final rest (1969). These stages, which are presented as normal responses, received wide acceptance and were then generalized to explain emotional responses to all types of significant losses. Intermittently, throughout these stages, appears a strand of hope, a wish for miraculous recovery. Kübler-Ross presented, in addition to the stage model, some typical problems that arise at each stage, with suggestions for resolving them.

The popular acceptance of this pioneering theory indicated a need for a guide in caring for the dying. The theory has been used in a simplistic and rigid manner, according to many critics, with an expectation that all dying patients should be helped to move through all stages to acceptance, in order to die well (Kastenbaum, 1991).

Practitioners should be aware that the stage theory is not accepted by other leading contributors, such as Schneidman, who described a "hive of affect . . . a constant coming and going . . . a constant interplay between disbelief and hope . . . a waxing and waning of anguish, terror, acquiescence and surrender" (cited in Peterson, 1980, p. 927). These observations are not necessarily of the elderly dying. Much of the literature on the special attributes of the elderly dying indicate that most elderly people do not fear death (Kalish, 1985; Silverstone & Burack-Weiss, 1983). Elders usually have experienced and coped with the deaths of many friends and relatives, as well as other significant losses. They are generally prepared, at least intellectually, for the inevitable end of the life cycle (Kastenbaum, 1987). But for some elderly people, the reality of a terminal condition will bring a long-repressed death anxiety to the surface, leading to a range of emotional reactions and depression. Each older dying person is confronted by a specific, often unpredictable response to the terminal illness and is affected differently by treatment choices and the kind of setting in which care is provided. Furthermore, the elder's reaction is influenced by ethnicity, lifestyle, and socioeconomic status. The caveat, as always, is to individualize in assessing each older client, particularly with respect to his or her readiness to deal with death, and to be prepared with appropriate interventions, such as counseling, life review therapy, support groups, and family therapy.

An important concern when working with the very old is not to assume they are near death by virtue of the "natural order." Many younger people may die of cancer, AIDS, congenital defects, accidents, violence, or disasters before the healthy octogenarians, who are presumably nearer mortality (Gadow, 1987). The major goal, therefore, in working with elderly people is not to help them die better but to help them live to the best of their abilities.

An area in which confusion sometimes interferes with rational assessment is the issue of communicating the news of a terminal illness. The social norm has moved from a "conspiracy of silence" to the ethic of the patient's right to know. In fact, some hospitals have written policies that require "the physician to confront the terminally ill patient with the diagnosis as soon as it [is] known, regardless of whether the patient want[s] to know or whether the physician perceive[s] full disclosure to be in the best interest of the patient" (Adler, 1989, p. 159). Experience with elderly people who have been told they have a terminal condition demonstrates a wide range of responses, from philosophical acceptance to severe depression and suicide. It is therefore important to stress the need for sensitive handling of such potentially devastating information and to call for an understanding of the particular person, including his or her personality, cultural expectations, and social supports.

Several physicians have written eloquently about the need for doctors to develop specific skills in communicating with the dying patient (Hogshead, 1978; Payne, 1967). It is seen not as an issue of telling or not telling but as an issue of how to tell, how often, how euphemistically, or how much beyond what the patient or family already knows. These physicians agree that without saying anything that is not true, the information can be presented in a manner that leaves the way open for retreat, if necessary. There is a consensus through all the literature on dying that hope should not be destroyed.

These principles apply to all practitioners working with elderly people and their families. The cues must come from the patient about how much information is bearable, and when.

Practitioners can learn a great deal about coping with death from their elderly clients. Most older people have developed a philosophical or spiritual style of accepting their own inevitable death. It is the loss of significant others that may overwhelm the fragile balance of the older client and that most challenges the practitioner. It may help to recall in the throes of grief that, for each of us, our turn will come.

Interventions with terminally ill elderly people. Before discussing interventions, it is necessary to clarify who can be identified as terminally ill. Researchers in this field speak of a death trajectory, the course of death from a particular illness. They speak of a lingering trajectory and expected or unexpected quick trajectories (Kastenbaum, 1991; Schulz, 1978). A pragmatic definition of who is dying might state that dying begins when nothing more can be done to prevent death, when the patient enters a living–dying stage. These formulations are vague by necessity, because there are often differences in professional opinions as to the prognosis of particular patients. There is still a great deal that is unknown about why, among patients with similar "fatal" conditions, some die quickly, some linger, and some spontaneously recover.

For elderly patients who are suffering depression in response to their diagnosis, counseling can be very helpful. Often the family of the older person is unable to provide the opportunity to talk out fears, guilt, and disappointments from the past. The family support system may be sparse or even nonexistent should the death prove to be a lingering one. Or the family may be suffering with its own anticipatory grief and therefore unable emotionally to permit the dying patient to express his or her deep feelings (Rando, 1986).

Counseling can take many forms, including brief supportive visits from a range of helpers—physicians, nurses, social workers, clergy, and psychologists. One approach in counseling the dying is the goal of facilitating the patient's ability to draw on his or her own inner strengths, through helping to restore self-confidence and provide a renewed sense of still being a valued and lovable person (Jackson, 1977).

One therapeutic approach that is unique to elderly people is the use of life review or reminiscence. Reminiscence helps elders maintain self-esteem and sense of continuity through past achievements. Although it is true that people of all ages reminisce, that activity is particularly associated with elderly people and has a distinctive function for them (Miller & Solomon, 1980). Most elderly people reminisce normally, some repetitiously, which can be tedious for those who are impatient with hearing the same stories of the past over and over. But reminiscence serves as an important part of the life review, which has been identified by Erikson as a necessary developmental task of late life—the acceptance of one's life as it has been lived, resulting in ego integrity (Erikson, 1959). It was first used therapeutically by the noted geriatric psychiatrist and first head of the National Institute on Aging, Robert Butler.

Through encouraging life review, the therapist provides the elderly patient with an opportunity to reexamine his or her life, which with skillful interpretation and clarification can result in a resolution of internal conflicts and the reconciliation of family relationships (Butler & Lewis, 1982). Life review as therapy is more structured than reminiscence and includes tape recording an extensive autobiography, or "oral history." Leaving such a legacy can be a therapeutic experience for the dying older person.

Life review is also applicable to groups and can be a life-affirming experience when shared memories reactivate past successes, and it can even help in coping with past failures.

Practitioners can creatively explore with dying elders which aspects of their lives they want to be remembered by. For example, they might be encouraged to write a statement of their cherished beliefs, or a "moral legacy" for their grandchildren (Bumagin & Hirn, 1990). This is an excellent method for validation or finding the meaning of one's life.

Practitioners should be alert to the concrete, practical needs of the dying elderly, as well as their emotional needs. Concerns about finances, funeral arrangements, unfinished business, and relationships may all require attention. Offering help with these practical issues, or when indicated advocating for direct services, may satisfy the patient's emotional needs simultaneously.

As stated previously, most elderly people say that they are not afraid of dying but are concerned with how they might die: in pain, isolated, out of control, and dependent. Practitioners provide an invaluable service through communicating to the dying that they will be cared for and that everything possible will be done to make them comfortable. Some elderly dying people need only reassurance that they will not suffer or be abandoned (Kalish, 1985).

One of the early contributions in the literature on dying and death was a model of five points to consider in psychological treatment of the elderly, which is still relevant today (Wahl, 1973). They include (1) a regular visiting schedule to instill a sense of security, (2) visits from patient's acquaintances to counter a sense of withdrawal, (3) use of brief visits to avoid the aura of a death vigil, (4) the therapist's listening for symbolic indicators of fears of death in order to help the patient resolve them, and (5) use of physical touching to impart a sense of comfort and acceptance of the dying patient.

Hospice care. One of the most important advances in serving the needs of the dying is the development of the hospice movement, dedicated to protecting the quality of life of the terminally ill and their families. The hospice philosophy of care derives from the St. Christopher model in England. St. Christopher's

Hospice is a small, freestanding facility that provides specialized, compassionate terminal care to dying patients in a homelike atmosphere, as well as service in the patient's home. Goals of the program are directed at palliative and supportive care, without treatment aimed at curing. Patients and their families are provided every opportunity for closeness, and pain and symptom control is a treatment goal.

In 1974 the Connecticut Hospice of New Haven became the first full-service hospice in the United States. Soon after, the hospice principle was instituted in several existing health care programs (Buckingham, 1983). The first hospice established as part of a nursing home appeared in New York in 1975 at the Isabella Geriatric Center, known for innovative programming and outstanding patient care. The hospice was developed in recognition of the fact that in focusing on an optimistic therapeutic milieu, the staff did not always tune in to those residents who were nearing death. The hospice philosophy emphasized staff education and self-awareness, as well as "bending the rules" of the institution to meet the individualized needs of the dying resident and his or her family (Safford, 1977).

There are now more than 2,200 hospices in the United States (Gordon, 1995), including hospital-based programs, home care programs, and freestanding facilities. Many are reimbursed through the National Hospice Reimbursement Act (Kastenbaum, 1991). It would seem that hospice care would be the ideal model for dying elderly people, with its emphasis on pain control and quality of life. But although a large proportion of the patients served by hospices are elderly, it is not as large a number as would be expected. The reason that elderly people are underserved by hospices is that hospices are not prepared to provide lengthy inpatient services, which are often required for the terminal problems of elderly patients. Furthermore, they are not set up to handle patients with mental impairment, and a significant percentage of elderly ill are also mentally impaired. Finally, hospices often prefer to care for patients who can be served in their own homes, through the hospice volunteer programs. These programs require that at least one available caregiver be in the home, a condition not often met by elderly dying persons (Kalish, 1985).

Practitioners should be both familiar with the benefits of getting their elderly clients into hospice programs and aware of the current shortcomings. Advocating, when appropriate, for admission of an elderly person to a hospice, rather than an acute care facility (where aggressive treatment is the rule), might ensure a more humane, comfortable, and dignified death.

Advance directives and terminal treatment. One of the greatest concerns of many elderly people is that they may be hooked up to ventilators and intravenous tubes, without their consent, when their condition is irreversible. This is also a concern for other age groups because medical technology has now made it possible to keep people alive, sometimes indefinitely, in a persistent vegetative state, who would have previously died of trauma or innumerable other causes. However, elderly people and their families are especially concerned because there is greater probability that they will be affected by such a medical catastrophe.

The issues involved with treatment of irreversible terminal conditions are complex, and although what has been called the "right-to-die" movement began only a little over a decade ago, the public debate and legal battles have been intense and lengthy (Hooyman & Kiyak, 1991). The controversy has led to the development of "advance directives," which are written documents executed by people while still healthy and capable, to express their wishes regarding treatment decisions should they become incompetent. The "living will" is the most widely known and is a document to be shared with responsible relatives or friends, and with the physician. It generally delineates which treatment is refused in the event of an irreversible terminal condition.

When someone becomes a patient in the health care system, the physicians in charge generally feel an ethical duty to treat the condition aggressively, regardless of the terminal prognosis. Use of aggressive treatment may be related to the changes in the patient–doctor relationship that have emerged with the shift toward ever-narrowing specialization and technology. This shift has led to increasing numbers of malpractice suits and thus forced many physicians to practice defensively (that is, to use more aggressive treatment). It is also related to the wishes of some families to "do everything possible," which is at times an expression of their inability to accept death.

As a result of these factors, increasing numbers of people are writing living wills, which are now respected by most institutions in helping to make rational medical choices. However, the interpretation of these wills varies from state to state (Crandall, 1991). An important issue that has been resolved is that tube feeding or hydration is now considered a medical treatment. In addition to a living will, executing a "durable power of attorney" for health care decisions, which names a trusted person to carry out one's wishes, is recommended by lawyers specializing in elderly issues, by medical ethicists (a new specialization), and by practitioners with concern for these ethical dilemmas. Many books are available to help the practitioner become more effective in educating the public about this timely issue. Two issues of *Generations* offer in-depth reviews of this challenging topic ("Autonomy and Long Term Care," 1990; "Ethics and Aging," 1985), as does a collection of articles, "End-Stage Medical Decisions" (1990), in *The Gerontologist*.

In December 1991 a federal bill titled the Patient Self-Determination Act took effect; it has had an impact on all health care institutions and the handling of advance directives and end-of-life decisions. A resource manual is available to aid practitioners in hospitals, skilled nursing facilities, home health agencies, hospice programs, and health maintenance organizations in developing procedures for implementing this legislation ("Concern for Dying," 1991).

Because of the extensive literature now available on the implementation of advance directives, physicians' attitudes toward end-of-life treatment, the use of institutional ethics committees, and the impact on the health care system of the high costs of medical treatment, the editors have included a new chapter specifically addressing these issues (see chapter 13).

Working with Bereaved People

Bereavement in old age. Bereavement in old age presents a paradox. Because elderly people are most experienced with losses and grief, one might expect that they would be able to cope more easily with bereavement in late life. However, elderly people are also more vulnerable to multiple depletions, such as physical frailty, decreased resilience, and fewer available supports. Elderly people tend to accumulate losses. The longer they live and form loving attachments, the more there is to lose. This phenomenon has been described as "bereavement overload"

(Kastenbaum, 1991). As a result of this overload, bereavement, which runs a difficult course in earlier life stages, may prove to be even more difficult for the elderly.

Although grief—the painful emotions in reaction to significant losses—is a normal response, it is also like an illness from which one must recover (Worden, 1982). Lindemann (1944), one of the early contributors to a theory of "grief work," based his findings on intensive psychiatric help to over 100 people (not elderly) who had lost close relatives in the Coconut Grove Nightclub fire in Boston. He identified five basic characteristics of bereaved people:

1. The syndrome of somatic distress, such as sighing, choking, shortness of breath, exhaustion, and digestive disturbances, is always present.
2. There is a preoccupation with the image of the deceased. Other people seem to recede into the background, unnoticed.
3. There are feelings of guilt and a profound sense of personal blame for the death—"What if I. . . ."
4. Hostile reactions, irritability and anger, and profound, confusing feelings are characteristic.
5. The pattern of conduct is lost. The death of a central person shakes up the family system.

In trying to help the bereaved person adjust to the loss, Lindemann identified the following tasks:

- The survivor must deal with the pain of facing the loss—one must cry with tears of inner despair.
- Each emotion that is felt—such as fear, anger, and guilt—must be expressed.
- Eventually, by admitting the separation through death, the grieving survivor must be free from bondage to the deceased—the image must fade; the guilt must be overcome.
- The grieving person must ultimately readjust to the social environment with new roles.
- New relationships must be formed.

Lindemann found that by facilitating "grief work," the period of bereavement could be shortened. He suggested that therapeutic intervention was most beneficial within the first six months, beginning between two and four weeks after the death.

This seminal work has been validated by many researchers on grief and bereavement, although other therapists have grouped the characteristics and tasks somewhat differently (Butler & Lewis, 1982; Parkes, 1972; Peterson, 1980; Simos, 1977; Worden, 1982). One formulation, for example, classifies two major tasks for the bereaved (Butler & Lewis, 1982):

1. to express, understand, and accept the feelings of loss.
2. to break ties with the deceased and learn new roles.

The most important theme is that the goal is to help the bereaved person mourn the loss and grieve adequately, not to cheer him up or help her get over the grief too quickly.

The practitioner must be alert, however, in considering these general guidelines for helping the bereaved, to the range of individual differences in handling grief, which are often obscured (Kastenbaum, 1991). One researcher on grief experiences has cautioned that acceptance of such concepts as "good grief" and "pathological grief" reflects integration of stereotypic notions of how people are expected to grieve. Such expectations lead to unrealistic limitations on the need for people to grieve in their own characteristic ways (Sanders, 1977). This need for individualized assessment of the impact of grief was supported in more recent research reported in *The New York Times*, headlined "New Studies Find Many Myths about Mourning" (1989). The article pointed out that the research (conducted at the University of Michigan by Camille Wortman) suggests a far wider range of reactions to grave loss than previously assumed.

Assessment of risk and interventions. Who among the elderly might require help with grieving? There seems to be general agreement that how one reacts to death depends on the strength of the relationship and degree of dependency, the supports available, and past coping patterns and health (Peterson, 1980). These principles are expanded on in an excellent article on counseling the bereaved, which, although it does not specifically address the special needs of elderly people, identifies a range of risk factors and specific skills and techniques in assessment and planning of care (Raphael & Nunn, 1988).

Those most in need of intervention can be spouses, sons or daughters, siblings, or nieces or nephews, depending on the definition of the loss. Among elderly people, the group most frequently in need of services is widows, because of current longevity patterns, and if the demographic trends continue, they will be ever older at the time of loss. Because there is growing evidence that stress has a direct effect on the body's immune system (Frederick, 1976, 1981) and very advanced age makes these widows even more vulnerable to somatic complications, they are doubly at risk for developing serious health problems. It is therefore essential that practitioners address the elderly bereaved person's physiological needs, such as adequate nutrition, fluids, and medical attention, as well as the psychological needs.

In one of the early studies of widowhood, often cited in subsequent research, Lopata (1973) identified five short-range needs of widows: grief work, companionship, solution of immediate problems, building of competence and self-confidence, and help in re-engagements. Again, although the study was not restricted to elderly people, its findings are applicable. One of Lopata's interesting contributions is the fact that many widows idealize the memory of the deceased, termed "husband sanctification." Lopata found that the process of idealization served as a memory support system after other available supports withdraw and while the widow is establishing a new status as a single person.

For those needing practical help, as well as those assessed as vulnerable to prolonged grieving, counseling is essential. A model for bereavement counseling that is relevant for elderly people is available in an article by Raphael and Nunn (1988), which is highly recommended for its specificity regarding counseling strategies. Other articles in the same volume (44) of *Journal of Social Issues* (1988) add valuable insights for bereavement counseling.

Another helpful manual for counselors working with the bereaved (of all ages) is *Grief Counseling and Grief Therapy: A Handbook for the Mental Health Practitioner* (Worden, 1982).

In addition to individual counseling, several group approaches have been found to be effective with the bereaved. Support groups are a form of self-help that has been found to be beneficial. They provide an opportunity to express grief in an accepting, understanding, and caring environment. They become a source of practical help and advice and an opportunity to establish new relationships. There are varying models of support groups, some led by professionals and others by "veterans" of the problem who can demonstrate successful resolution of grief (Caplan & Killilea, 1976; Parkes, 1980; Peterson, 1980; Vachon, Lyall, Rogers, Freedman-Letofsky, & Freeman, 1980). Hospices also provide help through support groups as an integral part of their services.

Another successful model is the "widow-to-widow" program developed in the United States by Phyllis Silverman through the Harvard Laboratory for Community Psychiatry. In this model, trained widows reach out to newly bereaved women and assist in their transitional crisis by providing information and teaching new skills while offering support (Silverman, MacKenzie, Pettipas, & Wilson, 1974).

Impact on Practitioners

Practitioners who work particularly with terminally ill patients are presumed to have a high rate of stress, leading to burnout and job turnover. However, some studies have shown that more stress was experienced from the work environment than from the direct work with dying patients and their families (Vachon, 1987). In addition, an empirical study of hospice nurses showed that burnout and staff turnover are relatively low, demonstrating the value of the hospice principle, which provides support for staff as well as patients (Turnipseed, 1987).

Regarding the stress experienced by counselors who work closely and intensely with dreaded losses, it is suggested that debriefing, case review with peers, supervision, supportive work groups, and ongoing education are helpful (Raphael & Nunn, 1988).

Research Issues

Although there is a massive body of research literature, much of it is more speculative than systematic, and results have been contradictory. One problem is the difficulty in controlling for the effect of age on bereavement or bereavement on age (Hansson et al., 1988b). It is important to separate the main effects (of aging or widowhood, for example) from interaction effects (of aging in combination with widowhood).

One suggestion for dealing with the research issue of the effects of individual differences on such a complex process as grief is the use of multivariate techniques, such as multiple regression analyses (Bettis & Scott, 1981). With the advances in research methodology available through computer technology, the knowledge for practitioners on issues of death and bereavement will be enhanced. For example, large, long-term longitudinal data sets are now available for repeated-measures analysis. The repeated-measures design checks for consistency within the measurements by comparing pre- and postevent assessments of key variables using analysis of variance to control for initial differences between groups, and repeats these analyses at regular intervals. Such repeated measures lead to more valid conclusions in understanding the long-term effects of bereavement among different groups (Hansson, Stroebe, & Stroebe, 1988a).

Practitioners can address many of the gaps in the knowledge by systematically collecting and analyzing data. Such gaps include the need to know whether family members of the elderly understand their rights to advocate for treatment or no treatment with respect to terminal illness, as well as the need for systematic evaluation of different counseling methods with regard to their effectiveness for specific phases of grief, for particular cultures or racial groups, or for particular individuals. As practitioners begin to evaluate their own methods systematically, and begin to share their results, we will move toward a better-informed helping community for the bereaved elderly population.

REFERENCES

Adler, S. S. (1989). Truth telling to the terminally ill: Neglected role of the social worker. *Social Work, 34*, 158–160.

Autonomy and long term care. (1990). *Generations, 14* (Suppl.).

Bettis, S. K., & Scott, I. G. (1981). Bereavement and grief. In C. Eisdorfer (Ed.), *Annual review of gerontology and geriatrics: Vol. 2* (pp. 144–159). New York: Springer.

Buckingham, R. W. (1983). *The complete hospice guide.* New York: Harper & Row.

Bumagin, V. E., & Hirn, K. F. (1990). *Helping the aging family.* New York: Springer.

Butler, R., & Lewis, M. (1982). *Aging and mental health* (3rd ed.). St. Louis: C. V. Mosby.

Caplan, G., & Killilea, M. (1976). *Support systems and mutual help*. New York: Grune & Stratton.

Concern for Dying. (1991). *Advance directive protocols and the Patient Self-Determination Act*. New York: Author.

Crandall, R. C. (1991). *Gerontology* (2nd ed.). New York: McGraw-Hill.

Death and bereavement [Special issue]. (1987). *Generations, 11*(3).

End-stage medical decisions [Special section]. (1990). *Gerontologist, 30*, 462–485.

Erikson, E. H. (1959). Identity and the life cycle. *Psychological Issues, 1*, 101–164.

Ethics and aging [Special issue]. (1985). *Generations, 10*(2).

Frederick, J. (1976). "Grief as a disease process. *Omega, 7*, 297–306.

Frederick, J. (1981). The biochemistry of acute grief. In O. Margolis (Ed.), *Acute grief: Counseling the bereaved* (pp. 111–117). New York: Columbia University Press.

Gadow, S. (1987). Death and age: A natural connection? *Generations, 11*(3), 15–18.

Gordon, J. (1995, November 29). "Medicare covers hospice" [Letter to the Editor]. *New York Times*, p. A18.

Hansson, R. O., Stroebe, M. S., & Stroebe, W. (Eds.). (1988a). Bereavement and widowhood [Special issue]. *Journal of Social Issues, 44*(3).

Hansson, R. O., Stroebe, M. S., & Stroebe, W. (1988b). In conclusion: Current themes in bereavement and widowhood research. *Journal of Social Issues, 44*(3), 207–216.

Hogshead, H. P. (1978). The art of delivering bad news. In C. Garfield (Ed.), *Psychological care of the dying patient*. New York: McGraw-Hill, 128–129.

Hooyman, N., & Kiyak, A. (1991). *Social gerontology: A multidisciplinary perspective* (2nd ed.). Boston: Allyn & Bacon.

Jackson, E. (1977). Counseling the dying. *Death Education, 1*, 27–40.

Kalish, R. (1985). Services for the dying. In A. Monk (Ed.), *Handbook of gerontological services* (pp. 531–548). New York: Van Nostrand Reinhold.

Kastenbaum, R. (1987). Death and bereavement [Editorial]. *Generations, 11*(3), 4.

Kastenbaum, R. (1991). *Death, society and human experience* (4th ed.). New York: Macmillan.

Kübler-Ross, E. (1969). *On death and dying*. New York: Macmillan.

Lindemann, E. (1944). Symptomatology and management of acute grief. *American Journal of Psychiatry, 101*, 141–148.

Lopata, H. A. (1973). *Widowhood in an American city.* Cambridge, MA: Schenkman.

Miller, I., & Solomon, R. (1980). The development of group services for the elderly. *Journal of Gerontological Social Work, 2*(3), 241–257.

New studies find many myths about mourning. (1989, August 8). *New York Times,* p. C1.

Parkes, C. M. (1972). *Bereavement: Studies of grief in adult life.* New York: International Universities Press.

Parkes, C. (1980). Bereavement counseling: Does it work? *British Medical Journal, 281,* 53–56.

Payne, E. (1967). The physician and his patient who is dying. In S. Levin & R. Kahana (Eds.), *Psychodynamic studies on aging, creativity, reminiscence and dying* (p. 135). Boston: Boston Society for Geriatric Psychiatry.

Peterson, J. A. (1980). Social-psychological aspects of death and dying and mental health. In J. Birren & R. B. Sloane (Eds.), *Handbook for mental health and aging* (pp. 922–942). Englewood Cliffs, NJ: Prentice Hall.

Rando, T. A. (1986). *Loss and anticipatory grief.* Lexington, MA: D. C. Heath.

Raphael, B., & Nunn, K. (1988). Counseling the bereaved. *Journal of Social Issues, 44*(3), 191–206.

Safford, F. (1977, November). *Introducing a hospice program to a long term care facility.* Paper presented at Gerontological Society Scientific Conference, San Francisco.

Sanders, C. M. (1977). *Typologies and symptoms of adult bereavement.* Unpublished doctoral dissertation, University of South Florida, Tampa.

Schulz, R. (1978). *The psychology of death, dying, and bereavement.* Reading, MA: Addison-Wesley.

Silverman, P. R., MacKenzie, D., Pettipas, M., & Wilson, E. (1974). *Helping each other in widowhood.* New York: Health Sciences Publications.

Silverstone, B., & Burack-Weiss, A. (1983). *Social work practice with the frail elderly.* Springfield, IL: Charles C Thomas.

Simos, B. G. (1977). Grief therapy to facilitate healthy restitution. *Social Casework, 58*(6), 337–342.

Turnipseed, D. J. (1987). Burnout among hospice nurses: An empirical assessment. *Hospice Journal, 3,* 105–119.

Vachon, M. (1987). *Occupational stress in the care of the critically ill, the dying, and the bereaved.* Washington, DC: Hemisphere.

Vachon, M. L. S., Lyall, W. A., Rogers, J., Freedman-Letofsky, K., & Freeman, S. J. J. (1980). A controlled study of self-help intervention for widows. *American Journal of Psychiatry, 137,* 1380–1384.

Wahl, C. W. (1973). Psychological treatment of the dying patient. In R. H. Davis (Ed.), *Dealing with death* (pp. 9–23). Los Angeles: University of Southern California, Andrus Gerontology Center.

Worden, J. W. (1982). *Grief counseling and grief therapy: A handbook for the mental health practitioner.* New York: Springer.

13 Advance Directives: Choices and Challenges

Florence Safford

The technological miracles of modern health care have benefited millions with longer lives and are therefore welcome and extolled. But for those suffering a terminal condition, these very technologies can ironically cause dreadful hardship, through the de facto prolongation of the process of dying. Furthermore, medical innovations have been developed and put into practice with such speed that our social institutions have not been able to keep up with the dilemmas created by the new choices.

Respirators and dialysis machinery can extend life indefinitely, even in the terminally ill, but for whose benefit? Patients who are in a vegetative state can be sustained through intravenous fluids or nasogastric or gastrostomy tube feeding, but at what cost to their humanity, and with what impact on their family?

Such increasingly complex moral questions have led to productive debates among health professionals, lawyers and judges, politicians, social workers, theologians, and ethicists. The issue is generally framed as concern for patient autonomy. This is particularly relevant for social workers, whose practice is based firmly on the value of client self-determination and advocacy for clients' rights. The National Association of Social Workers, in response to the controversial nature of these terminal care decisions, issued a policy statement, "Client Self-Determination in End-of-Life Decisions," to provide guidelines that are compatible with professional and personal ethics, legal parameters, along with respect for client self-determination (National Association of Social Workers, 1997). This publication is highly recommended for those with minimal knowledge in this area because it provides basic definitions of all relevant terms as well as a concise, yet comprehensive presentation of the issues (see appendix).

Several court cases have established precedents concerning the rights of patients and their families to refuse treatment or to discontinue treatment (Alessandroni, 1984; Steinbrook & Lo, 1984). The first, the Karen Ann Quinlan case, involved a 21-year-old admitted to a New Jersey hospital in 1975 in an irreversible coma, following a party at which she consumed alcohol and barbiturates. Her life was sustained thereafter by a respirator and tube feeding. Her family felt that she would not want to continue living in this manner, and her father had to apply to the court to be appointed guardian to have the respirator removed. He was opposed by Karen's physicians and the state attorney general, and his request was refused by a trial court. It took another year of anguish for the family before the New Jersey Supreme Court reversed the lower court ruling and required that the respirator be removed. However, the nasogastric tube feeding was not considered a medical treatment and it was therefore continued, keeping Karen Ann in a "persistent vegetative state" for nine more years.

The next very significant court case concerned 24-year-old Nancy Cruzan of Missouri, who in 1983 suffered permanent brain damage in an automobile accident. She was sent to a Missouri state hospital where she was sustained by tube feeding and, like Karen Ann, remained in a persistent vegetative state. After she had lived like this for several years, her parents petitioned the court to discontinue tube feeding, stating that their daughter would not want to be kept alive in that condition. The court ruled that there was no "clear and convincing evidence" as was required from formerly competent patients to discontinue treatment. The case went all the way to the U.S. Supreme Court in 1990, which supported the standard of "clear and convincing evidence" but at the same time established the principle that a competent patient has a constitutional right to reject unwanted medical treatment. The case then went back to the Missouri courts when some coworkers of Nancy Cruzan testified that she had told them she would never want to be kept alive if she were in a coma, thereby providing the type of evidence needed for the case to finally be resolved. The court ruled in favor of removing the feeding tube, and a few days later, Nancy Cruzan died.

These cases represented what Justice William Brennan referred to as "prisoners of technology."

As medical "heroics" became routine procedures, at the same time that health costs have become a serious social concern, there was a growing public awareness of the need for guidelines, although few would argue that financial incentives should influence ethical judgments.

DEATH WITH DIGNITY

Many states have now passed laws that expand the traditional definition of death to include brain death, or the irreversible loss of brain function, a most important criterion in this new era when machines can artificially maintain heartbeat and breathing ad infinitum. This important legal guide is but one indicator of the profound issues that confront health professionals when dealing with terminal illness. Decisions to treat or not to treat, whether to resuscitate, or when to allow death are handled by physicians who are empowered with this responsibility but lack guidelines and who arrive at these decisions inconsistently, with widely different practices the rule even within the same hospital (President's Commission, 1983a).

As a result of the growing concern for ethical principles in clinical decision making, several commissions at federal and state levels have been studying the issues, and in the past few years many academic and medical research results are becoming available (Current Opinions of the Council on Ethical and Judicial Affairs of the American Medical Association, 1992; American Nurses Association Task Force on the Nurse's Role in End-of-Life Decisions, 1992; Hastings Center, 1987; SUPPORT Principal Investigators, 1995; Life-Sustaining Technologies in the Elderly, 1987). One of the earliest and most significant was the President's Commission for the Study of Ethical Problems in Medicine and Research, headed by Morris Abrams in 1979, which published an extensive report in 1983(b) based on expert testimony from different regions of the country.

Paramount in its findings, the commission emphasized the right of patients to die in dignity. Its recommendations highlighted the following:

> If mentally competent patients want to forgo or end life-sustaining therapy, or resuscitation in a crisis, they should be able to do so, even if earlier death could result. If patients are incapable of making decisions, these should be made by their families or a designated representative. Doctors and hospitals should outline treatment options and assist patients in making decisions in their best interests. Hospital and nursing homes should establish ethics committees to review critical treatment decisions. (1983b, p. 34)

The commission supported the principle of shared decision making, based on informed consent derived from sensitive professional communication to the patient. This was viewed as a continuing collaborative process between patient and providers of care, with the goal of advancing the patient's interests in both health and self-determination. The commission argued that treatment decisions that best promote a patient's health and well-being must be based on the particular patient's values and goals—that no uniform objective determination can be adequate, whether defined by health professionals or by society.

LIVING WILLS AND HEALTH CARE PROXIES

Many professionals concerned with patients' self-determination recommend that older people write "living wills" while they are still competent (even in the early stages of Alzheimer's disease) that state what medical care they would accept or refuse in the event of terminal illness, at which point they may no longer be able to state their preference. Also recommended is the durable power-of-attorney for health care (DPAHC) in which a trusted relative or friend is then empowered to make such decisions as a proxy if the patient becomes incompetent (Dubler, 1984; High, 1993; Markson & Steel, 1990; Michelson, Mulvihill, Hsu, & Olson, 1991).

As the country became aware of the legal and ethical struggle of families like the Quinlans and the Cruzans to discontinue unwanted medical treatment, public opinion moved toward acceptance of the use of living wills and other advance directives. This was to provide "clear and compelling evidence" of a patient's preferences for nonheroic treatment in the event that the patient could no longer express his or her wishes. Advocacy of patient choice in treatment or no-treatment decisions came to be called "the right to die movement" (Hooyman & Kiyak, 1996).

The federal government's response was the passage of the Patient Self-Determination Act, which became effective in December 1991. This law requires that all health facilities that receive funds from Medicare and Medicaid inform patients of their rights to accept or refuse treatment and to prepare advance directives (Doukas & Reichel, 1993).

One purpose of this legislation was to educate health professionals and consumers about the living will and the DPAHC. A major problem with implementing the Patient Self-Determination Act is the timing of providing information to patients. As part of the admission process, all institutions offer written information about living wills to patients and their families, usually by a clerk, followed by discussion with nursing personnel. This is generally a period of high anxiety about the health problem for which the patient is entering the hospital, and obviously not the right time for explanation about advance directives in case of medical emergencies. Just as "informed consent" forms have no meaning in terms of validating the patient's understanding of the procedures to which they are consenting, the advance directive if signed on admission to the health facility is very questionable. There is an urgent need instead for community education *before* a medical crisis, to enhance understanding of the benefits of advance directives.

EDUCATIONAL PROGRAMS AND STRATEGIES TO INCREASE USE OF ADVANCE DIRECTIVES

Throughout the country, newspapers, magazines, health organizations, senior citizens groups, religious organizations, unions, and other civic gathering places have offered various types of information about advance directives. Some have been informational pamphlets, letters, and flyers explaining the purpose of living wills and health care proxies (DPAHCs). Many large hospitals with outpatient services have offered programs to the community to clarify the issues and provide forms to be filled out. The Department of Veterans Affairs, for example, has developed a wide range of materials for consumers and in-service training for professionals to increase understanding and implementation of directives, including the use of video programs. These educational efforts, however, do not report a high rate of completion of directives in response to the presentations. Even when physicians discuss with patients the need to plan for end-of-life treatment, patients do not write advance directives (La Puma, Orentlicher, & Moss, 1991).

To increase the comprehension and use of advance directives, many facilities have researched a variety of strategies. Rather than abstract information about the directives, case vignettes have been developed that provide several scenarios of health crises, and the participants are asked to consider what their preferences would be if they were in such a state.

For example, one large study from a health maintenance organization (HMO) in San Francisco demonstrated the effectiveness of mailing an educational pamphlet about the durable power-of-attorney for health care along with a DPAHC form. The pamphlet was designed for an elderly population and used a question-and-answer format and several thought-provoking case vignettes, such as:

> You have been suffering from Alzheimer's disease for years. Your condition has worsened and you are now unable to recognize people and speak understandably. You've developed severe pneumonia. Would you want to be hospitalized and treated with antibiotics? Or, would you choose to decline life-prolonging treatment and accept only care to make you more comfortable? Since you're unable to communicate your wishes, who should make these health care decisions for you?

The pamphlet described the DPAHC and its advantages. Patients were encouraged to discuss these issues with family members, friends, and health care providers. As a result, 18.5 percent of the experimental group completed a DPAHC form, with minimal involvement of the staff of the HMO (Rubin, Strull, Fialkow, Weiss, & Lo, 1994, p. 210).

Another study demonstrated the effectiveness of a program in which information about advance directives was offered as an interdisciplinary effort between a social worker, a physician, and other health professionals. The study reached 34 elderly patients in a geriatric outpatient clinic, and offered information and counseling over several months. This provided enough time for participants to develop trust, as well as an understanding of the documents and procedures described, at their own pace. As a result, 71 percent completed advance directives, which they had discussed with their family members. Although it took 60 to 90 minutes before completion of the directives, the project team felt that this much time was needed to discuss these emotionally laden issues. They were in agreement that the time was well spent in that it will probably facilitate the difficult process of making critical end-of-life decisions that will reflect the value of self-determination (Luptak & Boult, 1994).

Another study found that the best intervention in terms of the outcome of increasing completion of advance directives was one that provided both educational materials and help in filling out the forms (High, 1993).

Another area affected by the dilemmas of enhancing patient autonomy through education is in the field of home health care. Providers are also required by the Patient Self-Determination Act to inform clients of their rights in making treatment decisions. A survey of home health care agencies found that consistent policies are needed for social workers, nurses, and other staff to handle the ethical dilemmas surrounding decision making for the mentally impaired (Davitt & Kaye, 1996).

The importance of consumer comprehension in completing advance directives (also called "instructional directives" in some studies) cannot be overestimated. Several studies have shown that the manner of presenting information to patients can influence their stated preferences for life-sustaining treatment or no treatment. When treatments were described vividly, in harsh clinical terms, the treatments were 2.5 times more likely to be refused than when they were described in less threatening terms (Malloy, Wigton, Meeske, & Tape, 1992).

Some studies have demonstrated the value of presenting information through discussion of vignettes and using large graphics for illustration. Community-based and nursing home residents increased their understanding of enteral tube feeding (also known as g-tubes), leading some to discuss this medical intervention with their physicians as part of their advance directives (Krynski, Tymchuk, & Ouslander, 1994).

In addition to concerns about comprehension of medical interventions, a significant study that has increased the probability of capturing authentic preferences is the National Values History Project. A questionnaire was developed to gather information about nursing home residents' values as part of the institutional care plan (Gibson, 1990). This has been widely disseminated and incorporated into many projects. Its purpose is to increase communication about the deeply held beliefs and wishes of older people, and it has been found to be helpful because, although stated values may change over time, basic values are consistent. Collecting and evaluating a person's values is a means of enhancing autonomous decision making.

One values history model starts out with eliciting basic values as follows:

BASIC LIFE VALUES

Perhaps the most basic values in this context concern length of life versus quality of life. Which of the following two statements is the most important to you?

_____ 1. I want to live as long as possible, regardless of the quality of life that I experience.

_____ 2. I want to preserve a good quality of life, even if this means that I may not live as long.

QUALITY OF LIFE VALUES

Many values help to define the quality of life that we want to live. The following list contains some that appear to be the most common. Review this list (and feel free to either elaborate on it or add to it) and circle those values that are important to your definition of quality of life.

1. I want to maintain my capacity to think clearly.
2. I want to feel safe and secure.
3. I want to avoid unnecessary pain and suffering.
4. I want to be treated with respect.
5. I want to be treated with dignity when I can no longer speak for myself.
6. I do not want to be an unnecessary burden on my family.
7. I want to be able to make my own decisions.

8. I want to experience a comfortable dying process.
9. I want to be with my loved ones before I die.
10. I want to leave good memories of me to my loved ones.
11. I want to be treated in accord with my religious beliefs and traditions.
12. I want respect shown for my body after I die.
13. I want to help others by making a contribution to medical education and research.
14. Other values or clarification of values above. (Doukas & McCullough, 1991)

It is clear that using this questionnaire as the basis for discussion with a patient, a client, or another consumer will be time-consuming but can yield a multidimensional understanding of preferences, while helping the client develop a rationale for his or her decisions.

Another example of a frequently cited method to increase the use and usefulness of advance directives was developed by Linda and Ezekiel Emanuel, physicians and medical ethicists at Harvard Medical School. In response to some of the problems which became apparent in the implementation of advance directives, they devised four scenarios of severe medical problems in which patients would hypothetically choose from four treatment options with respect to 11 specific life-sustaining interventions. The scenarios described patients as

1. in a persistent vegetative state
2. in a coma with a small chance of full recovery
3. having severe dementia with no other life-threatening illness
4. having severe dementia with a terminal illness.

For each scenario the patient is asked which of the following he or she would choose: accept; decline; unsure; treatment trial; stop if not working for the following treatments:—antibiotics; blood transfusions; cardiopulmonary resuscitation (CPR); invasive diagnostics; artificial tube feeding; intravenous fluids; major operations; minor operations; dialysis; and mechanical respiration.

The practitioner–researchers found that testing this method on almost 500 outpatients produced the ability to predict patient preferences for specific treatments within given scenarios in relation to the stipulated prognoses. They found that decisions about CPR and mechanical ventilators, which are the most common directives elicited in current advance care directives, are not the most powerful predictors of whether the patient would want or refuse other treatment. As a means of increasing the value of advance care decisions, they recommend that, when talking about hypothetical medical situations, place more emphasis on a broader range of treatments, in particular preferences regarding antibiotics and major surgery, within specific illness states (Emanuel, Barry, Emanuel, & Stoekle, 1994).

The use of such a scenario and a treatment-specific instructional form requires a commitment to the value of authentic doctor–patient communication, which the Emanuels clearly exemplify.

LIMITATIONS OF LIVING WILLS AND HEALTH CARE PROXIES

Despite initial enthusiasm about the potential value of living wills as a means of respecting patients' wishes even when they are no longer competent, it became apparent that there were many obstacles to meeting that goal. First, there is a very small percentage of people who actually execute advance directives, ranging from 4 percent to 20 percent (High, 1993). This is not surprising when we consider that denial is a common defense against the fear of terminal illness and death. Furthermore, it should be recognized that the emphasis on the opportunity to make choices may be overlooking the fact that not everyone wants to state treatment preferences. Choosing not to choose must also be honored as a value (Wetle, 1994).

Second, even when put in writing, the wishes of patients may be overlooked or countermanded by the physician or by family members who are not ready to "let go." A significant research project, titled the Study to Understand Prognoses and Preferences for Outcomes and Risks of Treatment (SUPPORT), carried out at the Center to Improve Care of the Dying based at Georgetown University Medical Center, showed that the last wishes of patients are often ignored (Harrold, 1996). Another view is that the wishes are not so much ignored in favor of aggressive and often futile treatment as that the wishes are unclear, inconsistent, or misunderstood by physicians (Levinsky, 1996).

Because of the enormous complexity of clinical decisions in terminal care, the living will alone is often inadequate in stating that the patient would not want his or her life prolonged by artificial means, or would not want extraordinary treatment or heroics. Nor is a very detailed will better because there is a risk that a particular turn of events is not foreseen. Evidence also has shown that people do not always understand what they sign (Pearlman, 1994). When their preferences are elicited through open-ended questions, with an opportunity for clarification by a physician, misunderstandings of terms become apparent. Furthermore, the living will has been criticized as having a "fatal flaw" in that once it is signed, the patient gives up the protection of informed consent, leaving all health care decisions in the hands of the doctor who has the power to decide when the document goes into effect (Smith, 1994). Instead, it is recommended that a DPAHC be endorsed.

Through the use of a health care proxy, a trusted relative or friend accepts responsibility for treatment decisions. It is assumed that the patient's surrogate will be informed by the physician of the pros and cons of various options, and decisions can then be reached that the patient would have chosen (if known) or that are based on the "best interest" of the patient. Because advance care documents often require some interpretation as various diagnostic forks in the road are reached in the management of the very sick or elderly (Thorne, 1993), it is essential that a health care proxy (usually a relative) be involved. In addition, many studies of the wishes of older people as to who should make decisions for them in the event of their incapacity have shown that the family is the preferred surrogate, even when no advance directives are executed (High, 1988; Pearlman, Uhlmann, & Jecker, 1992; Shawler, 1992).

Family–Patient Communication

Despite the logic in advocating for the use of the DPAHC, there are several immediate problems in depending on families if the goal is to ensure that the wishes of the patient are carried out.

The first is that the proxy often does not know what the patient's preferences would be, because even among those who complete directives, there is little discussion of what they would want if they became terminally ill. There have been many studies that have demonstrated a lack of concordance between people and their health care proxies when they are asked for treatment preferences through use of vignettes of terminal care treatment decisions (High, 1988; Lurie, Pheley, Miles, & Bannik-Mohrland, 1992; Sansone & Phillips, 1995; Tomlinson, Howe, Notman, & Rossmiller, 1990; Zweibel & Cassel 1989). In other words, the designated family member or friend often does not choose the treatment options that the patient would have chosen.

In a study of 386 adults representing the diverse population of South Florida, it was found that 76.6 percent believed that the family should make treatment decisions for them if they could not, but that fewer than half (48.7 percent) had ever discussed their preferences with their friends or family (Safford, 1993). These studies clearly emphasize the need to facilitate communication about these issues before a medical crisis arises.

An additional concern is that even when there has been a conversation about preferences, in the emotional crisis at the time of imminent death, the relative may not remember what had been discussed. There is an urgent need to help families communicate about these emotional topics. A very useful resource is the book by Ahronheim and Weber (1992), and a chapter by George Burnell, "How to Talk to Your Family or Friends About Dying or Prolonging Life" (Burnell, 1993).

Family–Physician Communication

A second obstacle to the ability of a proxy to fulfill the decision-making role is that many physicians have demonstrated an unwillingness to forego life-sustaining treatment or to discontinue it (Solomon et al., 1993). Very often it is difficult for the physician to predict if death is imminent, or whether a chronic health condition has changed to a terminal one. Even when the family proxy is also a medical professional, familiar with the ethical issues involved, there has been resistance on the part of the medical establishment to respect his or her wishes. Poignant articles by physicians, nurses, lawyers, and newspaper editors, with titles such as "Why Won't the Doctors Let Her Die?" "They Tortured My Mother: Patronizing Doctors, Agonizing Care" and "Must They Tinker with the Dying?" (Feinstein, 1986; Hechinger, 1991; Lederman, 1993), testify to the widespread frustration and confusion of the family proxies as they try to have their relatives' dying process eased.

It is apparent that physicians and family members need to learn how to communicate with each other about life and death decisions. Many physicians have been trained to protect themselves from the pain of having their patients die by detaching themselves from the families' emotional upheavals. Detached concern is the stance that seems to allow empathy, without becoming ineffectual. This detachment, however, at times may lead to an inability to assess the validity of the families' requests for or against specific treatments.

FAMILIES AS DECISION MAKERS

Current discussions of the rights of patients to refuse treatment have moved to include the concept of the rights of families to be included in the assessment. It is argued that perhaps as a society, we have put too much emphasis on the value of autonomy and individualism as opposed to the competing values of family support and interdependency (Clark, 1991). It has been further argued that the family's ability to figure out the preferences of the patient is not the issue as much as the view that they are *entitled* to a role in decision making since the family is often affected by whatever decisions are made (Kapp, 1991). Another possible moral argument for acknowledging family authority to make decisions is the family's role as the primary social unit in providing care and intimacy. Because individuals and their values are shaped by the families in which they are reared, even if they are unable to express their treatment preferences directly, the family proxy can speak from the same context, and thus approximate the patient's wishes (Bailly & Depoy, 1995; Nelson & Nelson, 1994).

It is also important to stress that emphasis on family decision making is a way to respect the cultural values of particular groups. For example, medical decision making and the process of conveying bad news to a patient may be insensitive to his or her cultural heritage and fails to honor the role of the family in protecting the patient (Michel, 1994; Teno, Nelson, & Lynn, 1994). Many cultures believe that their relatives should not be told that they have a terminal illness, fearing that such information strips away hope and places additional burdens on patients and family. This may pose an ethical dilemma for the health care provider who stresses the dominant value of patient autonomy and the right to know. Such issues must be explored and analyzed in the context of the strength of their adherence to the culture's precepts, whether patients are in hospitals, long-term care facilities, or the community (Boyle, 1995; Rogers, 1997).

In support of families as decision makers, it is noted that most states now have surrogate–family decision making procedures as a backup for people who have not completed advance directives. These regulations give high priority to family members for substitute health care decisions (High, 1994). This is a reflection of the common practice in medicine for physicians to look to family members for a decision concerning the patient who lacks decisional capacity. When decisions are required to withhold or withdraw life-sustaining treatment for a terminally ill patient, there are state statutes that require, when adult children serve as surrogates, that either all or a majority of those available must be consulted (Areen, 1987).

This sometimes causes difficulties when there are disagreements among family surrogates or when family members do not make "good faith" choices. At the same time recognizing the authenticity of the family's right to make decisions for a patient who is no longer competent, professionals must be alert to situations in which the patient may be abused as a result of conflicting interest, or vulnerability to decisions based on misguided judgment (Teno et al., 1994). In such cases the professional is required to work toward implementation of choices that reflect the patient's autonomous interests, through counseling and negotiation. If the family is unresponsive to the professional's recommendations, legal protection for the patient may need to be invoked as a last resort (Kapp, 1991). For those situations in which family surrogates cannot agree on treatment decisions and they are resistant to compromise, a guardianship petition may need to be initiated to clarify the formal decisional authority of the family members. These troublesome dilemmas emphasize the value of the advance naming of a surrogate through the DPAHC. Where there is no satisfactory agreement, consultation with an institutional ethics committee may help resolve the conflict. For a provocative and helpful discussion of the controversies concerning the right to die, read the section "Should People Have the Choice to End Their Lives?" in Harry R. Moody's outstanding reader, *Aging: Concepts and Controversies* (1994).

INSTITUTIONAL ETHICS COMMITTEES

As a direct consequence of the illuminating report of the President's Commission for the Study of Ethical Problems in Medicine and Biomedical and Behavioral Research, many hospitals and some of the largest nursing homes have developed institutional ethics committees to provide guidelines, education, and consultation in difficult treatment decisions (Cranford & Doudera, 1984). These committees vary in membership but typically have representative physicians, nurses, and clergy and sometimes administrators, social workers, and ethicists. Ethics committees may include family members or surrogates when discussing particular patients.

Although many physicians and administrators may resist the formal involvement of patients' families, fearing their emotional reactions as obstructive, through education, counseling, and open communication, the surrogates' role in sharing responsibility for life and death decisions can be significant. An excellent participant–observer account of the very effective ethics committee of Hermann Hospital in Houston, Texas, is offered in *First, Do No Harm* (Belkin, 1993). Through the case histories of five patients of varied ages and conditions, with a sensitive discussion of the dynamics of decision making, the reader becomes deeply aware of heart-wrenching challenges and realities. In the most common scenario, the doctors decide nothing more can be done, and the family insists that the physician is not being aggressive enough. But half the time the situation is reversed, with the family wanting to withdraw care and the doctor refusing. Often, some family members agree with the doctor, and others disagree. The policy at the Hermann Hospital ethics committee is to invite the family to meet with the committee and to convince them that the patient would or would not want this particular treatment or surgery or decision to turn off the machines. The committee then makes recommendations that are not binding but are almost always followed.

An alternate model for resolving ethical dilemmas has been developed at the Jewish Home and Hospital of New York City in collaboration with Mt. Sinai Hospital and the Hastings Center. Targeting end-of-life treatment issues and informed consent for the frail elderly, a Center on Ethics in Long-Term Care was developed, which initiated ethics rounds as a method for case finding and discussion, service implementation, and education and research. This interdisciplinary effort has resulted in increased sensitivity to the everyday dilemmas of enhancing autonomy along the broad spectrum of services in the institution and home care (Olson et al., 1993).

Ethics committees may be particularly relevant for mentally impaired aged people, for although there is now general consensus that competent patients have the right to know their diagnosis and take part in decisions for or against treatment, there is no guide for informed and ethical decision making for victims of Alzheimer's disease and related disorders. This is part of the burden experienced by relatives of mentally impaired older people—they must assume responsibility for every aspect of care for these incompetents—a role for which they are not emotionally or socially prepared. Furthermore, the burden of responsibility for these terminally ill relatives now continues for many more years than in previous eras because of advances in medical care, typically falling to only one or two available family members.

These families, which are often wrongfully criticized as neglecting their older members, suffer from guilt, as though they are somehow deficient in not being able to restore their loved ones to their cognizant state. They may be overwhelmed physically and emotionally if they are caring for their loved one in the community or immobilized with guilt if their loved one is in an institution.

When inevitable additional illnesses occur, or when the deteriorating brain causes further impairment, decisions may be indicated in regard to the extent or limits of treatment. In fact, good practice might include such eventualities as part of an ongoing treatment plan, using history from the family to design an individualized program as well as the management of illness or crises in the future. Compassionate guidance from an ethics committee may help the responsible relative analyze the options available and try to come to an understanding of what the patient would want if he or she were competent to share in the decision. The committee can introduce the concept of "substitute judgment" as an ethical principle to guide the distraught relatives, who often struggle with ambivalent feelings, wishing for death, and then feeling guilty if the wish is interpreted as selfishly motivated (Alessandroni, 1984). Through the process of substituting the patient's presumed judgment for his or her own, the relative, with intimate knowledge of the patient's values and preferences when competent, can try to determine what the patient would consent to under the present circumstances.

One might try to project what the patient would have considered to be "death with dignity," for example. Would he or she want a nasogastric tube when no longer able to take nourishment by mouth? Or would a gastrostomy be considered extraordinary treatment? With no hope for a cure of the mental impairment, would the patient want a life sustained artificially, or would the choice be to let nature take its course and allow death to come. By interpreting the patient's own values and attitudes to the physician involved in treatment decisions, the relative can, in good conscience, request the withholding of treatment when this is the case.

Where the patient's preferences are not known, the ethical principle of "best interests" can be used, with responsible family members determining, with the guidance of the ethics committee, what course of action or inaction would be in the best interests of the patient. Since such determinations are always problematic, a partnership approach to what is the best interest of the particular patient, rather than the more common subjective concern for the quality of life, will reflect greater respect for the individual. Through this shared mechanism for decision making, the patient's rights to self-determination are more closely protected, with recourse to the courts if consensus within the family or with the staff cannot be reached.

One might reasonably ask at this point, "Is it really necessary to formalize the life and death decisions for incompetent patients? Isn't this merely an extension of the traditional process between physicians and family members?"

In many respects these decisions were traditionally made privately between the physician, who knew the patient for many years, and the family. Now that the majority of people with terminal conditions die in hospitals, treated by physicians who do not know them, the private decision is no longer feasible. Once hospitalized, patients are often treated aggressively, without regard for prognosis or previous quality of life.

The hospice movement is one response to the preference for palliative care rather than heroics when confronted with terminal conditions. It has contributed toward our awareness of our anxiety about death, and the task of accepting death as a natural event. But mentally impaired elderly people are not candidates for hospice care because of the lengthy duration of their terminal stage.

THE HOSPICE ALTERNATIVE

When patients have been diagnosed with a terminal condition from which death is predicted within six months, they may choose, with or without advance directives, to forego curative treatment and receive hospice care. As described in chapter 12, hospices provide comfort or palliative care. Patients are helped with medications to be free of pain and are made as physically and spiritually comfortable as possible, and this includes counseling for the family. They are free of the possibility of being tied to respirators and fed by tubes, unless it is felt to be necessary for their comfort.

Hospices provide most care at home, but there are several free-standing facilities, and some hospitals set aside beds for hospice patients. The hospice is not a place but more of a philosophy of care that accepts the dying process as a natural event and enables those who want to talk about death to do so. It offers emotional support and assistance in maximizing the quality of life that remains. The hospice does not support the practice of active euthanasia or assisted suicide. At present, about 400,000 patients a year choose a hospice for terminal care (Foreman, 1996).

A recent federal policy change that will lead to better care for dying people is that Medicare now will pay for palliative care for a terminal patient in the hospital, even when the person is not formally a hospice patient. Until October 1996 doctors could not bill Medicare for services that were aimed solely at comfort, not resuscitation or life extension (Glasheen, 1997). This has led to the practice of prescribing unnecessary diagnostic procedures and medical interventions as a strategy to justify hospitalization and to avoid having to discharge a dying patient to his or her home. Although the motivation for such a strategy may have been for the benefit of the patient and family, the results were an increase in the excessively high cost of terminal care and excessively burdensome treatments.

Social workers and other health care professionals can take part in educating physicians and patients' families about this new reimbursement policy that encourages palliative care. As doctors become more familiar with comfort care, hopefully they will refer more patients to a hospice, where their total needs will be more humanely met. Because physicians are not trained or accustomed to considering the hospice as an alternative to traditional clinical protocols, it may be necessary for social workers to advocate for referrals to a hospice.

PHYSICIAN-ASSISTED SUICIDE

The most recent ethical debate, which has been the subject of countless articles and programs, is the issue of assisted suicides. Brought to national attention by Jack Kevorkian, M.D., a Michigan pathologist, two cases have been before the U.S. Supreme Court that involve mentally competent people who have terminal conditions and who have asked their physicians to help them end their lives. Although the concept of suicide emphasizes self-determination and is therefore accepted as part of the right-to-die movement, physician-assisted suicide moves close to euthanasia, which makes the majority of Americans uneasy. Cases appear regularly in the press and are discussed on national television, with the finding that it is impossible to reach consensus on this matter, just as the abortion rights issue cannot reach consensus. The emotionally held values by the diverse groups in society do not permit agreement, but the right to choose, for competent people, has recently been decided by the Supreme Court (*Washington v Glucksberg*, No. 96-110, and *Vacco v Quill*, No. 95-1858, June 26, 1997). The Court decided that no constitutional right to aid in suicide has ever been asserted and upheld by a court of final jurisdiction, but left such determinations open to the states. Thus, the national debate will continue on a state-by-state basis, reflecting the ambiguity and ambivalence that prevail. In the meantime, the health community is aware that physicians and sometimes nurses will provide enough medication to relieve pain and suffering, even with the knowledge that the dosage will also cause death (Herald Wire Services, 1996).

Timothy Quill, the outspoken physician who has written of his decisions to assist some terminal patients to die more comfortably, justifies assisted suicide as a compassionate response to patients with intractable pain. He explains that when medications, such as morphine or barbiturates, are given to prevent suffering and in the process they hasten death, that is called a "double effect." The intent is to prevent suffering and not to cause death. Even the Catholic Church agrees with such procedures. A 1975 directive from the National Conference of Catholic Bishops stated, "It is not euthanasia to give a dying person sedatives and analgesics for the alleviation of pain even though they may deprive the patient of the use of reason, or shorten his life" (Preston, 1994, p. A15). Current doctrine of most churches and all three branches of Judaism supports the administration of pain medication, despite the possibility that increased doses may shorten the patient's life (Landers, 1994).

Most physicians are afraid to put themselves in jeopardy by prescribing in a way that could be considered illegal, and consequently many terminal patients suffer needlessly. Dr. Quill stated that hospice care is sometimes overromanticized, in that comfort care has limits, and in some cases death would be a welcome relief. A small percentage of patients have a difficult time with only palliative care, for example, developing delirium when pain medication has to be increased (Quill, 1996). Patients with AIDS often are tormented at the end of their dying process with dementia and blindness. Some patients with respiratory failure struggle to breathe and are often continuously coughing and bringing up huge amounts of mucus. Morphine can be used to treat the pain and ease their struggle, although at times it indirectly suppresses the breathing and therefore inadvertently hastens death (Quill, 1993). If the intent of the use of the particular medication is relief of suffering, it is well within the double effect principle.

The notion of physician-assisted suicide would not be necessary if most physicians were adequately trained to care for dying patients and to become skillful in pain relief.

EDUCATIONAL RESOURCES FOR CARING FOR DYING PEOPLE

As the results of major research into terminal care practice have been published in the past few years, it has become evident that physicians are woefully unprepared to meet the challenge of caring for dying people. One response has been the development of a project dedicated to improving end-of-life patient care (Educational Resource Document, 1996). The goal of the project was

> to identify and promote physician competency in the care of dying patients during internal medicine residency and subspecialty training "focused on" the elements of professionalism essential in caring for the dying and expected in interactions with patients and family, the requisite body of knowledge and core skills necessary to organize and deliver care, and strategies for evaluation. (p. i)

The resulting monographs are a model for educating not only physicians, but all members of the interdisciplinary health care team. They are comprehensive, practical, and sensitively written, including knowledge about physicians' roles and skills, palliative care, pain control, symptom assessment, hospice, role of the health care team, role of psychiatrist, and role of religion. This project should significantly improve the care available for the dying patient.

At present, it is still necessary for patients and their families to take an active role in controlling or influencing their end-of-life treatment decisions, first through family discussion and then through execution of advance directives.

AS GOOD A DEATH AS POSSIBLE

There is much confusion about what might constitute a good death. Even the attorney arguing for physician-assisted suicide in a recent Florida case stated that a lethal dose of drugs is preferable to the common method of giving patients pain killers and then letting them die of starvation and dehydration (Rozsa, 1997). The implication is that "letting" patients die of starvation is cruel neglect and inconsistent with medical ethics. There is a connotation about starvation or starving to death that is so horrifying that professionals, patients, and families must learn that this is a misleading term in the context of end-of-life care. People who are starving are those who are hungry but have no food available. People who are terminally ill lack a healthy appetite. For centuries people near the end of life have stopped eating and have died in this manner, painlessly and quietly (Ahronheim & Weber, 1992).

My own father died peacefully at age 85, after several years of mental deterioration, in precisely this manner, when he gradually stopped eating. He was offered all his favorite foods, but finally, after accepting only small portions of ice cream, indicated that he no longer had an appetite, and after a few days, he quietly passed away in no discomfort whatsoever. This was in 1976, fortunately before the widespread introduction of gastrostomies and g-tube feeding, so we were spared the agony of decision making, and my father was permitted to pass away naturally.

It is still common for physicians to recommend tube feeding when patients either stop eating for lack of appetite or become unable to swallow. There are countless anecdotes about the health professionals' assertion that "we can't let them starve to death." Patients' families must learn to counterassert that it is not starvation, but a natural and comfortable way to die, with the probability that the patient will lapse into a sleeplike state before death occurs.

Educating families and professionals in institutions and in the community about the extent of this fallacy about starvation is an appropriate role for social workers. We must be aware at the same time that there is also a financial interest in keeping patients alive with tube feeding. Enteral nutrition and the now prevalent ventilator industry in home care has become a billion-dollar business. Simply educating and advocating for the right to refuse such treatment or to have it discontinued may not be successful against such powerful profits.

The public and many professionals are unaware of the fact that high-tech home care has become the fastest growing sector of the entire health care economy, a result of the Medicare reimbursement policy in the late 1970s that began to pay for home parenteral and enteral nutrition, and then to the beginning of the diagnosis-related groups in 1983, when hospitals suddenly had a financial incentive to discharge patients earlier than under the former policy which paid them according to their costs. As sicker patients were discharged earlier, they tended to need continuing medical treatment and providers moved quickly to develop and market devices, drugs, and ancillary services. This rush for profits has occurred without any analysis of the consequences. The boundary between the intensive care unit in the hospital and the living room in the home is becoming blurred for increasing numbers of families." A significant gap is emerging between our home-based technical prowess and our ability to discern humane, just, and efficient use of this technology" (Arras, 1994, p. 52).

Thus, the social worker and other health professionals will face some formidable obstacles when trying to help those patients and families, who are burdened by this level of treatment, to understand and exercise their rights.

It must also be pointed out that many physicians and nurses are still unclear about their legal responsibility with regard to terminating treatment. The social worker has an important opportunity to provide information in this muddled area. There is no legal distinction between withholding treatment and withdrawing treatment once it has begun. The doctor does not risk exposure to a lawsuit for withdrawing treatment. In fact, doctors and hospitals are protected from liability for honoring good-faith decisions by the health care proxy who speaks for the patient and "has priority over every doctor and family member or close friend" (Clement, 1995, p. A16).

TOWARD A SUMMATION

The reader may reasonably feel overwhelmed by the complexities of these dilemmas and controversies, which are so contemporary that every week there are new aspects discussed in the media. *The New York Times* devoted two and one-half pages to one of the major themes discussed here—the need for families to communicate their wishes about terminal care long in advance.

The front page headline read "Failing to Discuss Dying Adds to Pain of Patient and Family" (Fein, 1997).

Social workers can help families and elderly people to overcome their reluctance to talk about dying by offering workshops, lectures, and training programs in a broad variety of settings. There are already excellent training materials available for in-service education of health personnel, such as a manual developed through the Southeast Florida Center on Aging and San Jose University, California, on enhancing autonomy in long-term care (Pelaez & David, 1992).

Some families may benefit from reading some of the excellent books now available on death and family decision making. Other families may find that the Internet offers an opportunity to communicate about these issues with the growing numbers of people throughout the country who are searching for answers to these existential dilemmas. Some of the websites, out of the thousands of links dealing with death and dying and physician-assisted suicide, are

- http://www.choices.org — Choice in Dying, a nonprofit organization that helps patients and families in decisions about end-of-life care
- http://www.islandnet.com/deathnet — the site of DeathNet, founded by author Derk Humphrey and the right-to-die movement
- http://www.nho.org — the site for information about hospices
- http://www.cyberspy.com/webster/death.html — the WEBster: Death, Dying, and Grief resources.

There are also many videos now available to facilitate discussion of life and death issues (see "Selected Resources" at the end of this chapter).

The entire issue of advance directives is a challenge and an opportunity for social workers to assume a leadership role in identifying the ethical issues as they affect elderly people and their families, the health care system, related social programs, and society as a whole; clarifying these ethical issues; and educating clients, peers, and other health professionals, including physicians.

Social workers should also seize the opportunity to share the legal facts about the right to refuse treatment or to request that treatment be withdrawn, when it is clear that there is no chance for recovery. They can also consider and discuss the possibility that the debate about advance directives and proxy decision making is "not about rights and the right to die, but instead about the quality of life and relationships in a medical and social community" (La Puma, 1995, p. 2). Because there is much ethical discomfort in assessing what is quality of life, recognizing that the parameters may change as the patient changes, it is essential for this basic value to be discussed from time to time, and recorded in advance directives that are reviewed annually. Earlier it was indicated that physicians are in the best position to discuss advance directives with their patients, and some laudable efforts have been made to test a variety of approaches. However, it has been reported that these discussions are rare—either the physician is reluctant to bring up a difficult subject, or the patient does not know if he or she can bring it up because visits with the doctor are usually brief and time limited.

Therefore, social workers are urged to accept the challenge in fulfilling their roles as counselors, educators, mediators, and advocates to get us all talking about our values and attitudes about end-of-life decisions. Advance directives are only one way of developing public awareness and getting people to indicate their preferences. But since passage of the Patient Self-Determination Act, many directives are signed in institutions, often without full comprehension, sometimes out of a depression related to the institutionalization, sometimes during a period of decreased mental competence caused by medications. It is important for social workers to be aware of these obstacles to appropriate decision making and include these issues as part of a thorough biopsychosocial assessment.

In addition to encouraging the use of advance directives to identify and clarify the ethical dilemmas and systemic contradictions, social work can be the profession that consistently advocates for fairness and justice in health care in all stages of life, not only in relation to terminal care decisions. We must be aware that we have moved from an era when there were incentives to treat aggressively to an era of cost containment within managed care. This has led to concern about limiting or rationing health care. Social workers and other health care professionals must argue for care based on individualized assessments, not on age or assumptions of preferences. Patients should not be burdened by unwanted care and should not be undertreated either. Our ideal might be stated as a quest for living life fully, as long as possible, but accepting death as an inevitable and natural outcome. By encouraging the life review and facilitating and validating the integrity of the life well lived, we respect life while we accept mortality.

REFERENCES

Ahronheim, J., & Weber, D. (1992). *Final passages: Positive choices for the dying and their loved ones.* New York: Simon & Schuster.

Alessandroni, M. (1984, Spring). Who decides for patients who can't? *Generations, 18*(1), 27–29.

American Nurses' Association Task Force on the Nurse's Role in End-of-Life Decisions. (1992). *Position statement on foregoing artificial nutrition and hydration.* Washington, DC: American Nurses' Association.

Areen, J. (1987). The legal status of consent obtained from families of adult patients to withhold or withdraw treatment. *JAMA, 258,* 229–235.

Arras, J. D. (1994). The technological tether: An introduction to ethical and social issues in high-tech home care. *Hastings Center Report, 24*(5), S1–S2.

Bailly, D. J., & Depoy, E. (1995). Older people's response to education about advance directives. *Health & Social Work, 20,* 223–228.

Belkin, L. (1993). *First, do no harm.* New York: Simon & Schuster.

Boyle, P. (1995). Multiculturalism in nursing homes. In E. Olson, E. R. Chichin, & L. S. Libow (Eds.), *Controversies in ethics in long-term care* (pp. 15–27). New York: Springer.

Burnell, G. (1993). *Final choices: To live or to die in an age of medical technology.* New York: Simon & Schuster.

Clark, P. (1991). Ethical dimensions of quality of life in aging: Autonomy vs. collectivism in the United States and Canada. *Gerontologist, 31,* 631–639.

Clement, M. D. (1995, November 29). Letter to the editor. *New York Times,* p. A16.

Cranford, R. E., & Doudera, A. E. (1984). *Institutional ethics committees and health care decision making.* Ann Arbor, MI: Health Administration Press.

Current opinions of the Council on Ethical and Judicial Affairs of the American Medical Association: Withholding or withdrawing

life-prolonging treatment. (1992). Chicago: American Medical Association.
Davitt, J. K., & Kaye, L. W. (1996). Supporting patient autonomy: Decision-making in home health care. *Social Work, 41*, 41–50.
Doukas, D., & McCullough, L. (1991). The values history: The evaluation of the patient's values and advance directives. *Journal of Family Practice, 32*(2), 145–153.
Doukas, D., & Reichal, W. (1993). *Planning for uncertainty: A guide to living wills and other advance directives for health care*. Baltimore: Johns Hopkins University Press.
Dubler, N. (1984, Winter). The ethics of research. *Generations, 9*(2), 18–21.
Educational Resource Document. (1996). *Caring for the dying: Identification and promotion of physician competency*. Philadelphia: American Board of Internal Medicine.
Emanuel, L., Barry, M., Emanuel, E., & Stoekle, J. (1994). Advance directives: Can patients' stated treatment choices be used to infer unstated choices? *Medical Care, 32*(2), 95–105.
Fein, E. B. (1997, March 5). Failing to discuss dying adds to pain of patient and family. *New York Times*, pp. A1, A14–A15.
Feinstein, A. R. (1986, October 6). Why won't the doctors let her die? *New York Times*, Op-Ed page.
Foreman, J. (1996, October 5). Survey: Most would seek hospice care over suicide. *Miami Herald*, p. 5D.
Gibson, J. M. (1990). National values history project. *Generations, 14* (Suppl.), 52–64.
Glasheen, L. K. (1997). A new frontier for care. *AARP Bulletin, 38*(3), 1, 19.
Harrold, J. K. (1996, January/February). Last wishes ignored: Why we must protect end-of-life decision making. *Aging Today*, 7–8.
Hastings Center. (1987). *Guidelines on the termination of life-sustaining treatment and the care of the dying*. Bloomington: Indiana University Press.
Hechinger, F. M. (1991, January 24). They tortured my mother: Patronizing doctors, agonizing care. *New York Times*, Editorial page.
Herald Wire Services. (1996, May 23). Compassion or complicity? Nurses admit aiding death. *Miami Herald*, pp. 1A, 9A.
High, D. (1988). All in the family: Extended autonomy and expectations in surrogate health care decision making. *Gerontologist, 28*, 46–51.
High, D. (1993). Advance directives and the elderly: A study of intervention strategies to increase use. *Gerontologist, 33*, 342–349.
High, D. (1994, November/December). Families' roles in advance directives. *Hastings Center Report*, Special Supplement, S516–S518.

Hooyman, N., & Kiyak, H. A. (1996). *Social gerontology* (4th ed.). Boston: Allyn & Bacon.
Kapp, M. B. (1991). Health care decision making by the elderly: I get by with a little help from my family. *Gerontologist, 31*, 619–623.
Krynski, M., Tymchuk, A., & Ouslander, J. (1994). How informed can consent be? New light on comprehension among elderly people making decisions about internal tube feeding. *Gerontologist, 34*, 36–43.
Landers, P. (1994, June 9). Facing our mortality. *Miami Herald*, pp. 1G, 3G.
La Puma, J. (1995). Are advance directives for the frail elderly? In E. Olson, E. R. Chichin, & L. S. Libow (Eds.), *Controversies in ethics in long-term care* (pp. 1–14). New York: Springer.
La Puma, J., Orentlicher, D., & Moss, R. J. (1991). Advance directives on admission: Clinical implications and analysis of the Patient Self-Determination Act of 1990. *JAMA, 266*, 402–405.
Lederman, N. M. (1993, January 16). Must they tinker with the dying? *New York Times*, Op-Ed page.
Levinsky, N. G. (1996). The purpose of advance medical planning—Autonomy for patients or limitation of care? *New England Journal of Medicine, 335*, 741–743.
Life-sustaining technologies and the elderly. (1987). Washington, DC: U.S. Congress, Office of Technology Assessment.
Luptak, M., & Boult, C. (1994). A method for increasing elders' use of advance directives. *Gerontologist, 34*, 409–412.
Lurie, N., Pheley, A., Miles, S., & Bannik-Mohrland, S. (1992). Attitudes toward discussing life-sustaining treatments in extended care facility patients. *Journal of the American Geriatric Society, 40*, 1205–1208.
Malloy, T., Wigton, R., Meeske, J., & Tape, T. (1992). The influence of treatment descriptions on advance directive decisions. *Journal of the American Geriatrics Society, 40*, 1255–1260.
Markson, L., & Steel, K. (1990). Using advance directives in the home care setting. *Generations, 14* (Suppl.), 25–28.
Michel, V. (1994). Factoring ethnic and racial differences into bioethics decision making. *Generations, 18*(4), 23–26.
Michelson, C., Mulvihill, M., Hsu, M. A., & Olson, E. (1991). Eliciting medical care preferences from nursing home residents. *Gerontologist, 31*, 359–363.
Moody, H. (1994). *Aging: Concepts and controversies.* Thousand Oaks, CA: Forge Press.
National Association of Social Workers. (1997). *Social work speaks: NASW policy statements* (3rd ed., pp. 59–62). Washington, DC: NASW Press.

Nelson, H. L., & Nelson, J. L. (1994, November/December). Preferences and other moral sources. *Hastings Center Report,* Special Supplement, S19–S21.

Olson, E., Chichin, E. R., Libow, L. S., Martico-Greenfield, T., Neufeld, R. R., & Mulvihill, M. (1993). A center on ethics in long-term care. *Gerontologist, 33,* 269–274.

Pearlman, R. A. (1994, November/December). Are we asking the right question? *Hastings Center Report,* Special Supplement, S24–S27.

Pearlman, R. A., Uhlmann, R. F., & Jecker, R. F. (1992). Spousal understanding of patient quality of life: Implications for surrogate decisions. *Journal of Clinical Ethics, 3*(2), 114–121.

Pelaez, M., & David, D. (1992). *Enhancing autonomy in long-term care: A training manual for home care.* Miami: Southeast Florida Center on Aging and San Jose State University.

President's Commission for the Study of Ethical Problems in Medicine and Biomedical and Behavioral Research. (1983a). *Making health care decisions.* Washington, DC: U.S. Government Printing Office.

President's Commission for the Study of Ethical Problems in Medicine and Biomedical and Behavioral Research. (1983b). *Summing up.* Washington, DC: U.S. Government Printing Office.

Preston, T. A. (1994, November 1). Killing pain, ending life. *New York Times,* p. A15.

Quill, T. E. (1993). *Death and dignity: Making choices and taking charge.* New York: W. W. Norton.

Quill, T. E. (1996). *A midwife through the dying process: Stories of healing and hard choices at the end of life.* Baltimore: Johns Hopkins University Press.

Rogers, P. (1997, February 26). When the dying don't get the facts about their fate: Some families' beliefs pose dilemmas for doctors. *Miami Herald,* pp. 1A, 12A.

Rozsa, L. (1997, January 14). Right-to-die case weighed. *Miami Herald,* p. 5B.

Rubin, S. M., Strull, W., Fialkow, M., Weiss, S., & Lo, B. (1994). Increasing the completion of the durable power of attorney for health care. *JAMA, 271,* 209–212.

Safford, F. (1993). Survey of knowledge and attitudes about advance directives. Unpublished research report. Florida International University, Miami.

Sansone, P., & Phillips, M. (1995). Advance directives for elderly people: Worthwhile cause or wasted effort? *Social Work, 40,* 397–401.

Shawler, C. (1992). Surrogate decision-making for elderly hospitalized patients. *Journal of Gerontological Nursing, 18,* 5–11.

Smith, W. J. (1994, May 5). The living will's fatal flaw. *Wall Street Journal*, pp. A14.
Solomon, M. Z., O'Donnell L., Jennings, B., Guilfoy, V., Wold, S. M., Nolan, K., Jackon, K., Koch-Wesser, D., & Donnelly, S. (1993). Decisions near the end of life: Professional views on life-sustaining treatments. *American Journal of Public Health*, *83*(1), 14–23.
Steinbrook, B., & Lo, B. (1984, June). Sounding board: Decision making for incompetent patient by designated proxy. *New England Journal of Medicine*, *310*, 1598–1603.
SUPPORT Principal Investigators. (1995). Study to understand prognoses and preferences for outcomes and risks of treatment (SUPPORT). A controlled trial to improve care for seriously ill hospitalized patients. *JAMA*, *274*, 1591–1598.
Teno, J. M., Nelson, H. L., & Lynn, J. (1994, November/December). Advance care planning: Priorities for ethical and empirical research. *Hastings Center Report*, Special Supplement, S32–S36.
Thorne, I. (1993, February 1). Doctor of the dying treads with care [Letter to the editor]. *New York Times*, p. A12.
Tomlinson, T., Howe, K., Notman, M., & Rossmiller, D. (1990). An empirical study of proxy consent for elderly persons. *Gerontologist*, *30*, 54–64.
Wetle, T. (1994, November/December). Individual preferences and advance directives. *Hastings Center Report*, Special Supplement, S55–S58.
Zweibel, N. R., & Cassel, C. K. (1989). Treatment choices at the end of life: A comparison of decisions by older patients and their physician-selected proxies. *Gerontologist*, *29*, 615–621.

FURTHER READINGS

Gillick, M. (1994). *Choosing medical care in old age: What kind, how much, when to stop*. Cambridge, MA: Harvard University Press.
Hackler, C., Mosely, R., & Vawter, D. (Eds.). (1989). *Advance directives in medicine*. New York: Praeger.
Hill, T. P., & Shirley, D. (1992). *A good death: Taking more control at the end of life*. Reading, MA: Addison-Wesley.
Kogan, B. (Ed.). (1991). *A time to be born and a time to die*. New York: Aldine de Gruyter.
Moller, D. (1990). *On death without dignity: The human impact of technological dying*. New York: Baywood.
Nuland, S. (1994). *How we die: Reflections on life's final chapter*. New York: Alfred A. Knopf.
Schneiderman, L., & Jecker, N. (1995). *Wrong medicine*. Baltimore: Johns Hopkins University Press.

SELECTED RESOURCES

Organizations

Choice in Dying (formerly Concern for Dying, and Society for the Right to Die), 200 Varick Street, 10th Floor, New York, NY 10014; (212) 366-5540

For information on advance directives in every state:

National Hospice Organization, 1901 N. Moore Street, Suite 901, Arlington, VA 22209; (703) 243-5900; Helpline: (800) 658-8898

For information on bioethical issues:

Hastings Center (National Bioethics Center), 225 Elm Road, Briarcliff Manor, NY 10510; (914) 762-8500

Videos

A Fate Worse than Death, Lori Hope, King Broadcasting Company. This 50-minute documentary shows several families involved in terminal care decisions. Relatives, doctors, nurses, attorneys, and ethicists comment on the complex moral and legal dilemmas.

The Way We Die, Jonathon Mednick. This 25-minute discussion with medical professionals and terminally ill patients is designed to develop treatment plans in accordance with needs, values, and wishes of the particular patient and family.

The Right to Decide, Peter Walsh, New World Media Alliance. This 43-minute exploration of treatment choices is presented through patient–physician interviews.

For information on any of these videos, contact Fanlight Productions, 47 Halifax Street, Boston, MA 02130, (800) 937-4113, www.fanlight.com.

14 Impact of the Elderly on the Health Care System and Its Implications for the Delivery of Social Services

George I. Krell

The practice and management of social work in the hospital and health care field have been greatly affected by the needs of the elderly population, the miracles of modern medicine, the public programs of Medicare and Medicaid, private health care insurance, new methods of health care delivery, and mechanisms of third-party reimbursement. Medical social work in hospitals, which was originally humanitarian in concept and performance, is now an integral part of the big business and multiservice complex of the modern health care industry (Clarke, 1983).

Social work has spread to virtually every hospital, with its services geared not only to the problems of the poor but also to the continuing care needs of all patients, especially elderly people. This spectacular growth does not reflect a newfound national conscience related to assisting the sick as much as it does the use of the social work professional to help safeguard health care dollars within the framework of a restrictive national definition of health care—a definition that excludes social problems and needs from health care dollar reimbursement in spite of the relatedness of social factors, physical well-being, and recovery from illness and posthospital care.

Social work meets the need of the industry to redirect the sector of the public that uses health care inappropriately or at a level of care that is costlier than the appropriate level. Social workers provide the bridge for the industry to those community resources that their patients and their families require.

Through its casework techniques, social work assists those patients and families to deal with their health-related problems.

Social work can guide the patient from one part of a health or social care service to another in a delivery system that is so complex that, by its nature, it creates its own high costs and inefficiencies, in addition to questionable levels of service quality (Rehr, 1985).

HOW THE SYSTEM WORKS

To better understand how the delivery of health care services is affected by elderly people and how those effects in turn determine the nature of the social services that can be provided to them, it is helpful to examine first the organizational structure of a major health care program—in this instance, Medicare. Following this examination, some mechanisms used by Medicare/ Medicaid and private insurance companies to restrict reimbursements and to ensure quality of care controls are discussed.

The Medicare Program

Medicare is a program that provides health care services primarily for those aged 65 years or older through a social insurance program within the social security system. It was established by Congress in 1965, exists under law, and is administered by a federal agency with regulatory responsibilities. Operationally for social work, the program is important as a resource for health care services for a large population of older people.

Under Medicare, a "beneficiary" is someone who is eligible to participate in the program after meeting its requirements, primarily someone 65 years of age or older. Other categories of beneficiary exist that are subject to change. Current information on the regulations is available from any social security office. Social work concerns itself with assisting beneficiaries, those eligible to become beneficiaries, and those who are not eligible as beneficiaries but who need help to meet their health care needs in another way, that is, through other public programs and community resources.

"Benefits" are the health care services the Medicare program will provide; for elderly people, these are primarily physician services, hospital care, out-of-hospital care, nursing home care, hospice care, and home health care. Social work helps the consumer use these benefits to resolve or adjust to his or her health care problem. Social work coordinates, integrates, and case manages the beneficiaries' involvement with the benefits to which they are entitled.

"Benefit qualifications" are used to determine whether a beneficiary needs a hospital benefit, that is, whether the beneficiary needs to be in the hospital. A nursing home benefit is allowed provided the patient requires a "skilled level" of nursing home care; other levels of nursing home care do not qualify. All program benefits have qualifications—qualifications that can, and do, change frequently to reflect new legislation or administrative devices usually related to reducing program costs. Social work in a hospital assists the patient with personal problems related to or caused by these benefit qualifications. The patient who no longer needs to be in the hospital but who cannot go home, the patient who needs a nursing home but not at a skilled level, and the patient who needs more home health care than the program will provide are all in need of discharge planning assistance because of qualification problems. Social work, through discharge planning assistance, mobilizes and guides the individual and his or her significant others to achieve their medical care goals through Medicare and other resources as required and as available.

A "provider" can be an individual (such as a physician) or an agency (such as a hospital) that provides a program service. In order to participate in Medicare, regardless of the services to be offered, it is necessary for a provider to meet the "conditions of participation" as set down by the regulatory agencies. Therefore, a hospital must meet the conditions set forth for hospitals and be "certified" in order to participate in the program. Social work services appear in provider conditions. For example, a hospital must provide discharge planning assistance, and social workers are on the list of professionals required to provide the service. Hence to participate in the hospital field and to have one's services paid for requires, or is enhanced by, being included in the conditions. For social work to be there "to do its thing" is dependent to a great degree upon these conditions. Although the conditions do indicate a need for a social work presence, they do not set a standard for staffing, that is, the number of professionals required to do the job.

"Provider requirements" are the specific guidelines and standards for ensuring that the provider works within the framework of the program's intentions, in terms of both the law and the regulations. Social work is concerned with provider requirements, especially those that place a stress on patients and their families and that, if not met, result in a loss of reimbursement revenue to the hospital as a provider.

"Program monitoring implementation mechanisms" affect the beneficiary as well as the provider. Major agencies in this category are the U.S. Department of Health and Human Services and its Health Care Financing Administration (HCFA), the federal agencies responsible for implementing the overall program and for its financing. The Professional Review Organization (PRO), a federal agency that is regionally based, is responsible for monitoring the monitors, that is, for ensuring that the appropriateness of the provider's implementation of benefits and service quality are being maintained by the utilization review committee/staff of each provider. The "fiscal intermediary," a private organization under federal contract that pays the providers' bills for the program, also screens the appropriateness of the bills. The state agency (in each state) has the role of supervising the conditions of participation and Medicare involvement as it affects the state and state programs. Also involved is the Joint Commission on Accreditation of Hospitals (JCAH), a privately financed consortium of hospitals and physician groups that sets standards for hospital accreditation used in the conditions of participation. Social work must be knowledgeable about these mechanisms as they affect the patient and family and as they influence the development of social work service priorities and staff utilization within the institution in the delivery of social work services.

Restrictions on Reimbursements and Quality of Care Controls and Their Effects on Hospital Social Work

From the beginning of Medicare, there have been provider requirements involving a mechanism for cost control purposes built into the program of each hospital known as "utilization review." Its purpose was to ensure that if hospital days were being paid for, the patient really needed to be in the hospital. Since 1966, the basic provider requirement for both Medicare and Medicaid (and for private insurance companies, too) has evolved from simply attesting to a need for a hospital stay to providing comprehensive review of each patient admitted, which covers the appropriateness of admission, the length of stay, extended stay, and the validity of discharge criteria. Over the years, the greater the federal concern with program costs, the more complex, tortuous, and benefit-excluding the review definitions have become.

In hospitals, these required reviews are carried out within 24 hours after patient admission by a review team composed usually of nurses who work with a physician adviser. This mandated internal mechanism is further monitored, as previously indicated, by the regional PRO and the fiscal intermediary to ensure that it is functioning properly. Patients who do not meet the criteria for level of care are required to be informed that after 48 hours Medicare will no longer pay for their stay and they will be liable for the full costs. They are informed at the same time of their right to a fair hearing if they disagree with this determination. The hospital must bill these patients directly for their stay after their receipt of such a communication. The hospital can be penalized if it does not meet these responsibilities. It must work within a certain percent of review accuracy in order to maintain its standing. There is no restriction on how long a patient stays in a hospital as long as the patient can pay for it.

There are patients' rights under Medicare, Medicaid, and the JCAH that attempt to protect the patient during a hospital stay. These rights range from the right of patients to know about the medical treatment being provided to that of appealing decisions by the providers of services as well as by the monitors of the providers. Social work has a traditional interest in these rights and has a role to play in assisting the patient and his or her family in achieving those rights in the hospital setting. This is an area in which a conflict of interest can occur between carrying out the social work code of ethics and fulfilling the obligation of staff loyalty expected of a hospital employee.

In the mid-1980s, Medicare/Medicaid initiated the diagnosis-related groups (DRGs), whereby a specific dollar rate is assigned to each of some 468 diagnostic categories of illness and disease. The hospital is paid the prospective, or prearranged, set dollar figure for the primary category that best fits the patient's medical condition, regardless of the actual length of the patient's stay; hence the shorter the patient's stay, the more the hospital earns (Grimaldi & Michelettia, 1985).

It is obvious that the above two mechanisms used to carry out the policy of restricting what constitutes appropriate medical care for reimbursement purposes have had a tremendous impact on discharge planning. Since 1966, assisting the patient and family has expanded from being a humanitarian, medical-care-oriented service, solely the purview of the social work profession, to being directly related to maintaining Medicare, Medicaid, and private insurance cost controls (Austin, 1986).

One effect of the DRGs on medical practice has been to require organized medicine to do more procedures on an outpatient basis and, when patients are hospitalized, to ensure that the level and pace of treatment and tests are consistent with those required of a hospital.

Program policy and practice procedures such as these have dramatically highlighted the social issues and problems that are directly related to health care. The patient inappropriately admitted to the hospital is likely to be an elderly person who is sick, but not sick enough for hospital care and without adequate resources or family supports (Krell, 1977).

Social work, after years of being nice but not necessary to have around, has been discovered by the health care industry as the only profession that has any experience in dealing with problem patients, especially those who have no resources or inadequate resources. Social work, however, was not prepared for this opportunity; as a profession it did not enjoy adequate staffing and financial support in the health care field, and as a group it was not unanimous in its desire to participate in such mundane activities as discharge planning. However, in the past 20 years, the combination of patient/family need, industry need, and an aggressive approach by the Society of Hospital Social Work Directors (SHSWD) of the American Hospital Association, with the full support of that organization, has resulted in the emergence of health care as the field in which the greatest number of social workers with a master's degree now work (Kane, 1985).

PATIENT RIGHTS IN LONG-TERM-CARE FACILITIES

Of ongoing concern to social work has been the treatment in long-term-care facilities of elderly people who are in need of long-term care. Nursing homes and adult congregate living facilities (ACLFs) have been disparaged as "warehouses" for the infirm elderly, where resident choice and autonomy are often absent.

The Omnibus Budget Reconciliation Act of 1987 (OBRA) is a giant step toward the recognition of residents' rights and the need for control of the quality of care in long-term-care facilities. Basically financed through Medicaid to serve the needs of all nursing home patients, this joint federal–state program also encourages states to broaden their patient rights actions to include nonmedical facilities such as ACLFs.

OBRA sets forth the goal that each long-term-care facility is responsible for protecting and promoting the rights of each resident, emphasizing the rights to a dignified existence, self-determination, and communication with and access to persons and services (OBRA, 1987). Institutional licensing and provider certification requirements under Medicaid and Medicare attempt to ensure that the resident rights provisions are being carried out.

The following illustrations are just a few examples of the scope of the OBRA approach: the need for institutions to provide written and oral material to residents and staff on rights and responsibilities; the need for institutions to provide notices to residents on getting a new room or roommate or on discharge or transfer; and the need to provide procedures for complaints, grievances, privacy, and confidentiality. In addition, a number of quality of care nursing and medical service requirements further strengthen patient rights.

OBRA allows states to develop and receive financing for an ombudsman program. *Ombudsman* is the Swedish word for a person who acts as a citizen representative. For example, in Florida,

> the primary duty of an ombudsman is to protect the rights of individuals by investigating and resolving problems and grievances, providing information, and working with institutions, organizations, and agencies to increase their responsiveness to the people they serve. An ombudsman acts on behalf of persons who need assistance in advocating their own cause. The goal of the ombudsman program is to improve the quality of life for long-term-care facility residents. (State of Florida, 1991)

In Florida the program is carried out by a group of citizen volunteers who are appointed by the governor. The ombudsman works through district councils, with each council having at least 15 members, including a physician, a social worker, a nurse, a nursing home administrator, an ACLF administrator, a pharmacist, a dietitian, an attorney, and consumer advocates, including institutional residents. In the ombudsman program, social work has a key role in line with its long tradition as a client advocate in clinical practice and as a provider of psychosocial services.

TYPES OF CLINICAL PRACTICE WITHIN THE SYSTEM AND IMPLICATIONS FOR MANAGEMENT

The type of practice that emerges from a Medicare package of benefits is primarily short-term crisis intervention. The needs of the hospital and skilled home health care programs are for short-term contacts of an intense nature to establish as quickly as possible the needs of the patient; the patient's level of functioning; available supports such as family, friends, and community; and the requirements of the medical problems and the treatment plan being followed (Roberts, 1989). This pertinent information is usually established after two to three patient/family contacts plus collateral contacts, at which time a continuing care plan is formulated and implementation initiated. This type of intervention is somewhat akin to medical emergency room triage in that cases requiring an immediate and intensive relationship in order to achieve successful discharge are sorted out from cases requiring minimal assistance, such as providing resource information.

Short-term crisis intervention requires great skill, because the hospital social worker has to achieve the discharge planning goal within the patient's brief hospital stay. Unlike long-term counseling, there is no future session to rectify what was not achieved in an earlier session.

Case management is another major area of practice in health care. Case management implies an ability not only to guide the patient but also to see that services are received as required by the patient. However, too often what is promoted as case management is nothing more than old-fashioned social casework, with its goal of coordination and integration of community services and patient advocacy.

The power to control or to channel services distinguishes case management from basic case work, as discussed in chapter 6. When these criteria are used, the number of settings in which case management is actually taking place is quite reduced. The federally and state financed National Long-Term Care Channeling Demonstration Projects for the elderly, which had the means within the program itself to provide all levels of long-term care required of home maintenance, was a true case management program (Austin, 1983). The nature of existing Medicare programs tends to block case management because the patient's counselor carries authority only within his or her own program and can advocate only with other Medicare programs, which have the right to accept or reject this advocacy (Loomis, 1988; Moxley & Buzas, 1989).

Other areas of practice that are emerging relate to support groups, which are most important and very marketable in today's health care setting. Group sessions with patients and/or caregivers with common illnesses and health-related problems—such as cancer, diabetes, Alzheimer's disease, renal diseases, and AIDS—are greatly needed. Traditional techniques in the group work field are strengthened and refined in order to meet these group session demands in health care settings. Respite and day care for impaired elderly people are growing programs that also require social work services.

Another important service is the role of social work in health education, that is, in providing the type of information that individuals and their families require and that the doctor does not have the time nor the inclination to provide. Such instruction can be carried out with individuals or in groups.

The nature of the health care field and the needs of elderly people require social work to maintain an adequate level of staffing. Social work does a disservice both to itself as a profession and to elderly people whom it attempts to assist by not resolving such basics as the number of social workers required for hospitals and the educational level needed for the services to be provided. Because the profession does not aggressively speak to this issue, it is not social work administrators who make the staffing determinations that influence the delivery of social work services.

In view of the "big business" nature of health care for elderly people, the social work manager in a hospital must develop a management information system that not only covers discharge resources but also shows which agencies are receiving the hospital's business and to what extent (Karuza, Calkins, Duffey, & Feather, 1988). Social work departments are in a position to obtain vital information on the psychosocial needs of their clients as these needs interface with medical care costs and the purposes of provider programs within hospitals, nursing homes, home health care agencies, and hospices. Data now being obtained by social work departments in hospitals in such areas as the number of patients with psychosocial problems and the nature of these problems; the number of discharge placements to nursing homes, rehabilitation facilities, home health care agencies, ACLFs, and mental health and substance abuse programs; and referrals for financial assistance and community social service support programs are all of great significance to health care. Such data can form the basis of studies and research that would directly relate to health care costs, as well as increase our knowledge of health-related needs, gaps in community resources, and how to plan programs to meet these needs.

In this regard, hospital social work, through the SHSWD, is attempting to implement a nationwide uniform data collection system via a computer software package. Current blocks to implementation lie in costs, staff and personnel limitations, weaknesses in financing for social work, uneven levels of practice from institution to institution, and lack of support from and indifference of hospital administration.

The social work manager and his or her staff, in view of their discharge planning role, find themselves being courted by all manner of providers. The social work profession for the first time in its long, altruistic history finds itself in a close working relationship with a profit-making field. Strange bedfellows indeed!

INFLUENCE OF MANAGED CARE ON SERVICES TO THE ELDERLY

One of the most recent phenomena in health care is the rapid move toward managed care in an attempt to contain out-of-control costs. These costs have risen to a trillion dollars a year in 1996. The primary force to control such astronomical costs has been from the business world, overwhelmed by the expense of health insurance for employees, not from federal or state regulations. Giant private health care organizations are revolutionizing the health care system into managed care networks of patients, doctors, hospitals, and insurers. There is concern that these "multistate megacorporations" will focus more on cost control than on quality of care, and that the most vulnerable to inadequate treatment are the poor and elderly (Boyd, 1996).

Several studies have shown that poor and elderly patients with chronic diseases have had significantly worse health outcomes in managed care than have similar patients in fee-for-service systems. Other studies have had contradictory findings (Besdine, 1996/1997). As many states are moving their Medicaid recipients into managed care, some studies are evaluating the outcomes. With respect to cost containment, it appears that the costs of health maintenance organizations (HMOs) are artificially adjusted through shifting of expenses rather than elimination of administrative tasks (Enthoven, 1993). With respect to quality of care, however, some studies indicate that for the population receiving Medicaid, which has had disproportionately poorer access than has the population receiving Medicare, the effect of managed care may be beneficial: health outcome measures indicate no harmful effects of enrolling elderly people in prepaid plans rather than fee-for-service care. In fact, managed care provided slightly better access with quality care roughly equal to that offered under Medicaid fee-for-service (Landers, 1995).

There are now so many health care options for older Americans that health care professionals have a responsibility to update their knowledge of the various models. A useful resource is a special report by the American Association of Retired Persons (AARP, 1996), which explains the different types of plans such as HMOs, point-of-service plans, preferred provider organizations, and physician networks. The report defines commonly used terms, such as *capitation,* (a system of prepaying doctors and hospitals a set fee to provide health care for each enrollee, regardless of the type or number of services provided), *coinsurance, copayments, gatekeeper, pre-existing conditions,* and so forth.

Rosalie Kane, noted geriatrician and analyst of long-term care, pointed out that managed care "is neither a panacea nor a disaster" (Kane, 1996, p. 9). It can be a benefit for elderly patients if it coordinates interdisciplinary long-term chronic as well as acute care, and if it provides additional in-home benefits, emphasizes prevention, and includes medications, eyeglasses, dentures, and prostheses. She advises that a balance be found between an overly optimistic view of increased benefits and excessive worry about the limitation of services nervously referred to as "managed scare."

Another balanced view was offered by Fox and Fama (1996) who see managed care for elders as inevitable and as a potentially positive development. They do caution that federal and state governments need to be vigilant with regard to newly generated problems, and to be protective of the rights of beneficiaries at the same time.

The debate about the impact of managed care organizations is just beginning. Health care advocates must be wary of the intrusive effects of the for-profit surveillance of insurers on the professional judgments of physicians and social workers, for example. Social workers have ethical concerns about the threat to confidentiality for clients when records are exposed to many administrative handlers, as well as obligations to advocate for services that have been reduced although deemed necessary ("Ethics, Meet Managed Care," 1997).

The trade-off for elderly clients is lower out-of-pocket costs, for perhaps less satisfaction and quality. However, in an era when patients may have been subjected to excessive medical procedures driven by financial incentives, in a system of specializations, and minimal patient–doctor relationships, some older people may derive more satisfaction from the managed care option. Health care professionals must take part in the debate, based on a search for the facts about managed care, managed costs, or managed competition, and how well it may offer appropriate geriatric care, including mental health services.

NEED TO INCORPORATE SOCIAL WORK SERVICES MORE EFFECTIVELY INTO THE HEALTH CARE SYSTEM

Nowhere can one better witness the current revolution in the delivery of health care than in the hospital setting. Patient length of stay from admission to discharge in an acute care hospital has been greatly reduced over the past 20 years. Hence the time frame allowed patients and their families to work out their medically related social problems has been drastically reduced. In addition, the nonprofit community service hospital is in fiscal difficulty, and some 300 multihospital commercial corporations now run more than half the hospitals in the United States.

The needs of an aging population, the high levels of chronic illness among elderly people, and the wonders of modern health care have explosively created a gigantic home health care industry, which interfaces with the hospital and its patients. Home care, which until recently was characterized by small, voluntarily supported visiting nurse services and tax-supported public health nursing, is now primarily the domain of big business conglomerates. As people live longer, a support business geared to maintaining elderly people at home has become quite profitable.

Homes for the aged and specialty institutions, which once were primarily under sectarian, nonprofit, or local government auspices, are also outnumbered now by a huge profit-oriented nursing home industry.

Hospital discharge planning and related arrangements for the patient's continuity of care no longer focus on patient and family needs but on the needs of the provider and the regulatory agency. Because of the dollars involved, the time allowed the family for their participation in the discharge planning process has been greatly shortened. The institutional pace of getting a patient out of the hospital has been accelerated: from the moment of arrival (and even before) the patient is evaluated, assessed, and prepared for discharge. The actual ability to achieve timely discharge is related to family resources, patient eligibility for benefit programs, the requirements of outside providers, and the availability of community resources as well as a discharge planning mechanism (Smeke, Weele, & Weatherley, 1989; Wolock, Schlesinger, Dinerman, & Seaton, 1987).

The current status of discharge planning in a hospital too often involves social work negotiations with providers based on dollar considerations. The discharge planner knows that the nursing home operator seeks a patient case mix that favors low-level-of-care cases with good personal resources over high-level-of-care cases with limited resources.

In addition to these outside pressures due to negotiating on behalf of patients within the chaos of the health care marketplace, social work finds itself caught by comparable pressures in its own work setting. Institutional health care providers pigeonhole the social work director at a middle-management level, a rather low slot in a power structure controlled by a management hierarchy from the business and financial world (Ortiz & Bassoff, 1988). Whereas in the past the chief executive officer was likely to have been a physician, or, if not, to have had a full-time medical director, more often now he or she is an executive with a business background that is not focused on human needs and who is not supported by a career medical director. Social work's relationship to this power structure lies in the fact that the human needs in health care defy the product-oriented approach, and the industry finds that it requires social work's approach if it is to function effectively. The industry does not view itself as a social services institution and reluctantly backs into social intervention as required. As one hospital administrator succinctly stated: "Social workers would be a lot happier if they would learn to be discharge planners first and social workers second."

Social work with no voice on the governing board of health care institutions and with no managerial power functions primarily in a dependent role. Social work functions are often compromised by an administration that stresses the self-serving limited goals and interests of the provider rather than the needs of the patient and family. There are no staffing standards in the industry, and enough leeway exists for management not only to limit social work's role but also to substitute employees other than social workers in that role. The true losers in all of this are elderly people, for one of their best advocates, the social work profession, finds that it cannot even influence its workplace in order to better meet their needs and interests.

Although current federal law (OBRA) appears to open the door for a broader role and authority for social workers by allowing clinical social workers to become direct providers and to file claims for diagnostic and therapeutic services, it unfortunately contains limiting provisions. These limit the place of practice by the exclusion of social work performed in hospital inpatient and outpatient programs and in nursing facilities when the nursing facility is obligated to provide such services as part of their Medicare/Medicaid participation. Such exclusions reduce the ability of social work to function freely on behalf of the patient in critical health care programs.

Patients and families have also been frustrated by the fragmented approach, which requires them to relate to many different providers of limited and specialized services that are restricted in terms of time and the narrow goals of each program. Fragmenting programs, including federally supported services, according to categories is an inherent weakness in health care, which by its nature requires a total care approach. In addition to sacrificing quality of patient care by separating services, the current approach is costly to maintain (Zawadaski, 1984).

The health care industry has a responsibility to develop social needs data because these data have an impact on costs and patient care needs. The opportunity to organize data collection and develop significant studies and a meaningful research program on the social factors inherent in health care is being overlooked by the health care industry, an unfortunate omission in view of the importance of such data to the industry and the public it serves.

These identified phenomena are pushing the delivery of health care toward an organized, systematic approach. Social work, caught up in this frantic pace and a necessary alliance with a commercial industry, has the opportunity to play a key role as a bridge between patient/family needs, hospital needs, and the providers of services. The health care industry, government, and the social work field have to integrate and formalize their delivery methods within the framework of multiservice entities. The freestanding, independent hospital is already on the way out as it moves toward being one component of a package of programs. It is moving in this direction as it begins to formalize arrangements with home care agencies, which include durable medical equipment and "high-tech" services, nursing homes, ACLFs, rehabilitation centers, physician groups, hospices, and so on. Hospitals are also developing umbrella services under their own corporate ownership and management.

A SOCIAL SERVICES AGENCY FOR THE BENEFICIARIES OF MEDICARE AND MEDICAID

Although Medicare and Medicaid are nationally viewed as medical care programs, a substantial amount of their program costs, as noted above, come from the social factors involved in illness and physical well-being. These factors range from the way individuals use health care programs and the nature of their personal resources to the psychosocial requirements of beneficiaries. These are patients' social problems that providers must face by nature of their being health care providers.

Currently, under the Medicare program the hospital is required to maintain social services for at least discharge planning purposes. Medicare requires the home health care agency to provide social work assessment and to implement community connections. It requires nursing homes to have social services available for admission purposes and counseling intervention for the personal needs of their patients. Medicare also provides some degree of case management and psychosocial counseling and planning for those on dialysis, in a hospice, or in special HMOs serving the frail elderly population, and so on. The requirement that each institutional provider, that is, hospital or nursing home, must build in its own institution a social services capability is not only very costly to the Medicare system but also leads to the fragmentation of services that occurs when a patient moves from one benefit provider to another. The patient advocate and public interest role of social work is blocked by these settings, which can and do have a provider self-interest built into them.

One might ask how a nursing home can be an open-door facility for long-term cases when the provider running the facility needs to keep the beds at a high level of occupancy for year-end profitability. The nursing home patient has the right to wonder if the effort being expended to get him or her out of a nursing home facility and back into the community is the same expended to get him or her into the facility.

Hospital social work is limited to offering services to the patient that are primarily geared to getting him or her out of the hospital. Hospital social work is not financed to provide support to the patient when he or she leaves the hospital. Monitoring the continuing aftercare needs of a patient and providing the necessary ongoing support assistance after hospital discharge over a significant time frame are not seen as the role of the hospital or, therefore, of the hospital social worker.

Home health care uses social work in a limited manner and usually for only one or two patient contacts. Home care, which should be viewed as the key service in attempting to maintain individuals outside the institution, makes no significant use of social work because of program cost concerns and the nursing focus of the service. Skilled home health care is offered as a medical-nursing model and offers only a token response to the psychosocial factors involved in home care and in maintaining the individuals at home.

In view of the social problems, consumer issues, and public needs associated with Medicare and Medicaid, it appears that there would be great value in developing a social services support agency as a formal part of the Medicare/Medicaid system and financed by that system. Such an agency under professional social work directorship could do the following:

1. Provide a social services support system to cover the social services requirements of the Medicare/Medicaid program through one agency. This agency would service those program beneficiaries who have continuity of care problems and provide case management assistance to those beneficiaries who cannot use their benefits appropriately.
2. Provide the social work services component to small- and medium-size nursing homes on a mandated basis and to large nursing homes, which generally have professional social work departments, on an optional basis. A social work nursing home team from the support agency would cover the homes on a scheduled basis, providing advocacy, counseling, and discharge-planning services. These patient-oriented services on behalf of patients would come from outside the institution and, as such, would be protective of patient rights and representative of patient needs. In fact, from a cost and patient interest view, there would be real value for Medicare in experimenting with providing all support services to nursing homes from an outside support agency covering the homes on a scheduled basis. Nursing homes served by these outside support mechanisms would not be required to maintain their own social services and would be reimbursed accordingly.
3. Provide discharge planning to small- and medium-size hospitals on a mandated basis and to large hospitals on an optional basis. Once again, a team from the support social services agency would cover a number of hospitals on a

scheduled basis; the hospital would not be required to maintain its own social work department for discharge-planning purposes.

4. Provide continuing care case management to Medicare/Medicaid cases meeting social need requirements upon discharge from a hospital or nursing home. Provide special case management services to individuals who overuse Medicare benefits and/or who give an indication that psychosocial factors are directly related to the improper use of their benefits.
5. Provide the social work component for the skilled home health care agencies.
6. Coordinate and integrate, as required, private and community social services programs to better meet the needs of elderly people and those with special problems. Help the community to develop a 24-hour, seven-day-a-week response system in order to meet elderly care needs; provide such a seven-day response through the contract agency.
7. Use existing social welfare programs to connect with medical care programs; for example, use the protective service agencies for elderly people to contract for screening and treatment services related to elder abuse situations identified in the health care system.
8. Offer schools of social work and other professional teaching institutions opportunities for internships with the agency.
9. Provide a conduit for national research on social factors related to health care treatment and costs, research on short-term crisis intervention in medical emergencies, and case management in the use of Medicare benefits.

At present, financing for social work activities, Medicare Part A and Part B (that is, OBRA), does not allow for the existence of a social services support agency. Redirecting current Medicare expenditures to social work for such a program should be more than adequate to finance the program and as a by-product could result in considerable cost savings both in services delivery and in program benefits.

The health care field has a significant interest in whether our communities develop social resources that would complement the special health care wants of the public it serves. The voluntary social services system needs to organize itself if it is to play an important role in serving the health care field. The typical private agency tends not to be a force in this area and by its current nature adds to the fragmentation of social services delivery.

A growing aging population characterized by chronic illness is a key factor in the revolution now taking place in health care and the delivery of services. This revolution requires a full partnership between medical/nursing programs and social services agencies. A joint partnership requires the use of health care dollars to finance social services support agencies and a formal systematic involvement in the delivery of care. It also requires traditional social services to integrate and coordinate its own delivery system and to become more meaningful to the health care needs of an aging population.

REFERENCES

American Association of Retired Persons. (1996, November). Managed care [Special report]. *AARP Bulletin,* pp. 9–12.

Austin, C. D. (1983). Case management in long term care: Options and opportunities. *Health & Social Work, 8,* 16–30.

Austin, C. D. (1986). D.R.G.'s and the elderly: Pro's and con's. *Health & Social Work, 11,* 69–70.

Besdine, R. W. (1996/1997). Managed care and older Americans: Opportunity and risk. *Generations, 20*(4), 64–68.

Boyd, R. (1996, November 10). Backlash against managed care spurs health system's evolution. *Miami Herald,* p. 21A.

Clarke, S. S. (1983). Hyman J. Weiner's use of systems and population approaches: Their relevance to social work practice in health care today. *Social Work in Health Care, 9*(2), 5–14.

Enthoven, A. C. (1993). Why managed care has failed to contain health costs. *Health Affairs, 12*(3), 27–43.

Ethics, meet managed care. (1997, January). *NASW News,* p. 7.

Fox, P., & Fama, T. (1996). Managed care and the elderly: Performance and potential. *Generations, 20*(2, Summer), 31–36.

Grimaldi, P., & Michelettia, J. (1985). *Prospective payment: The definitive guide to reimbursement.* Chicago: Pluribus.

Kane, R. A. (1985). Health policy and social workers in health: Past, present and future. *Health & Social Work, 10,* 258–270.

Kane, R. (1996, July/August). Assessing managed care: Is it healthy for elders? Striking a balance. *Aging Today, 9,* 12.

Karuza, J., Jr., Calkins, E., Duffey, J., & Feather, J. (1988). Networking in aging: A challenge, model and evaluation. *Gerontologist, 28,* 147–155.

Krell, G. I. (1977). Overstay among hospital patients: Problems and approaches. *Health & Social Work, 2,* 113–178.

Landers, T. (1995). Medicaid managed care: A brief analysis. *Journal of the NYS Nurses Association, 26*(3, September), 7–11.

Loomis, J. F. (1988). Case management in health care. *Health & Social Work, 13,* 219–225.

Moxley, D. P., & Buzas, L. (1989). Perception of case management services to elderly people. *Health & Social Work, 14,* 196–203.

Omnibus Budget Reconciliation Act (OBRA). P.L. 100-203; 1330 Stat. (1987).

Omnibus Budget Reconciliation Act of 1987 compliance checklist for long term care facilities. (1989). *Federal Register, 54*(21).

Ortiz, E. T., & Bassoff, B. Z. (1988). Proprietary hospital social work. *Health & Social Work, 13,* 114–121.

Rehr, H. (1985). Medical care organizations and the social service connection. *Health & Social Work, 10,* 245–257.

Roberts, C. S. (1989). Conflicting professional values in social work and medicine. *Health & Social Work, 14,* 211–218.

Smeke, J., Weele, T. V. D., & Weatherley, R. (1989). Delayed discharges for medical and surgical patients in an acute care hospital. *Social Work in Health Care, 14*(1), 15–31.

State of Florida. (1991). Regulations, Chapter 400, Nursing Homes and Related Health Care Facilities, Part I—Nursing Homes, Part II—Adult Congregate Living Facilities.

Wolock, I., Schlesinger, E., Dinerman, M., & Seaton, R. (1987). The post hospital needs and care of patients: Implications for discharge planning. *Social Work in Health Care, 12*(4), 61–76.

Zawadaski, R. (Ed.). (1984). Community-based systems of long term care. New York: Haworth.

15 A Recapitulation of Workplace Guidelines

George I. Krell

The primary focus of this book is gerontological knowledge of use to the practitioner working with elderly people. Although this book is not specifically designed as a "how-to" manual for the practice of social services within a hospital, nursing home, or other health care setting, it does cover numerous principles and guidelines of universal applicability. In this concluding chapter, these practice principles, which can be viewed as workplace guidelines regardless of setting, are recapitulated.

RECIPIENT OF SERVICE

Each elderly recipient of service is unique. Recipients from certain ethnic, racial, cultural, or religious groups require special considerations, sensitivity, and competency in the provision of services. Clients may manifest cultural rules that define the acceptable way of being ill, acceptable illnesses, and the mode of expressing those acceptable illnesses, as pointed out in chapter 8. Professionals must learn these cultural rules.

Chronological age is not a factor in determining the capability of an older person to approach and resolve a problem. Self-determination and autonomy are vital to human dignity and must be respected. Clients may be financially well-to-do with adequate personal resources, or poor, underserved, and lacking health benefits. Materially poor clients may be persons with great inner strengths and adjustment abilities, and materially wealthy clients may be persons with inner weaknesses and a lack of coping abilities.

Physiological changes and an increase in multiple pathologies are characteristic of the aging process. The elderly client requires a holistic approach by those who are providing services if the client's needs are to be meaningfully understood and dealt with.

THE FAMILY

The family has long been recognized as an important force in health care practice. Family relationships must always enter into the professional's consideration of a case. First, family members can provide information about the psychosocial background of the client, which is germane to each care plan. Second, it is necessary to evaluate family relationships to determine if the family offers a meaningful resource and vital support. Finally, the family possesses legal or quasi-legal power to influence case plans.

From the view of providing a social service, the level of a client's physical and psychosocial needs relates to the level of family involvement. The client with a totally disabling chronic illness needs a level of care that can be handled only by assistance from others—primarily the family or significant others (such as friends and neighbors). How the family is actually involved will depend on the client, the service setting, the available resources, and the nature of the particular problem.

Significant others can and do play the role of family when they have a close relationship with the client and a willingness to assume responsibilities. Often an elderly client may have a more meaningful relationship with a significant other than with the family members. However, the practitioner must be aware that certain legal or regulatory limitations can restrict the full use and effectiveness of the significant other as an informal resource.

Ethnic, racial, cultural, and religious factors are important in considering the role of the family and significant others. Variations in expectation of family responsibility do exist among groups and must be recognized.

Health crises tend to bring out the best in families and, unfortunately, the worst. Deciding which son or daughter is to take care of the ailing parent can become the true test of the strengths and weaknesses in a family. An extreme in dysfunctional family relationships is evident in adult abuse and neglect situations, wherein the elderly client may be in need of protection from his or her own kin. Service providers must become attentive to clues of psychological or financial abuse within a family. This frequently hidden problem can be exposed through exploration if the practitioner is sensitive to the reluctance of family members to share shameful secrets with outsiders.

The elderly client whose children are also old presents intervention problems unique to our aging society. The practitioner today may find on any given case that he or she has two elderly groups to relate to; that is, the client and the client's children.

PRACTICE METHODS

Case finding, differential assessment, diagnosis, treatment plan, implementation, monitoring the results of intervention, and case closure are the basic steps characteristic of practice in most settings. The steps, however, will differ in scope, emphasis, and applicability according to the health care setting.

Case Finding

Clients reach the professional through a referral, which can be the result of an organized approach of case finding. One hospital social work department may see only clients who are referred by a physician or nurse, whereas another department may have a system that screens patients on the basis of set criteria, such as all patients admitted from a nursing home or all patients who are over 65 years of age. Conversely, a nursing home with a long-term resident population could have its social worker see all of its residents on an ongoing basis.

Hence, in terms of reaching the client who needs assistance, similar settings vary in their approach, and dissimilar settings vary among themselves. The willingness of the facility to reach out and make its services accessible is related to such factors as the purpose of the program, administrative intentions, adequate staffing and funds, and competency of staff, as well as the "caring atmosphere" of the facility. How we make services readily available to all elderly people who are in need is a challenge to practitioners in each work environment.

Differential Assessment

Assessment of the aging client requires a knowledge and understanding of health and illness, including physiological changes; characteristics of disease, medications and their effects; biopsychosocial factors; as well as cultural and ethnic differences, preferences, and strengths. Assessment is made more systematic by intake forms and reevaluation forms, which require tools such as checklists and questionnaires. Accurate assessment also requires the practitioner to be skillful in administering and interpreting at least one of the mental status examinations.

Comprehensive assessment involves careful medical and psychosocial history taking as well as collection of pertinent information from medical examinations and evaluations. Contributions and input by all members of the interdisciplinary care team are a necessary part of this process.

Diagnosis, Treatment Plan, and Implementation

The diagnosis, the development of the treatment plan based on the diagnosis, and the subsequent implementation of this plan constitute practice in all settings. Most hospital-based social work consists of short-term contacts with acutely ill patients, which limits the depth of diagnostic evaluations and treatment plans. The specialized purpose of the hospital also has an impact on the nature of the social work exploration, which is often crisis-oriented and therefore strengthened by limiting goal setting to the problems at hand. On the other hand, the case manager or any practitioner with an ongoing client relationship can focus in greater depth on the totality of the client's problems and develop a broader range of treatment approaches.

Treatment can involve client counseling, either short-term and problem-oriented or long-term and in-depth; the counseling of family members or of significant others; and advocacy on behalf of the client. Advocacy may include educating the physician, nurse, other health care professionals, and outside community resources as to the special needs of the aging client.

One of the most challenging and frustrating roles of health care professionals in acute care hospitals is that of discharge planner. Administrative pressure to discharge the elderly patient quickly for financial reasons runs contrary to a basic principle of working with elderly people, namely, the need for a slower pace. Since many frail elders lack the social supports and resources needed to buffer the effects of illness, the discharge plan frequently requires more time than is dictated by the diagnosis-related groupings of Medicare/Medicaid. Practitioners must develop techniques that lead to rapid, accurate assessment and up-to-date knowledge of the resources that can be put together as an effective home care plan. Skill in networking with community services is essential to facilitate use of necessary resources. The professional's reward for an effective discharge is the immediate satisfaction obtained in feedback from the appreciative client and his or her family.

Other aspects of treatment involve the education of the client and family regarding the nature of the specific illness and disease, as well as the complexity of the aging process; the medications required; and their shared tasks in aftercare needs. Involving the client or family members in self-help or educationally oriented groups can be a most significant intervention.

The amount of time spent by the practitioner in working with family members can vary by setting. The hospital-based social worker involved in discharge planning may spend more of his or her casework time working with family members to effect a timely discharge than with the sick patient himself or herself. Conversely, the nursing-home-based social worker may spend more time with the patient who is a long-term resident than with family, who may only be keeping in touch. In the former instance the hospital may view the family's involvement as essential, and in the latter instance the nursing home may view the family's involvement as desirable.

The nature of health care problems calls for a broad scope of community services if the needs of elderly people are to be adequately met. Counseling alone will not suffice for the client and supporting family in need of food, housing, money, or a certain level of care for which a facility is not available. Matching individual need to the appropriate service is a challenge to the practitioner working within our system of fragmented programs and complex benefit structures.

Paradoxically, obtaining some resources may lead to widely divergent results depending on the setting. For example, in the hospital setting one resource, such as Medicaid, may be a means to facilitate discharge, and in the nursing home the same resource may be a means to maintain the patient in the facility.

Obtaining the required resources can strongly enhance a client–practitioner relationship and often "opens the door" to the resolution of the less concrete problems faced by the client. In such a situation the case manager is then provided with an opportunity through the therapeutic relationship to maximize the potential of the elderly client and his or her family, friends, and resources, even at the last stage of the life cycle.

Although case management is not a role that can be achieved in every setting, the holistic, coordinating, and empowering approach characteristic of the case manager should be attempted by all practitioners regardless of the setting.

It must be emphasized that the term *case management* has become popularized in the health field, and its meaning somewhat diffused, in recent years. For example, case managers are now being used by health insurers and other third-party payors and tend to be oriented more toward program benefits than focused on the client. They strive to decrease the cost of health care programs through management of services, sometimes overlooking the needs of frail elders. The efficient clinical case manager is oriented toward client service but does not overlook the need for accountability and cost effectiveness.

Monitoring the Results of Intervention

Monitoring the effectiveness of professional intervention goes hand in hand with good practice. Each setting should have some means of follow-up that attempts to evaluate how well the needs of a client and the client expectations have been met.

Quality assurance has become, through many of the regulatory requirements of Medicare and Medicaid and provider insurance contracts, an important part of practice. The necessity for each health care discipline to set practice standards criteria and to meaningfully monitor how well it meets these standards should now be viewed as a norm in all settings. The development of a data collection system geared to gathering ongoing information on the services being provided and on the effectiveness of this service delivery to the elderly population is a must for all settings. A formalized system of data collection enables a setting to carry out research and study projects, which can produce information essential to our understanding and treatment of elderly people.

A feature of practice that is shared by the health care field and gerontology is the interdisciplinary nature of these fields. In no other area of personal service do so many disciplines bring their unique contributions to bear on an individual's personal problems. Working as a team should be seen as a common goal for all service settings. The initiation and coordination of this joint collaboration constitute a natural role for the social work profession, which by its essential character functions as a bridge or unifying link among all disciplines. Clients can best be served when all disciplines view a case in its totality and when assessment, diagnosis, and treatment bring together the knowledge of all disciplines and all function in concert with each other.

Case Closure

Case closure, or the completion of a service, should not be seen in a literal way by those who work with elderly people. Too often, upon case closure professionals fail to develop connections for their clients to other resources that could further enhance their clients' well-being and complement the services just completed. The multifaceted nature of health and social welfare services and the multiproblem characteristics of the elderly require the movement of clients with continuing needs to other settings. A case that may be officially closed should not actually be relinquished until the client with continuing needs is in the "safety net" of another program. The achievement of continuity of care for elderly people in our current system of services delivery is perhaps one of the greatest challenges to practice and undoubtedly one of the most frustrating.

WORKPLACE DILEMMAS

Health care organizations are guided by internal policies and goals as well as external regulations and third-party payment controls. Therefore, the practitioner may face ethical dilemmas in the workplace as he or she is caught between the organizational structure and the individual client, whose personal requirements or expectations may conflict with that structure.

Practice must accommodate both the realities of the setting and the client as an individual. What is right and proper in practice need not be inconsistent with the stated public goals of the setting or the needs of the client, if the judgments being used are valid professional judgments. The hospital social worker faced with the stress of making immediate discharge arrangements should be aware that there is no regulation requiring an inappropriate aftercare plan to placate the setting. To the contrary, regulations mandate the appropriateness of patient care and discharge plans as an institutional condition for continued participation in government-funded programs.

The practitioner who is concerned with how individual needs may best be met is on proper ground when the older person is viewed, as stated in chapter 9, as a subject and not an object—a subject with a right to control his or her destiny when possessed of the wherewithal to do so. Advance directives such as health care proxies and living wills, which now enable individuals to decide how they are to be treated in life-saving situations, are significant legal instruments through which the practitioner can promote self-determination and allow the elderly person to maintain his or her dignity to the end.

A FEW FINAL WORDS

Being a good practitioner involves more than being an effective clinician; it also involves influencing one's work setting and the health care field itself. Elderly people need the meaningful input and active participation of practitioners who promote the concept of human services delivered in a humane manner. The professional is not just a service instrument of the workplace but is also a force that reflects the values of his or her profession and the rights, dignity, and needs of the recipient of service.

To succor the health care needs of elderly people is an endeavor that can bring to the practitioner personal reward and professional satisfaction. It is the authors' hope that this practice guide will assist you, the reader, to achieve that end.

Appendix

NASW Policy Statement: Client Self-Determination in End-of-Life Decisions

BACKGROUND

End-of-life decisions are the choices made by a person with a terminal condition regarding his or her continuing care or treatment options. These options may include aggressive treatment of the medical condition, life-sustaining treatment, palliative care, passive euthanasia, voluntary active euthanasia, or physician-assisted suicide. For the purposes of this policy statement, these terms are defined as follows:

Terminal and irreversible condition means a continual profound comatose state with no reasonable chance of recovery or a condition caused by injury, disease, or illness, which, within reasonable medical judgment, would produce death within a short time and for which the application of life-sustaining procedures would serve only to postpone the moment of death. There is no universally accepted definition of "a short time," but in general it is considered to be less than one year (American Hospital Association, 1991).

Client self-determination means the right of the client to determine the appropriate level, if any, of medical intervention and the right of clients to change their wishes about their treatment as their condition changes over time or during the course of their illness. Self-determination assumes that the client is mentally competent.

Incompetent means lacking the ability, based on reasonable medical judgment, to understand and appreciate the nature and consequences of a treatment decision, including the significant benefits and harms of and reasonable alternatives to any proposed treatment decision.

Advanced health care directive is a document in which a person either states choices for medical treatment or designates who should make treatment choices if the person should lose decision-making capacity. Although the term "advance directive" generally refers to formal, written documents, it may also include oral statements by the patient (American Hospital Association, 1991).

Life-sustaining treatment is a medical intervention administered to a patient that prolongs life and delays death (American Hospital Association, 1991).

Medically inappropriate life-sustaining procedures means life-sustaining procedures that are not in accord with the patient's wishes or that are medically futile.

Palliative care is medical intervention intended to alleviate suffering, discomfort, or dysfunction but not to cure (American Hospital Association, 1991).

Passive euthanasia is the withholding or withdrawing of life-sustaining treatment. It is the forgoing of treatment, sometimes called "letting die." The right-to-die rulings such as in the Karen Ann Quinlan case establish the right under certain circumstances to be disconnected from artificial life support.

Voluntary active euthanasia is a physician's administering a lethal dose after a clearly competent patient makes a fully voluntary and persistent request for aid in dying. This is the active termination of a patient's life by a physician at the request of the patient.

Physician-assisted suicide is a patient's ending his or her life with the means requested of and provided by a physician for that purpose. The physician and the patient are both involved. Nurses or significant others may also be involved, but the physician has the responsibility for providing the means. In all cases, the patient will have been determined competent to make such a decision.

Some argue that little distinction exists between euthanasia and physician-assisted suicide other than mechanical or technical difference as to who—the patient or the physician—triggers the event. Others (for example, Quill, 1991) maintain the difference is significant in that in assisted suicide the final act is the patient's; the risk of subtle coercion from doctors, family, or other social forces is reduced; the balance of power between patient and physician is more equal; and there is less risk of error, coercion, or abuse.

There has been a proliferation of state legislation related to assisted suicide, including Washington State's "Death with Dignity" initiative, which was narrowly defeated in a referendum in 1991, and bills that were in progress in 1993 in California, Iowa, Maine, Michigan, and New Hampshire state legislatures. (The Michigan bill required social work counseling to qualified applicants for assisted suicide.) Currently, 37 states outlaw actively helping a patient to die (Brody, 1992).

The Patients' Self-Determination Act of 1990, included in the Omnibus Budget Reconciliation Act of 1990, requires all hospitals participating in Medicare or Medicaid to ask all adult inpatients if they have advance directives, to document their answers, and to provide information on state laws and hospital policies. Other health agencies such as home health and hospice have instituted similar requirements (American Hospital Association, 1991). In many of these facilities, social workers are called on to work with patients regarding advance health care directives and end-of-life decisions.

ISSUE STATEMENT

Advances in medical capabilities and technology have made it possible to extend life through artificial means that were heretofore unimaginable. Although this level of care often provides enormous benefits for patients, it may also present difficult and increasingly complex ethical choices for patients, their families, and health care professionals. Inappropriate or unwanted utilization of medical technology may lead to lessened quality of life, loss of dignity, and loss of integrity of patients.

State and federal legislation related to advance health care directives has raised public awareness about the right of patients to participate in medical decision making, including end-of-life decisions. The individuals most immediately facing end-of-life decisions are those with a terminal and irreversible condition, a progressive chronic illness, or chronic intractable pain.

As advocates for the rights of individuals; as providers of mental health services; and as workers in hospitals, hospices, nursing homes, and crisis centers, social workers regularly deal with quality-of-life issues and choices related to life and death. Social workers have requested guidelines that are compatible with professional and personal ethics, legal parameters, and respect for client self-determination. Furthermore, other professionals look to social work for guidelines on these complex issues:

> Social work values, our traditional role as advocates and enablers, and our self-awareness and conscious use of self should serve as justification for engaging people in open and honest debate, recognizing the biases that society and the health care system have had with respect to the backgrounds, lifestyles, and illness of different groups of patients. . . . The social work community has the opportunity and the obligation to educate, organize, and advocate for a more widespread and extensive debate of these life and death matters. (Mizrahi, 1992)

In acknowledging and affirming social work's commitment to respecting diverse value systems in a pluralistic society, end-of-life issues are recognized as controversial because they reflect the varied value systems of different groups. Consequently, NASW does not take a position concerning the morality of end-of-life decisions, but affirms the right of the individual to determine the level of his or her care.

It is also recognized that de facto rationing of health care based on socioeconomic status, color, ability to pay, provider biases, and government policy differentially affects people's right to choose among viable service alternatives and their ability to give truly informed consent. The social worker should work to minimize the effect of these factors in determining the care options available to individuals.

In examining the social work role in working with clients concerning end-of-life decisions, the following issues must be addressed:

- the legal parameters that affect social work practice (for example, limits of confidentiality, state laws prohibiting assisted suicide, the potential for civil liability)

- the potential conflict of social work values with those of other health care professionals
- the emerging pressures for cost control and rationing of health care (for example, temptation of health care institutions and insurers to encourage use of end-of-life practices to control costs)
- the possibility of patients feeling obliged to choose death rather than becoming a burden (Brock, 1992)
- the society limits on individual self-determination and autonomy
- the necessity to define safeguards to protect individuals and society in the implementation of end-of-life practices.

POLICY STATEMENT

NASW's position concerning end-of-life decisions is based on the principle of client self-determination. Choice should be intrinsic to all aspects of life and death.

The social work profession strives to enhance the quality of life; to encourage the exploration of life options; and to advocate for access to options, including providing all information to make appropriate choices.

Social workers have an important role in helping individuals identify the end-of-life options available to them. This role must be performed with full knowledge of and compliance with the law and in accordance with the *NASW Code of Ethics* (NASW, 1996). Social workers should be well informed about living wills, durable power of attorney for health care, and legislation related to advance health care directives.

A key value for social workers is client self-determination. Competent individuals should have the opportunity to make their own choices but only after being informed of all options and consequences. Choices should be made without coercion. Therefore, the appropriate role for social workers is to help patients express their thoughts and feelings, to facilitate exploration of alternatives, to provide information to make an informed choice, and to deal with grief and loss issues.

Social workers should not promote any particular means to end one's life but should be open to full discussion of the issues and care options. As a client is considering his or her choices, the social worker should explore and help ameliorate any factors such as pain, depression, need for medical treatment, and so forth. Further, the social worker should thoroughly review all available options including, but not limited to, pain management, counseling, hospice care, nursing home placement, and advance health care directives.

Social workers should act as liaisons with other health care professionals and help the patient and family communicate concerns and attitudes to the health care team to bring about the most responsible assistance possible.

Because end-of-life decisions have familial and social consequences, social workers should encourage the involvement of significant others, family, and friends in these decisions. Social workers should provide ongoing support and be liaisons to families and support people (for example, caregivers, significant others) with care to maintain the patient's confidentiality. When death occurs, social workers have an obligation to provide emotional and tangible assistance to the significant others, family, and friends in the bereavement process.

Social workers should be free to participate or not participate in assisted-suicide matters or other discussions concerning end-of-life decisions depending on their own beliefs, attitudes, and value systems. If a social worker is unable to help with decisions about assisted suicide or other end-of-life choices, he or she has a professional obligation to refer patients and their families to competent professionals who are available to address end-of-life issues.

It is inappropriate for social workers to deliver, supply, or personally participate in the commission of an act of assisted suicide when acting in their professional role. Doing so may subject the social worker to criminal charges. If legally permissible, it is not inappropriate for a social worker to be present during an assisted suicide if the client requests the social worker's presence. The involvement of social workers in assisted suicide cases should not depend on race or ethnicity, religion, age, gender, economic factors, sexual orientation, or disability.

NASW chapters should facilitate their membership's participation in local, state, and national committees, activities, and task forces concerning client self-determination and end-of-life decisions. Education and research on these complex topics should be included in the social work role.

Policy statement approved by the NASW Delegate Assembly, August 1993. For further information, contact the National Association of Social Workers, 750 First Street, NE, Suite 700, Washington, DC 20002-4241. Telephone: (202) 408-8600 or (800) 638-8799.

REFERENCES

American Hospital Association. (1991). *Put it in writing.* Chicago: Author.

Brock, D. W. (1992). Voluntary active euthanasia. *Hastings Center Report, 22*(2), 10–22.

Brody, J. E. (1992). Doctor-assisted suicide: Ever acceptable? *New York Times.*

Mizrahi, T. (1992). The direction of patients' rights in the 1990s: Proceed with caution. *Health & Social Work, 17,* 246–262.

National Association of Social Workers. (1996). *NASW code of ethics.* Washington, DC: Author.

Patients' Self-Determination Act of 1990, P.L. 101-508, 104 Stat. 1388 et seq.

Quill, T. (1991). Death and dignity: A case of individualized decision making. *New England Journal of Medicine, 324,* 691–694.

Index

The Editors

Florence Safford, DSW, one of the first home care practitioners in the United States, has been a medical social worker for more than four decades. During her 15 years as director of social work at the Isabella Geriatric Center in New York City, she developed an innovative training program for families of mentally impaired elderly people. This program led to one of the first support groups for families struggling with Alzheimer's disease and related disorders. Dr. Safford is a professor emeritus in the social work department at Florida International University, Miami, where she had been chair of the Concentration in Services to the Elderly program.

George I. Krell, MS, has had a distinguished career in the health care field. He served as an assistant deputy commissioner for the Boston Department of Health and Hospitals, which involved social services, utilization review, and physician relations for the system's acute hospital, long-term-care facilities, emergency services, and the community outreach clinics. He was the first director of social services for the State of California's Medicaid program. Before retirement, he was director of social work for the Mount Sinai Medical Center, Miami Beach, Florida.

The Contributors

Terry Conward, DSW, is division director, Community Outreach Services, Metro-Dade Department of Youth and Family Development. She has more than 20 years of social work experience in the areas of child welfare services to the blind and services to elderly populations. As long-term-care administrator for the state of Florida, she regulated nursing homes and adult congregate living facilities. She was formerly on the faculties of Howard University School of Social Work, Washington, DC, and the Department of Social Work at Florida International University, Miami.

Mary Helen Hayden, MSW, is assistant professor and undergraduate (BSW) program coordinator in the social work department at Florida International University. She has worked in the area of addictions, both as a clinical social worker in a rehabilitation program and as a chief trainer for the National Institute on Drug Abuse Southeast Regional Training Center.

Gema G. Hernandez, DPA, is associate professor at Nova University, Fort Lauderdale, director of Social Work Services at Little Havana Activities and Nutritional Centers in Miami, and a consultant to various private and public organizations. She is a member of the American Society on Aging, National Council on Aging, Older Women's League, National Coalition of Hispanic Health and Human Services Organizations, American Association of University Professors, and the American Association of Public Administrators.

Jordan I. Kosberg, PhD, ACSW, is professor and coordinator of the PhD program in the School of Social Work at Florida

International University and faculty associate in the university's Southeast Florida Center on Aging. He was previously the Philip S. Fisher Professor and director of the Centre for Applied Family Studies in the School of Social Work at McGill University, Montreal, and professor of Gerontology at the University of South Florida. Dr. Kosberg is a Fellow of the Gerontological Society of America and was appointed to the Subcommittee on Aging for the National Institute of Mental Health.

Carol R. Odell, MSW, is associate professor and director of field instruction at the School of Social Work at Florida International University, and a consultant to several Miami-area nursing homes. She was formerly on the faculties of Florida State University and Barry University School of Social Work, Miami Shores.

Mary O'Donnell, RN, MHM, was a pioneer of the hospice movement in South Florida in the mid-1970s and is currently associate director of Hospice Care of Broward County, Inc., and adjunct professor at Florida International University and Broward Community College. She is known nationally as a lecturer on issues of loss, grief, and growth and is the recipient of numerous awards in that area of interest.

Martha Pelaez, PhD, is associate director of the Southeast Florida Center on Aging at Florida International University, with overall responsibility for the center's education and training programs. She is on the health care administration faculty of the university, where she teaches Ethical Decision Making for Health Managers. Dr. Pelaez has developed a variety of training programs on ethical issues in long-term care, has presented papers on the topic at numerous professional conferences, and is co-principal investigator on the project, "Training Practitioners to Enhance Autonomy on Long-Term Care." Most recently, she has been the regional advisor on aging to the Pan American Health Organization in Washington, DC.

James H. Riley, MSW, is director of Social Services at Heartland of Boca Raton, a skilled nursing facility that provides a range of progams from rehabilitation to long-term care for all age groups. He previously was a case manager for people with AIDS at Center One, Fort Lauderdale, and now is in the PhD program at Florida International University.

Karen M. Sowers-Hoag, PhD, is professor and dean of the College of Social Work at the University of Tennessee, Knoxville, and she also oversees the Social Work Office for Research and Public Service and the Mental Health Research Center. Prior to her appointment she served as director of the School of Social Work at Florida International University. She is a member of the board of directors and chair of the nominating committee for the National Association of Deans and Directors of Schools of Social Work. Dr. Sowers-Hoag is nationally known for her research and scholarship in the areas of case management with the frail elderly population, child welfare, cultural diversity, and culturally effective intervention strategies for social work practice.

Gerontology for Health Professionals
A Practice Guide
2nd Edition

Cover design by The Watermark Design Office

Composed by Christine Cotting,
UpperCase Publication Services,
in Palatino and Lucida Sans

Printed by Graphic Communications, Inc.,
on 60# Windsor